THE CONSTITUTIONAL RELEVAN(
DOMESTIC AND EUROP

The publication of this Volume has been made possible with the kind support of

 Regione Umbria
Consiglio Regionale

Centro Studi Giuridici e Politici

THE CONSTITUTIONAL RELEVANCE OF THE ECHR IN DOMESTIC AND EUROPEAN LAW

An Italian Perspective

Edited by

Giorgio REPETTO

intersentia

Cambridge – Antwerp – Portland

Intersentia Publishing Ltd.
Trinity House | Cambridge Business Park | Cowley Road
Cambridge | CB4 0WZ | United Kingdom
Tel.: +44 1223 393 753 | Email: mail@intersentia.co.uk

Distribution for the UK:
NBN International
Airport Business Centre, 10 Thornbury Road
Plymouth, PL6 7 PP
United Kingdom
Tel.: +44 1752 202 301 | Fax: +44 1752 202 331
Email: orders@nbninternational.com

Distribution for the USA and Canada:
International Specialized Book Services
920 NE 58th Ave. Suite 300
Portland, OR 97213
USA
Tel.: +1 800 944 6190 (toll free)
Email: info@isbs.com

Distribution for Austria:
Neuer Wissenschaftlicher Verlag
Argentinierstraße 42/6
1040 Wien
Austria
Tel.: +43 1 535 61 03 24
Email: office@nwv.at

Distribution for other countries:
Intersentia Publishing nv
Groenstraat 31
2640 Mortsel
Belgium
Tel.: +32 3 680 15 50
Email: mail@intersentia.be

The Constitutional Relevance of the ECHR in Domestic and European Law. An Italian Perspective
Giorgio Repetto (ed.)

© 2013 Intersentia
Cambridge – Antwerp – Portland
www.intersentia.com | www.intersentia.co.uk

Artwork on cover: Les trois poètes, Marcoussis Louis (1878-1941) © Musée national d'Art moderne – Centre Georges Pompidou, MNAM-CCI, Dist. RMN-Grand Palais / Jacqueline Hyde

ISBN 978-1-78068-118-4
D/2012/7849/96
NUR 820

British Library Cataloguing in Publication Data. A catalogue record for this book is available from the British Library.

ACKNOWLEDGEMENTS

As editor, I would like to thank all the colleagues and friends who made the publication of this volume possible.

First of all, I am grateful to the book's authors, who supported and encouraged me during the early stage of the initiative, and whose contribution, far beyond the articles published here, played an enormous role in the conception of the book. I wish to thank Eric Steven Dennis for his linguistic expertise and his sensitive approach to legal language.

Secondly, I am indebted to the two Institutions that supported the publication: *Centro studi giuridici e politici della Regione Umbria* and its President, avv. Marco Lucio Campiani, who aided us with a financial grant, and *Dipartimento di Diritto pubblico* at the Università di Perugia (Research Unit on 'The Effectiveness of Rights in the Light of the European Court of Human Rights Case Law', https://diritti-cedu.unipg.it), for its organizational and financial support.

Thirdly, I am grateful to Ann-Christin Maak of Intersentia and the anonymous reviewers, who helped me clarify the book's main thesis and allowed me to realize this project.

And last but not least, I wish to acknowledge all the people who gave me precious suggestions for every aspect of the book's preparation: Luisa Cassetti, Francesco Cerrone, Silvia Niccolai, Cesare Pinelli and Mauro Volpi.

CONTENTS

CONCLUDING REMARKS

The Constitutional Relevance of the ECHR in Domestic and European Law.
General Assessments

LIST OF AUTHORS

Gianluca Bascherini
Assistant Professor of Constitutional Law, Department of Law, University of Rome "La Sapienza", Italy (gianluca.bascherini@uniroma1.it)

Andrea Buratti
Assistant Professor of Public Law, Department of Public Law, University of Rome "Tor Vergata", Italy (buratti@juris.uniroma2.it)

Antonello Ciervo
Research Fellow in Public Law, Department of Public Law, University of Perugia, Italy (anto.ciervo@hotmail.it)

Alessandra Di Martino
Assistant Professor of Comparative Constitutional Law, Department of Law, University of Rome "La Sapienza" (alessandra.dimartino@uniroma1.it)

Andrea Guazzarotti
Associate Professor of Constitutional Law, Department of Economics and Management, University of Ferrara, Italy (andrea.guazzarotti@unife.it)

Marta Mengozzi
Assistant Professor of Public Law, Department of Public Law, University of Rome "Tor Vergata", Italy (marta.mengozzi@uniroma2.it)

Mariangela Montagna
Associate Professor of Criminal Procedure, Department of Public Law, University of Perugia, Italy (montagna@unipg.it)

Cesare Pinelli
Professor of Public Law, Department of Law, University of Rome "La Sapienza", Italy (cesarepinelli@tiscali.it)

Oreste Pollicino
Associate Professor of Comparative Public Law, Department of Law, Bocconi University, Milan, Italy (oreste.pollicino@unibocconi.it)

Giorgio Repetto
Assistant Professor of Public Law, Department of Public Law, University of Perugia, Italy (giorgio.repetto@unipg.it)

Ilenia Ruggiu
Associate Professor of Constitutional Law, Department of Law, University of Cagliari, Italy (iruggiu@unica.it)

Angelo Schillaci
Research Fellow in Constitutional Law, Department of Public Law, University of Teramo, Italy (aschillaci@tin.it)

Diletta Tega
Assistant Professor of Constitutional Law, Department of Domestic and International Law, University of Milano-Bicocca, Italy; Clerk at the Italian Constitutional Court (diletta.tega@unimib.it)

Alberto Vespaziani
Associate Professor of Comparative Constitutional Law, Department of Law, University of Molise, Italy (alberto.vespaziani@unimol.it)

Simone Vezzani
Assistant Professor of International and EU Law, Department of Public Law, University of Perugia, Italy (simone_vezzani@libero.it)

INTRODUCTION

THE ECHR AND THE EUROPEAN CONSTITUTIONAL LANDSCAPE: REASSESSING PARADIGMS

Giorgio REPETTO

1. THE ECHR AND THE IDEA OF 'CONSTITUTIONAL RELEVANCE'

In recent years, the debate over the constitutionalization of the European legal landscape has gained relevance and expanded its focus. After the outstanding reflection that preceded and accompanied the failure of the Draft Treaty establishing a Constitution for Europe between 2003 and 2005, much of the scientific discussion concerning the emerging constitutional paradigm has been compelled to narrow its ambitions, while at the same time reassessing its paradigms of inquiry.

While the dream of a unitary, progressively inclusive constitutional framework for Europe under the aegis of the EU's political contribution was fading, the claim to a broader and more complex pattern of constitutional legitimacy entered the scene. No one denied that the EU was the leading actor in this process, but the intrinsically weak constitutional legitimacy revealed the need for a broader framework, in which the EU's law and policies ceased to stand on their own, encompassing, in the European setting, a wider set of policies and sources of legitimacy. Therefore, it should come as no surprise that the Council of Europe, and particularly its crown jewel, the European Convention on Human Rights (ECHR) along with its judge, the European Court of Human Rights (ECtHR), was able to play a significant role in the process of reassessing this constitutional framework.

In the second half of the 2000's, the ECHR's machinery emerged from a deep transformation process. On the one hand, the institutional revolution triggered by the entry into force of Protocol No. 11 in 1999 conferred on the Court a stronger capacity to deal with its role as overseer of the European public order in the field of human rights, since its procedural action was strengthened by a more coherent set of remedies and admissibility tests. In so doing, the disappearance of the European Commission of Human Rights augmented the role of the Court as the only reference in the pan-European system of human rights protection. On the other hand, this institutional reassessment sidestepped the increasing difficulties that the ECHR had to face after Eastern European enlargement and the overwhelming number of applications it was called upon to decide. Both these aspects led scholars and public opinion to take the constitutional potential of the ECHR more seriously than in the past, since its growing success, as shown by the increase of Member States to the current number of 47, led it to progressively claim to have become Europe's true Constitutional Court, and the ECHR was called upon to become the core of a trans-European Constitution designed to ensure respect for a basic standard of human rights.[1]

Despite this, the enthusiasm surrounding the constitutional rhetoric on the ECHR soon began to show its inevitable limits.

First of all, the Court ended up being a victim of its own success, since the steadily growing number of applications showed the impossibility of it to becoming a true source of coherence and foresight in the arrangement of the pan-European public order. It has rightly been claimed that this weakness is due not only to the limited number of applications that pass the admissibility test (currently around 2%), but also to the unprincipled criteria that lead to the selection of cases deserving to be decided by the Court. Given that formal admissibility criteria are not sufficient to provide a meaningful basis of action for the Court, exposed as it is to casuistry that is hard to foresee, the Court should claim for itself a much clearer constitutional *allure*, by formulating trends of judicial policy able to limit its decisions to those cases 'of principle' that have the capacity to offer sound guidelines for national judicial authorities called upon to do the 'hard work', i.e. that of applying the rights and principles enshrined in the Convention, while occasionally disregarding domestic law.[2]

Secondly, the ECHR system has largely failed to maintain an autonomous constitutional role because of the progressive resistance shown by national public spheres to its case law and the unpredictability of its substantive interpretive criteria. In recent years, the Court's growing success in setting up a system of human rights control for those Member States which traditionally show a low degree of compliance (in particular, countries with well-established trends of massive violations, such as Turkey and Russia as regards the persecution of internal minorities), has been accompanied by strong criticism

---

[1] A. STONE SWEET, 'Sur la constitutionalisation de la Convention Européenne des droits de l'homme: cinquante ans après son installation, la Cour Européenne conçue comme une Cour constitutionnelle' (2009) 80 *Revue trimestrielle des droits de l'homme* 923, 933.

[2] L. WILDHABER, 'A Constitutional Future for the European Court of Human Rights' (2002) 23 *Human Rights Law Journal* 161, 164. For a functional critique see J.-F. FLAUSS, 'La Cour européenne des droits de l'homme est-elle une Cour constitutionnelle?' (1998) 36 *Revue française de droit constitutionnel* 711, 720–728.

from its traditional 'western' Member States, whose public opinions have often dealt critically with Strasbourg decisions that call into question basic internal value choices grounded upon long-standing traditions.[3]

Both these factors reveal the limits of a strongly committed constitutional rhetoric for the ECHR, centered upon the progressive elaboration of 'hard' constitutional values, since the enlarged spectrum of Member States has led the ECtHR to progressively abandon the most extreme tenets of a 'countermajoritarian' bias. It is therefore hard to grasp in the ECtHR case law a strong set of values capable of defining a common denominator in the field of fundamental rights: the same emphasis on 'democracy', which is often considered one of the cornerstones of the European machinery enshrined in the ECHR, has been correctly understated, since its basic features in the jurisprudence of the Strasbourg Court show a narrow prescriptive model, whose components are limited to the formal requirements of regular and free elections and to the vertical relationships between citizens and the State.[4]

The inability of more enthusiastic rhetoric to provide a useful account of the constitutional potential of the ECHR has been carefully taken into account and amended by the more recent theoretical strain toward the European constitutional heterarchy or (to put it better) pluralism. The widespread scepticism regarding the ECtHR's ability to progressively extract from national constitutional traditions a set of values and principles in the field of human rights, as if it were meant to be the emerging core of a European federalism in the field of human rights, has been reversed in the direction of a less ambitious, while theoretically more comprehensive, target. In a reconstruction of this kind, the impossibility of recasting true order is replaced by the effort to establish a meta-theoretical framework – an order of (dis-)orders – in which the 'relationships of the constituent parts are governed not by an overarching legal framework but primarily by politics, often judicial politics',[5] and where it is hard to find a common set of norms at the top that allows resolution of conflicts or would at least be the framework in which to argue about conflicts. The undecided question of authority at the top of the scale and the emphasis on the positive virtues of national backlashes and contestations contribute both to endowing the system with the ability to transform itself, and to providing, by its inner logic, the flexible solutions for dealing with impasses and conflicts, since in a system of this kind 'contestation might be easier to circumnavigate than in

---

3   For an insightful overview see K. Dzehtsiarou and A. Greene, 'Legitimacy and the Future of the European Court of Human Rights: Critical Perspectives from Academia and Practitioners' (2011) 12 *German Law Journal* 1707.

4   S. Marks, 'The European Convention on Human Rights and its "Democratic Society"' (1995) 66 *British Yearbook of International Law* 209, 212–214.

5   N. Krisch, *Beyond Constitutionalism: The Pluralist Structure of Postnational Law*, Oxford University Press, Oxford 2010, p. 111.

a constitutional order built on the ideal that these questions are settled in one way or another'.[6]

The pluralist strain has undoubtedly provided a more realistic account of the ongoing transformation in the order of European human rights[7], essentially by reversing the inescapable loss of sovereignty and authority at both the national and supranational level, into a virtuous model of interaction, in which the assessment of plausible reactions is encompassed by a dialogical framework shaped by the ideal of the contestability of constitutional solutions.

Despite this, or probably because of the intention to fill every gap left by the constitutional approach, the heterarchical literature has in some aspects gone too far in its effort to provide a more realistic description of the relationships between the model and sources of protection of fundamental rights: it has indeed progressively shaken off every trace of hierarchy and, in so doing, has limited itself to justifying, through meta-rational foundations, the effectiveness of the power balances between national and supranational entities. In other words, its effort to remedy the illusion of a 'thick' constitutional model has paved the way for an excessively 'thin' pluralist arrangement, whose founding premises risk fading into a merely procedural rationality that consciously and by default renounces the collective dimension of the moral foundations of policies and, in our field, substantive value-choices for human rights.[8]

While the 'constitutional' literature on the ECHR has failed to encompass the role played by national constituencies in the enhancement of judicial policies on human rights in Europe, mainly by overstating the unifying potential conferred to the ECtHR, the 'heterarchical' strain too early dismantles the hierarchical dimension of legal discourse in establishing an operational code for ECHR rights, by leaving the 'order of orders' in the hands of (mainly legally unbound) judicial politics.

Because of the limits shown by these two governing approaches to the constitutional role of the ECHR, the approach used in this volume seeks to combine the theoretical contributions from both, and to reassess them in light of the keywords 'constitutional relevance'. In our view, constitutional relevance should be meant as a broader set of codes and approaches to dealing with the ECHR, in that they encompass the action of national and supranational polities within a unitary framework, which is led neither by a top-down legitimacy (as in the more blatant cases of 'constitutional' rhetoric) nor by a bottom-up legitimization (as in the more extreme pluralist views), but rather by multiple interactions between judicial actors, whose actions should be grasped through

---

6   N. KRISCH, *supra* n. 5, p. 152.

7   In the more recent literature see M. AVBELJ and J. KOMÁREK (eds.), *Constitutional Pluralism in the European Union and Beyond*, Hart, Oxford/Portland, 2012.

8   Some of these critical stances are held by J.H.H. WEILER, 'Dialogical Epilogue', in G. DE BÚRCA and J.H.H. WEILER, *The Worlds of European Constitutionalism*, Cambridge University Press, Cambridge 2012, 302 and 304.

both the unintentional effects of decisions and the effort to strive for new constitutional (power) balances guided by law and its rationality.

The inescapability of complexity and pluralism, in other words, should not be understood as renouncing the ability of legal discourse to arrange new operational codes: it only means we are called upon to find new ones. As Sionaidh Douglas-Scott convincingly asked: 'Must we give up on this role for law just because we are apparently dealing with something overly complex because more than one legal system is at issue?'[9]

In so doing, one should be aware that every effort to imagine a 'strong' constitutional role for the ECHR is from the outset mitigated by the fact that the ECtHR's action should not be emphasized with regard to its constitutional ambitions, since it 'has no conclusive purposive theory of its own legal order, unlike the ECJ'.[10] At the same time, the integrated model of human rights protection in Europe is composed of different layers and standards, whose continuous interaction is marked by accommodation strategies as well as by friction, which gain a concerted constitutional relevance when they contribute, each on its own, to defining a proper sphere of action. In other words, national judges and the ECtHR act 'constitutionally', and their actions thus gain 'constitutional relevance', when they claim for their own a piece of the European mosaic by providing a rationale for their competence, while at the same time interactively defining the residual competence of other actors.[11]

This means that the notion of 'constitutional relevance' describes a situation in which, in Popper's terms, the more emphasis this quality is given, the more the inner and outer boundaries of constitutional actors (both national and supranational) are continuously falsified and reassessed, and the more judicial actors are engaged in a process of contestation and of setting new boundaries.[12]

In this light, the 'constitutional relevance' of the ECHR can be more fruitfully ascertained insofar as its role is analysed 'in action', i.e. beginning from controversial situations, where the boundaries of its judicial action are more vigorously called into question, rather than by *a priori* theoretical assessments.[13] This requires a contextual analysis, which dismisses the ambition to make a general statement about the essence of 'the' constitutional in the ECHR machinery, and instead attempts to conquer isolated fragments of constitutional significance when dealing with the individual issues being debated.

---

[9]   S. DOUGLAS-SCOTT, 'Europe's Constitutional Mosaic: Human Rights in the European Legal Space – Utopia, Dystopia, Monotopia or Polytopia?' in N. WALKER, J. SHAW and S. TIERNEY (eds.), *Europe's Constitutional Mosaic*, Hart, Oxford/Portland 2011, p. 130.

[10]   S. DOUGLAS-SCOTT, *supra* n. 9, p. 112.

[11]   S. DOUGLAS-SCOTT, *supra* n. 9, p. 116.

[12]   K. POPPER, *The Logic of Scientific Discovery*, Routledge, London 2002, p. 18.

[13]   For a similar approach see N. WALKER and S. TIERNEY, 'Introduction. A Constitutional Mosaic? Exploring the New Frontiers of Europe's Constitutionalism', in N. WALKER, J. SHAW and S. TIERNEY (eds.), *supra* n. 9, p. 12.

The composite nature of this framework therefore relies upon the impossibility of exhausting all paths of interaction between judicial actors and, on a deeper level, of foreseeing the solutions to be given to the most controversial issues concerning human rights. The term 'relevance', in this light, refers to a semantic universe in which there is no given *a priori* answer to controversial questions, and consequently the role of the actors (either judicial or scholar) should not be confined within a voluntaristic (or, rather, realistic) fallacy, i.e. within the statement according to which the more a legal assertion is true, the more it will be confirmed by future judicial decisions.[14]

The incompleteness of the European constitutional landscape, on the other hand, seems particularly suited to such an approach, which aims at providing a truthful account of the existing situation, without losing its ability to invoke plausible transformations when the (im)balance between the different constituencies at stake produces disharmonies in granting a composite and integrated system for the protection of human rights.

For all these reasons, the editor and the authors of the volume have decided to deal distinctly with the different facets of the 'constitutional relevance' of the ECHR by separating two major fields of inquiry, which reflect the fundamentally different angles from which the topics at stake merit investigation.

In the first part of this volume, the constitutional potential of the ECHR is analysed from the point of view of its increasing influence within domestic law. Beginning with the setting of the Italian legal order, which in our opinion provides a fruitful example of the European laboratory, the authors investigate the transformations that affect the internal role of the ECHR, starting from different perspectives: its rank within the system of legal sources; its contribution to the changing paradigms of legal and constitutional interpretation; its influence on the protection of a particularly sensitive right, such as that to a fair trial; and, lastly, its trajectory within a comparative survey. All these different perspectives are unified by the emphasis placed on the virtues and friction arising from the ECHR's increasing constitutional ambitions in domestic law.

In the second part of this volume, the 'constitutional relevance' of the ECHR is examined from the perspective of its role as a truly trans-European constitutional order. In this light, more than from the standpoint of specific judicial trends, what is at stake here are the dynamics lying behind the boundary-setting fostered by the ECtHR with Member States and the EU, with particular reference to the balance to be achieved in the protection of controversial rights and interests with the former, and in the framework governing relationships with the latter.

---

14 This idea of 'relevance' is inspired here by the works of the Italian philosopher of law Alessandro Giuliani, above all by his *Riflessioni in tema di esperienza giuridica*, Giuffrè, Milano 1957.

2. THE ECHR'S CONSTITUTIONAL DIMENSION IN DOMESTIC LAW

Many recent comparative overviews have demonstrated the multiplicity of factors that contribute to determining the effects of the ECHR in domestic law. Far beyond the consolidated theoretical premises enshrined in the alternative between the dualism and monism of domestic law *vis-à-vis* international law, the question concerning the ECHR's impact in national legal orders has proven to be a test bench for a wider range of scholars than in the past, since it involves issues that call into question the interactions between different jurisgenerative practices at both the international and national levels. Comparative inquiries like those conducted by Helen Keller and Alec Stone-Sweet[15] or Oreste Pollicino and Giuseppe Martinico[16] share the view that European law is progressively marked by a 'conflict of laws' trend, in which the line to be drawn between the 'national' and the 'European' is progressively blurring, to the point of encompassing areas and spheres restricted until now to their own scientific realms. How are we to deal, for example, with the phenomenon of the increasing compliance with the ECtHR's judgments in those countries traditionally showing a dualistic rather than monistic approach, which leads scholars to state that the dualistic or monistic approach of a legal order is no more so relevant as to the impact of the ECHR?[17] On the other hand, how are we to reconcile the traditional image of a Strasbourg Court devoted to intervening subsidiarily in the case of human rights violation, i.e. after domestic remedies have been exhausted, with the recent practice of pilot judgments, which operates as *a priori* judgment regarding an unpredictable number of cases entailing a systematic violation of a certain right?

In these circumstances, national legal systems have been called upon to face the complexity of the ECHR's impact simply by expanding the channels of interaction from Parliaments to judges (either constitutional courts or the judiciary) and by articulating judicial discourse on the ECHR as a form of internal dialogue between judicial actors. In so doing, the constitutional relevance of the ECHR in domestic law stems from an internal process of contestation and continuous reassessment of competences and boundaries, which reproduces at an internal level the responsive pluralism highlighted in the previous paragraph.

---

[15]   *A Europe of Rights: The Impact of the ECHR on National Legal Systems*, Oxford University Press, Oxford 2008.

[16]   *The National Judicial Treatment of the ECHR and EU laws. A Constitutional Comparative Perspective*, Europa Law, Groningen 2010.

[17]   A. Keller and A. Stone-Sweet, 'Assessing the Impact of the ECHR on National Legal Systems', *supra* n. 15, p. 686: 'The assumption that dualistic States have, a priori, an unfriendly attitude towards international law, and will, therefore, generate a relatively poorer rights record, is untenable'.

The functions of Parliaments, constitutional courts and the judiciary as to the incorporation of the ECHR are difficult to keep separate, since in many countries that traditionally have a centralized system for the protection of fundamental rights (like Italy or Germany, among others), the growing interaction between constitutional and ECHR rights has enmeshed form and substance of judicial protection.[18] This enmeshment has often called for a new balance among judicial actors, which are – although in very different ways – called upon to consider the impact of ECHR rights (as well as of ECtHR rulings) when seeking to ascertain the violation of a right enshrined in the Constitution. The 'duty to take [the Convention] into account' (*Pflicht zur Berücksichtigung*) imposed by the German Constitutional Tribunal upon the courts when they are called upon to apply rights and guarantees influenced by the ECHR, or the duty of Italian courts to provide an interpretation of domestic law that is consistent with the Convention, are two clear examples of the growing constitutional potential that the ECHR deploys beyond its well-established formal limits and the question of the strict compliance with its judge's rulings. Whether its contribution is contested or accepted, the ECHR has gained in any case a growing relevance in national legal systems, since it has deeply influenced the ways in which national fundamental rights are interpreted and enhanced.

Nonetheless, it should be clear that this influence is not *per se* synonymous with better or higher protection for national rights. While it is well known that the 'subsidiarity imperative' limits the ECHR's action to protecting a minimum standard of rights, it should not be forgotten that the rationale for the national protection of fundamental rights is multi-faceted, since it is not limited to the mere protection of individual claims and encompasses a certain idea of 'the' public and 'the' social, as demonstrated by the proliferation of 'social rights' in the post-WWII constitutions. The commitment to subsidiarity has undoubtedly helped the Strasbourg Court gain legitimacy before national constituencies, since through this it has respected the basic features of national identities; on the other hand, however, it has not prevented its case law from calling into question some basic assumptions of constitutional models, above all by endorsing a constitutional scenario in which the State and the individuals are often deemed to be mainly in conflict.[19]

The constitutional potential of the ECHR in domestic law should therefore not be identified only in the contribution the former can make to raising the level of protection of a certain right afforded by the latter: this is only part of the story. This contribution often creates conflicts (or better, meta-conflicts), since a higher protection for a given individual right often limits a public interest that is

---

[18] P. RIDOLA, 'La giustizia costituzionale e le sfide del "diritto costituzionale europeo"', in *Scritti in onore di Alessandro Pace*, vol. III, ESI, Napoli 2012, 2418.

[19] With regard to property right, a similar critical position is held by D. NICOL, *The Constitutional Protection of Capitalism*, Hart, Oxford/Portland 2010, 136.

not directly associated with a given right: for example, what about the value of definitive judicial decisions when a process must be reopened because a violation of the right to a fair trial has occurred? What about the commitment to generally accepted restrictive policies in criminal law when a more lenient law is called upon to be retroactive in accordance with Article 7 ECHR?

In our opinion, within this clash between the (mainly) more individualistic and reactive tenets of the 'model of rights' assumed by the ECHR and the (mainly) more social and proactive function of national rights, lies the heart of the problem concerning the ECHR's 'constitutional relevance' in domestic law. The theory and practice of its incorporation should be aware that it often poses problems that involve recasting the basic value-premises that define the image of the 'public good' and of society enshrined in a Constitution.

3. THE TRANS-EUROPEAN CONSTITUTIONAL RELEVANCE OF THE ECHR

While the growing impact of the ECHR in domestic law is progressively transforming the Member States' internal constitutional domain, the other perspective from which the constitutional relevance of the ECHR can be grasped is that of how and to what extent the Convention is deemed to establish a pan-European constitutional order with regard to Member States and the EU.[20]

According to the above-mentioned premises, this quest for relevance should not be intended as a bold elaboration of a substantive theory of human rights by the ECtHR, since that would mean dismissing the basic tenets of the role of the ECHR as a complementary instrument for protecting rights. In this light, Luzius Wildhaber (former President of the Strasbourg Court) and Jonas Christoffersen, among others, have convincingly linked the ECHR's constitutional character to a clearer delimitation of the boundaries between the action of the ECtHR and the Member States. The contribution of the latter is indeed essential to the proper function of the judicial action of the former, on the one hand because national authorities are considered the first-instance guardians of the application of the ECHR, and on the other hand because the Convention system 'does not purport to impose uniform approaches to the myriad different interests which arise in the broad field of fundamental rights protection'.[21] On these premises, the effort has been made to isolate those interpretive principles called upon to embody that sort of 'right distance' that should govern the relationships between the ECHR

---

[20] A. STONE SWEET, 'The European Convention on Human Rights and National Constitutional Reordering' (2012) 33 *Cardozo Law Review* 1859, 1864.

[21] L. WILDHABER, *supra* n. 2, p. 162, J. CHRISTOFFERSEN, 'Individual and Constitutional Justice: Can the Power Balance of Adjudication be Reversed?', in J. CHRISTOFFERSEN and M.R. MADSEN (eds.), *The European Court of Human Rights Between Law and Politics*, Oxford University Press, Oxford 2011, pp. 190–202.

and the Member States. According to the meaningful reconstruction by Steven Greer, principles like those of 'effective protection of rights' and of 'legality/rule of law', 'democracy' and 'priority of rights' operate as primary constitutional principles in that they offer a yardstick against which to evaluate compliance with the assumptions enshrined therein by the remaining interpretive criteria, i.e. 'secondary constitutional principles', or those of 'dynamic/evolutive interpretation' and of 'margin of appreciation', among others.[22]

Precisely because this distinction does not entail support for judicial action offered by a given political morality, the assessment of these basic principles implies a 'constitutional role' for the ECtHR since its interpretive criteria are variously called upon to balance a 'rights-privileging' approach with the commitment to enhancing democratic values.[23] Although this balancing assumes different contours in the different categories of the ECHR's rights (on a scale rising to the most privileged guarantees enshrined in Articles 3, 4(1) and 7(1), and descending to the weakest right, i.e. the right to the peaceful enjoyment of possessions pursuant to Article 1 of Protocol No. 1), one is tempted to say that the most controversial branch of the conventional adjudication is that concerning Articles 8–11 of the Convention or rights like those to free elections and to education (Articles 2 and 3, Protocol No. 1), where the texture of rights and public interests reflects the composite nature of the ECHR's constitutional action.[24]

In this light, the ECHR's ability to establish a pan-European constitutional order in the field of human rights is closely related to the construction of an ordered pluralism with the different constituencies entitled to concur with the Strasbourg Court, in particular for those rights that do not embody a clear-cut preference for individual protection over pursuit of public interest. The constitutional agency of the ECHR is indeed not essentially discussed when the Strasbourg Court is called upon to ascertain most violations of Article 3 of the Convention, because the European consensus on the values enshrined therein is widely shared. The more its judicial action is contested because of the lack of consideration for respecting basic (cultural, historical, ethical, political) national interests, as occurs in relation to the most debatable claims arising under above mentioned rights, the better can its 'constitutional relevance' be understood, starting in particular from the consideration the Court will give to those national claims and interests.

The focus on margin of appreciation with regard to the Member States and on the changing interactions with the EU thus represents a key element for such an inquiry, in that through this a clearer and more comprehensive account can

---

[22]   S. GREER, *The European Convention on Human Rights. Achievements, Problems and Prospects*, Cambridge University Press, Cambridge 2006, pp. 195–226.

[23]   S. GREER, *supra* n. 22, p. 208.

[24]   S. GREER, *supra* n. 22, pp. 209–211.

be given of the sphere of influence the ECHR can claim in a context where multiple judicial actors contribute to the construction of a 'Europe of rights'.

In this volume's conception, margin of appreciation must be intended not only as the technique used by the Court to draw a line beyond which it is not entitled to call into question discretionary choices made by national authorities, but rather as a more comprehensive reasoning that outlines the influence that national specificities can exercise on Strasbourg judicial practice, as well as, conversely, the feedback that the latter produces on the former.[25]

A similar approach may be used to reassess the relationships with the European Union. Although the EU is not yet formally Member of the ECHR, even if the Lisbon Treaty has paved the way to accession and negotiations are currently in progress, the judicial and institutional interactions between the two European Courts is likewise able to influence the constitutional shape of the ECHR to come. In recent years, the debate over the competition between the ECtHR and the ECJ for the role of European constitutional court has been a standard among scholars, while the recent evolution shows that it is first of all a false problem. Constitutional conversations between Luxembourg and Strasbourg have grown in intensity and frequency through cross-citations and a sort of diplomatic comity, so that it is hard to say that current relationships do not have a crucial importance for the role and the position of both Courts. The necessary coexistence between these two systems of protection of fundamental rights should therefore call for an inquiry into the form and substance of judicial interaction as a necessary counterpart to the interaction the ECtHR shows with national constituencies.[26]

If the actual debate over constitutionalization in Europe is aware of the need to move beyond the epistemic premises of 'holistic constitutionalism',[27] it is also necessary to take into account how and to what extent these frequent judicial interactions, even though outside a given legal framework, foster the constitutional relevance of the ECHR, in that they define the breadth and depth of Strasbourg's jurisprudence.

---

[25]   M. DELMAS-MARTY, *Towards a Truly Common Law*, Cambridge University Press, Cambridge 2002, pp. 71–74. An insightful survey of the problems and virtues related to margin of appreciation is that of C. VAN DE HEYNING, 'No place like home: Discretionary space for the domestic protection of fundamental rights', in P. POPELIER, C. VAN DE HEYNING and P. VAN NUFFEL (eds.), *Human rights protection in the European legal order: The interaction between the European and the national courts*, Intersentia, Cambridge – Antwerp – Portland 2011, pp. 83–94.

[26]   The need of an integrated approach toward the European human rights compound is stressed by W. VOERMANS, 'Protection of European human rights by highest courts in Europe: The art of triangulation', in P. POPELIER, C. VAN DE HEYNING and P. VAN NUFFEL (eds.), *supra* n. 25, pp. 375–378.

[27]   N. WALKER, 'Beyond the Holistic Constitution', in P. DOBNER and M. LOUGHLIN (eds.), *The Twilight of Constitutionalism*, Oxford University Press, Oxford 2010, 303.

Starting from an inquiry into the relationships that the ECtHR has with both the Member States and with the EU and the ECJ, this book assumes that the constitutional role of the ECHR in the European legal landscape can be ascertained primarily through an inquiry into the contextual relationships with this broadest set of actors, thanks to which the rationale for its action, as well as its actual limits, should be revealed.

4. THE 'ITALIAN' PERSPECTIVE

Before briefly outlining the content of the single chapters and the structure of the volume's parts, it is worth providing some account of the reasons that encouraged the editor and authors to choose the book's subtitle: 'An Italian perspective'.

On the one hand, and more evidently, we have been driven by our common affiliation with Italian legal culture. In our view, this affiliation does not merely reflect the common background of our legal education, since it is intended for a academic purpose, i.e. to offer to the debate a contribution stemming from within a constitutional culture that, unlike on EU topics, has been largely unable to share its contribution on the ECHR beyond national borders.[28] This inability is due to the ECHR's low impact on internal legal dynamics until recent years, when a constitutional amendment (in 2001) and a reversal of course by the Constitutional Court (in 2007) paved the way for its incorporation on a supralegislative rank. Since that time, the ECHR has played a steadily increasing role before the Constitutional Court and the judiciary, ascribing almost every claim concerning fundamental rights to a question concerning the violation of the ECHR's rights. For these reasons, the internal status of the ECHR and, more generally, the dynamics surrounding the increasing role of the ECtHR, became one of the most debated scholarly topics in constitutional law, as shown by the commitment to the issue by many of this volume's authors.

On the other hand, our intention is to demonstrate the utility of a perspective of inquiry that is situated within a single legal culture (extensively, but not at all exclusively taken into account in Part I), but aims at the same time to investigate problems and issues involving most national legal systems. The transition from a situation of low impact to one of higher impact (i.e. incorporation at a quasi-constitutional level), and the problems traditionally arising from the limited compliance by national authorities with ECtHR rulings, make the Italian perspective particularly useful for investigating the transformations of the internal constitutional status of the ECHR, as shown by the dilemmas accompanying the judicial enactment of the ECHR at the internal level. More

---

[28] A significant exception is the recent volume of O. POLLICINO and G. MARTINICO, *The Interaction Between Europe's Legal Systems*, Edward Elgar, Cheltenham/Northampton 2012.

generally, what this book aims to offer is a perspective that, likewise with regard to the ECHR's trans-European profiles, is shaped by methods and tools of inquiry that seek to accompany a national academic community's long-standing embeddedness by making an effort towards a dialogical and intrinsically comparative attitude to legal research. To sum up, we argue that Italy and its constitutional scholarship can be a fruitful laboratory for investigating the more general transformations affecting European constitutionalism in the field of fundamental rights.

5. OUTLINE OF CHAPTERS

According to the approach described above, the volume is divided into two parts, whose main focus is to deal separately with the domestic and the supranational profiles of the ECHR's constitutional relevance.

In the Volume's Part I, devoted to '*Establishing a Constitutional Dimension for the ECHR in Domestic Law*', the authors seek to deepen understanding of the different ways in which the ECHR is progressively reshaping the domestic constitutional orders, with a particular focus on the dynamics pertaining to the Italian legal system.

In Part I.A ('*The Renewing of a Constitutional Culture: the ECHR in Italian Domestic Law*') Diletta Tega, Giorgio Repetto and Andrea Guazzarotti reflect upon the trends in the *Corte costituzionale*'s case law in order to highlight the background of the 2007 revolution as well as the problems and inconsistencies it actually raises. Diletta Tega, starting from the theoretical alternatives to the relationships between domestic and international law that could be derived from Articles 10 and 11 of the Constitution, highlights three phases in the jurisprudence of the Constitutional Court, which has evolved from a traditional dualism in the initial stage to a final duality, in a transformation through an intermediate dualism that she defines as 'more modern'. The essential contours of this evolution are influenced by the evolving interactions between, on the one hand, a model of adjudication originally driven by the effort to reduce the impact of treaties (like the ECHR) simply by stating their legislative rank, and, on the other hand, the quest for a far more substantial approach able to encompass a broader set of interpretive trends, above all the attribution to the ECHR of the capacity to influence the interpretation made by the judiciary of domestic law. On these premises, Giorgio Repetto analyzes the basic features of the 2007 revolution by highlighting the elements of both continuity with, and departure from, the previous approach. In particular, behind the twin cases nos. 348 and 349 of 2007, a single phenomenon is seen at work, according to which the constitutional relevance of the ECHR is bound by the interpretive action of the Constitutional Court, which reserves for itself the task of deciding the breadth of and limits to its incorporation. Nonetheless, subsequent judicial experience has shown that this ambition can be frustrated by the need for deeper interaction between constitutional and conventional guarantees, which spur the *Corte costituzionale* to revise the basic premises of its established interpretive approach to fundamental rights. In the last contribution to Part I.A, Andrea Guazzarotti focuses on a narrower but no less important topic, which is the contribution to the evolution of Italian judicial practice that may be derived from the use of Strasbourg's precedents. Starting from the expanding relevance of the ECHR in domestic judicial practice, the author focuses upon the 'cultural' path of dependency on a blatantly rhetoric use of judicial precedent: both in judicial practice and in constitutional adjudication, precedents are normally invoked in order to confirm a decision that has already been taken for other reasons. The growing internal impact of the ECHR should rather lead the Constitutional Court to elaborate a more conscious theory of judicial precedent, or otherwise its jurisprudence will be condemned to managing Strasbourg's decisions without principle, with the effect of either carrying them out or opposing them without reasonable justification.

In Part I.B ('*The Most Dangerous Breach? The Right to a Fair Trial and the Quest for Effectiveness*'), Mariangela Montagna and Marta Mengozzi both focus on the ECHR's impact on the protection of the right to a fair trial, with which the Italian legal system has traditionally shown an outstanding difficulty to comply – a difficulty only partially overcome by the introduction into the Constitution in 1999 of a clause (Article 111) concerning the right to a fair trial that is clearly inspired by the guarantees enshrined in Article 6 ECHR. The aim of these contributions is to provide two examples, relating to criminal and to administrative trial, of the various elements that contribute to adapting the input originating from Strasbourg into the standard operational code fundamental to a certain constitutional order. With reference to two highly debated issues concerning criminal process, i.e. trial *in absentia* and right to a public hearing, Montagna explores the different and concurrent elements that led Parliament and judicial actors to provide for a solution to a repeated violation of Article 6 ECHR, and demonstrates that in a complex field like this one, where different normative layers contribute towards protecting the same right, reliance on the ECtHR's decisions implies an adaptation process that seeks compatibility between the invoked solution and the basic tenets shaping the internal model of protection. On several occasions, cases of resistance to full compliance should thus be considered in light of the structural, i.e. systemic, obstacles raised by a deeply rooted theory and practice of rights protection on the internal level. In the same vein, Marta Mengozzi analyzes the influence of the ECHR on the problems linked to the impartiality of the administrative judge. An institutional and historical peculiarity of the Italian model (i.e. the inclusion within the administrative trial of judicial and governmental functions) epitomizes the backlash that may arise from within a legal order when the ECtHR establishes a model of protection aimed at setting a common minimum standard: to what extent is the Strasbourg Court entitled to call into question, for the sake of protecting an individual right, an institutional balance between judiciary and government that has a long-standing tradition? The author's position is that the dialogue in recent years does not eliminate some basic contrasts, even if a mutual consideration between national judges and the Strasbourg Court has paved the way for a fruitful evolution in this area.

In Part I.C ('*ECHR in National Constitutions: Comparative Perspectives*'), the perspective of inquiry goes beyond national borders to investigate the comparative trends concerning some basic aspects of the ECHR's impact on European constitutional systems. It is worth noting that in this part, the authors, starting from the comparative overviews that have been widely published in the last years, aim to offer both a cross-European comparison of the national judicial treatment of ECHR and EU law (Oreste Pollicino) and a state-to-state comparison between Italy and Germany regarding the role played by the ECHR in constitutional adjudication (Alessandra Di Martino). The reason for this choice is to combine two different approaches (extensive and intensive) in order to highlight the different levels under which the transformations affecting the internal status of the ECHR are occurring. The contribution by Oreste Pollicino seeks to link these transformations to the changing attitudes of the Luxembourg and Strasbourg Courts after the enlargement phase: whereas the latter has in the last decade shown a particularly aggressive approach to national constituencies, the former has refrained from expanding to Central and Eastern Europe's new Member States its traditional 'majoritarian activism' in order to safeguard a principle of constitutional tolerance. These opposing trends have nonetheless led to a convergence between the ideas purported by the ECtHR and the ECJ as to the internal effects of EU law and of the ECHR, which had several repercussions in the case law of national constitutional courts. The rich analysis of the jurisprudence of several European countries shows that behind the intricacy of different models and standards lies a growing consensus on the impossibility of relegating supranational law (be it EU law or the ECHR) to a simple legislative degree, since judicial practices have a basic convergence in the effort to raise its relevance. Despite the existing differences between the States more inclined to progressively equating EU law with the ECHR (such as the Czech Republic and Slovakia, among others) and the States that show a resistance towards a limitless enforcement of Strasbourg jurisprudence (such as Italy or the United Kingdom), Pollicino argues that the time has come to reflect upon the elements of a 'unitary theory of supranational law'. The comparative analysis between Italy and Germany by Alessandra Di Martino starts from the assumption that the these two countries' common (i.e. dualistic) approach, strengthened by a legal scholarship that has traditionally gone hand in hand with establishing a theoretical framework for these issues (since Triepel and Anzilotti), encourages investigation into the reasons behind the diverging outcomes for the ECHR's incorporation into domestic law. According to Di Martino, the greater attention shown by the German *Bundesverfassungsgericht* than the Italian *Corte costituzionale* to the construction of national fundamental rights in harmony with the ECHR is due to the more evident emphasis placed by the former on the axiological dimension of the ECHR, which has found fertile ground in a more sensitive constitutional theory for fundamental rights.

The Volume's Part II (*'Inner and Outer Boundaries: The Relationship of the European Court of Human Rights with Contracting States and with the EU'*) is devoted to investigating the supranational profiles of the ECHR's constitutional relevance and starts, as mentioned above, from the assumption that the most viable approach to doing this is to deal separately with the constitutional interactions the ECtHR fosters with Member States through the doctrine of margin of appreciation (Part II.A), and with the EU (Part II.B).

The contributions in Part II.A (*'Just Deference? The Multiple Facets of the Doctrine of Margin of Appreciation'*) focus on different aspects of the protection of highly debated human rights enshrined in the ECHR; the main aim of this part is to call into question, more so than in many other cases, a continuous constitutional conversation (and occasionally a conflicting one) with Member States, due to their cultural, ethical and political weight.

In their contributions, Alberto Vespaziani and Ilenia Ruggiu discuss two different aspects of the problems concerning freedom of teaching, both positive and negative, and the influence of religion. Vespaziani focuses on the Strasbourg Court's judicial trend on the issue of the teaching of religion, in order to present a sceptical thesis according to which margin of appreciation is 'neither a legal doctrine nor a filter argument, but rather an argumentative black hole in which the constitutional antimatter collapses, a Hegelian night in which all the appreciations are grey'. Starting from the analysis of cases like *Folgerø v. Norway* and *Hasan and Eylem Zengin v. Turkey*, Vespaziani argues that the Strasbourg Court has not yet been able to develop a unitary approach, since it is appears biased by a highly questionable 'selective liberalism': the balancing between the religious feelings of the majority and the duty to protect minority rights has no clear yardstick, in that it is outweighed by an excessive deference to deeply-rooted religious beliefs. The main focus of Ruggiu's contribution, on the other hand, concerns the use of the margin of appreciation doctrine in the ECtHR's decisions relating to the presence of the crucifix in school classrooms. Starting from analysis of the well-known *Lautsi* cases, Ruggiu seeks to emphasize the inconsistencies lying behind the Strasbourg Court's reasoning, since the effort to deal with the balancing tests remained basically driven by an excessively weak and unprincipled legal argumentation. Conversely, the author, while not condemning *per se* the use of the margin of appreciation doctrine, argues that the Court's reasoning should be inspired in these issues by a more selective approach, which she draws from the recent literature from North America on the so-called 'cultural tests'.

In a similar vein, margin of appreciation is invoked by Antonello Ciervo as the main interpretive instrument the Strasbourg Court has relied upon in order to maintain an extremely cautious approach to national measures restricting the enjoyment of rights related to 'bio-law'. With regard to both the beginning of life (as in the cases concerning medically assisted procreation or abortion) and the end of life (as for euthanasia or assisted suicide), the highly complex and multi-faceted issues emerging from bio-law cases have been, according to Ciervo, hidden behind the argumentative shield of margin of appreciation, particularly in those cases where the ECtHR took the consequences of a more 'liberal' approach into critical account. In the last contribution of Part II.A, Andrea Buratti reflects upon the place held by historical argument in the case law of the Strasbourg Court. After having identified the most important cases in which the Court referred to historical considerations in order to ascertain the contours of the influence that the claims by the common interest had on the enjoyment of human rights enshrined mainly in Articles 8–11 ECHR, or related to political rights (such as *Sejdić and Finci v. Bosnia-Herzegovina* for the limits upon being elected for those belonging to a certain ethnic group, or *Garaudy v. France* with regard to positions on Holocaust denial), the contribution highlights a certain restraint by the Court when calling into question values and interests that limit human rights, by reason of a deep historical rootedness. At the heart of the critique of such a deferential approach, which hypostatizes those values and interests only because of their deep historical underpinning, Buratti argues that the Court should enrich the catalogues of its historical arguments, moving from the mere protection of 'selected historical narratives as traditions and foundations of the democratic order' to a critical historical method, which it could deploy from the most sensitive strains in the historical literature.

In sum, these contributions highlight, albeit from different perspectives, a common criticism of the use of the margin of appreciation doctrine, in that its theoretical haze risks placing in the Court's hands an interpretive tool that is almost *bon à tout faire*, which can endanger the enjoyment of rights in all those cases when the nature of the invoked right should rather call for a countermajoritarian bias. In so doing, margin of appreciation ceases to convey constitutional solutions capable of enriching the argumentative pathways of the ECtHR, and becomes an argument that obscures the catalogue of reasons and arguments that should, to the contrary, provide a meaningful constitutional dialogue.

Lastly, the contributions in Part II.B ('*Cooperation in Need of Coordination. European Court of Human Rights and the EU*') deal with three different aspects of the relationships between the ECHR's machinery and the EU. The authors' purpose is to show that a careful account of these ongoing constitutional interactions should take different perspectives into consideration.

In his contribution, Gianluca Bascherini starts from a most concrete perspective: i.e. the different but progressively converging approaches of the ECtHR and the ECJ towards protecting immigrants' family life. For these claims, characterized by a deep enmeshment of both personal and economic interests, the Strasbourg Court's recent case law has promoted a progressive attitude, particularly because of the will to protect some basic values such as those related to preserving family ties and protecting the child's interest. On the other front, the ECJ's case law has highlighted in this field the need to give due consideration to the immigrant's family rights, starting from their status as migrant workers. Despite this mainly economic assessment, the ECJ's case law has proved itself capable of enriching and broadening the basic traits of this protection by expanding, also with the aid of several directives and of the Nice Charter, the scope and action of the guarantees at stake, but without dismantling the original economic background. These trends therefore show a certain convergence between two systems, since the Strasbourg Court's action aimed at limiting the most blatant restrictions of immigrants' family rights has been strengthened and enhanced by the case law of the ECJ, in that it encompassed within the regulatory framework of the EU a broader set of claims and interests that otherwise risked remaining outside the realm of full-blown protection.

From a more theoretical approach, Angelo Schillaci's effort sets out an assessment of the relationships between the ECHR and the EU through the lens of 'cooperation'. It is well known that the absence of an institutional link has from the outset characterized these organizations' mutual influence within a cooperative framework, whose main channel is the judicial action of the ECtHR and of the ECJ. For different but converging reasons, even if not restricted to this, both Courts have relied upon one another's jurisprudence, and in so doing have quite unintentionally framed a constitutional scenario that has been strengthened by the entry into force of the Nice Charter (which referred to the ECHR as a stable means of interpretation of the EU's fundamental rights) and whose main features will probably soon be confirmed by the EU's accession to the ECHR. 'Cooperation', in the author's view, thus provides a fruitful perspective, since it highlights the inability of formal requirements to grasp the various forms of interaction between the ECHR and the EU, while at the same time not neglecting to take into account their mutual contribution to the constitutionalization of the European legal landscape.

The institutional aspects of the future standing of the EU and its Member States before the ECtHR after accession are at the core of the contribution by Simone Vezzani. Starting from a critique of some current assessments as resulting from the ongoing negotiation between the EU and the COE, Vezzani highlights the intricacy of the procedural machinery that will be required when the EU becomes a Member of the ECHR, because of the need to give due weight to the decisions of Brussels' political institutions while at the same time allowing the Member States to defend their own views when they act as *longae manus* for enforcing and applying EU law. Behind the different options concerning the EU's ability to stand before the Strasbourg Court, one may easily discern some basic features of the forthcoming cooperation between the two Courts, mainly because the alternatives at stake not only raise issues of consistency and efficiency, but also influence the capacity of both the EU and its Member States to provide justifications for the infringement of ECHR rights.

In the final chapter, Cesare Pinelli draws the Volume's conclusions, focusing chiefly on some basic tenets of the ECHR's constitutional relevance. In the author's view, the ECHR can contribute towards fruitfully enriching the European constitutional scenario insofar as its role eschews one-sided reconstructions. While old-fashioned state-centered settings are progressively losing any methodological appeal, critical account must be taken of the positions of those scholars who stress the need for national legal systems to be open to ascension to the ECHR, which is deemed to have become a sort of European paramount law in the field of human rights. On the one hand, a *caveat* of this kind is linked to the need not to downgrade allegiance to rules, since they reflect the original commitment of both constitutional courts and the ECHR to their respective political counterparts, i.e. Parliaments and High Contracting Parties. In both cases, this allegiance should not call for a liberation from formalism, but rather for a 'weaker version of formalism', which has a strong underpinning since it results 'from judicial deference towards the popularly elected authorities' will as legally enacted' and has, through sophisticated interpretive tools, influenced both the national and Strasbourg Court (such as tests of proportionality and balancing), albeit in different forms. On the other hand, a similar quest for a more coherent and comprehensive constitutional role played by the ECHR within the European legal landscape requires its action to be grasped within the theoretical framework of 'ordered pluralism', in that the increasing relevance of the ECHR (as well as of the ECtHR's jurisprudence) is not meant to modify the *raison d'être* of constitutional adjudication, but rather to favour forms of interaction that, by renouncing the struggle for supremacy, make a mutual influence between constitutional courts and the ECHR possible. However, according to Pinelli, this overall complex institutional balance should make the Strasbourg Court more sensitive to claims arising from, and deeply rooted in, national legal systems, which the Court has in some occasions overstepped by means of a highly debatable creative interpretation of the ECHR.

PART I

ESTABLISHING A CONSTITUTIONAL DIMENSION FOR THE ECHR IN DOMESTIC LAW

PART I.A

THE RENEWING OF A CONSTITUTIONAL CULTURE: THE ECHR IN ITALIAN DOMESTIC LAW

THE CONSTITUTIONAL BACKGROUND OF THE 2007 REVOLUTION

The Jurisprudence of the Constitutional Court

Diletta TEGA

1. THE VALUE OF THE EUROPEAN CONVENTION ON HUMAN RIGHTS IN THE SYSTEM OF NATIONAL SOURCES: DOCTRINAL RECONSTRUCTIONS

Two of the major issues related to the existence of international treaties on fundamental rights are the application of these treaties to national law and the position that these documents have in the system of sources of law in the member States (with particular regard to the ECHR, this may be seen in some of the member countries as a constitutional source, in others as sub-constitutional, in others as ordinary, and so forth). Nowadays, however, in addition to these two aspects, a third must be considered: namely, the conflict between the formal value of ordinary law accorded in Italy to the international Charters of Rights (at least until 2007 as regards the ECHR) and their 'irresistibly constitutional' content. This assumption is the starting point for analyzing how the Italian Constitutional Court has considered and used these documents, with particular attention to the ECHR.

The Italian legal system shows a clear preference for the instrument of ordinary law to implement the international documents on human rights. The reference to international Charters of Rights in constitutional case law has been, in a sense, a constant, and since as early as 1960 the courts have used it without interruption. The Constitutional Court, at the request of the referring courts, gave attention to the suitability of the Charters of Rights, in particular the ECHR, for 'integrating' the parameter in the judgment of constitutionality. So long as the Constitutional Court considered pre-eminent the fact of choosing ordinary law as the instrument of ratification and implementation of the Charter of Rights, integration was ruled out. In fact, the Italian system has no provision on the domestic value of international treaty law, or an article, such as 10, paragraph 2 of the Spanish Constitution, according to which constitutional freedoms must be interpreted in the light of international rights documents ratified by the State.

In an effort to enhance the 'constitutional' content of the Charters of Rights, in particular of the ECHR, legal scholarship has developed four different theories aimed at according the Charters of Rights a higher value than that of ordinary law,[1] starting from reflection on the value to be assigned to formal sources that implement those documents on the basis of the commitment the Italian system makes at the time of ratification.[2]

(a) Those who maintain the so-called internationalist principle affirm that Article 10, paragraph 1 of the Italian Constitution,[3] in stating that the legal system conforms to the norms of generally recognized international law, influences the hierarchical aspect of the rules for adapting to treaty law. Well-known in this regard is Quadri's position, arguing that this constitutional provision introduces into the Italian legal system a provision of adaptation to the rule *pacta sunt servanda*.[4] Criticism of this minority doctrine is based on the assumption that the production of the rules of international treaty law is due to the execution order, affirming that they have the same position in the system of sources and are placed accordingly, depending on the form the execution order takes.[5]

(b) This contrasts with the position of those who, like Barbera, referring to the so-called 'personalist' principle, recognizes Article 2 of the Constitution[6] as an 'open clause' that prepares constitutional protection for those inviolable

---

[1] See A. Cassese, 'Commento agli artt. 10 e 11, Principi fondamentali', in G. Branca (ed.), *Commentario della Costituzione*, Zanichelli-Foro Italiano, Bologna-Roma 1978, p. 491.

[2] That distinction is typical of all legal systems, like the Italian one, that are based on the dualistic interpretation of the relationship between internal and international orders. See, among others, G. Morelli, *Nozioni di diritto internazionale*, CEDAM, Padova 1967 pp. 89–90; A. D'Atena, 'Adattamento del diritto interno al diritto internazionale', in *Enciclopedia Giuridica*, Ist. Enciclopedia Italiana, vol. I, Roma 1988, p. 1; L. Paladin, *Le fonti del diritto italiano*, Il Mulino, Bologna 1996, pp. 413–419.

[3] Article 10, paragraph 1, states that 'The Italian legal system conforms to the generally recognised principles of international law'.

[4] See the different positions on Article 10, paragraph 1, maintained by R. Quadri, 'Diritto internazionale pubblico', Priulla, Palermo 1949, p. 46; and Id., 'Diritto internazionale pubblico', Liguori, Napoli 1968, p. 68; by P. Barile, 'Rapporti tra norme primarie comunitarie e norme costituzionali e primarie italiane' (1966) *La comunità internazionale* 15–16, who prefers the expression *pacta recepta sunt servanda*; and by A. D'Atena, 'Problemi relativi al controllo di costituzionalità delle norme di adattamento ai trattati internazionali' (1967) *Giurisprudenza costituzionale* 614.

[5] Italian legislation adapted an international convention, by a constitutional law in the case of constitutional law 21 June 1967, no. 1, only with regard to the Convention on the Prevention and Punishment of the Crime of Genocide, Adopted by Resolution 260 (III) A of the UN General Assembly on 9 December 1948.

[6] Article 2 states that 'The Republic recognises and guarantees the inviolable rights of the person, both as an individual and in the social groups where human personality is expressed.

rights not explicitly granted in the Constitution, but that emerge from the evolution of social consciousness and are proclaimed in international documents,[7] with a function subsidiary to the catalogue of the rights specifically mentioned from Article 13 onwards. The Constitutional Court particularly emphasized this interpretation, especially in 1988 and 1992, in recognizing the so-called right to housing and the right to expatriation through the parameter of Article 2 of the Constitution, read alongside the Charters of Rights.[8]

(c)   Those who adhere to the so-called pacifist principle, through the reference to Article 11 of the Constitution, consider the Charters of Rights on a par with the treaties devoted to establishing 'an order that ensures peace and justice among Nations'.[9]

(d)   The reform of Title V of the Constitution in 2001 introduced Article 117, paragraph 1, which provides that 'the legislative power is vested in the State and the Regions in compliance with the constraints deriving from EU and international obligations.' This provision has become, by the Constitutional Court's cases no. 348 and 349 of 2007, the exclusive reference, confirming the thesis according to which the ECHR and the other Charters of Rights, like all treaties whose ratification is authorized by law or which may be implemented by law, may be considered interposed rules in judgments on the constitutionality of laws.[10]

2.   THE JURISPRUDENCE OF THE CONSTITUTIONAL COURT

The reconstructions made above clearly show the doctrinal attempts to address the issue. However, if the impact of the Charter of Rights on the jurisprudence of Constitutional Court[11] is considered, it appears clearly that the traditional settings do not any longer offer a satisfactory solution to the issue.

The Republic expects that the fundamental duties of political, economic and social solidarity be fulfilled'.

[7]   A. BARBERA, 'Commento all'art. 2 Cost.', in G. BRANCA (ed.), *supra* n. 1, p. 59.

[8]   Cases no. 404 of 1988 and no. 278 of 1992.

[9]   See N. CARULLI, *Il diritto di difesa dell'imputato*, Jovene, Napoli 1967, p. 201; P. MORI, 'Convenzione europea dei diritti dell'uomo, Patto delle Nazioni Unite e Costituzione italiana' (1983) *Rivista di diritto internazionale* 306.

[10]   See among others A. D'ATENA, 'La nuova disciplina costituzionale dei rapporti internazionali e con l'Unione Europea' (2002) *Rassegna Parlamentare* 923; G. SERGES, 'Commento all'art. 117, primo comma', in R. BIFULCO, A. CELOTTO and M. OLIVETTI (eds.), *Commentario alla Costituzione*, UTET, Torino 2006, p. 2213.

[11]   The judgments of the Constitutional Court are available at www.cortecostituzionale.it. A few leading cases are translated into English every year.

The very debate about the outcome of the Strasbourg Court's case law in the national legal systems and the bills, presented in all legislatures, aimed at introducing a new source of revision of the criminal process,[12] prove that the focus is now no longer on the same point – the Charters of Rights' place in the system of legal sources – but on the content of these documents and, with regard to the ECHR, its interpretation by the ECtHR. A way that is also worth evaluating, by deviating from the criteria of hierarchy or competency, formulates the relationship between the Charters of Rights and constitutional principles from the point of view of the criterion of content.[13]

An initial element emerging from examination of the case law is that the Constitutional Court has, in almost sixty years of activity, made frequent reference to the ECHR, incorporated by ordinary law no. 848 of 4 August 1955, as well as to the International Covenant on Civil and Political Rights, incorporated by ordinary law no. 881 of 25 October 1977, and on rare occasions to the Universal Declaration of Human Rights (not officially incorporated in the Italian legal system) and, even more rarely, to other Charters of Rights (since 2002, the Court has begun to cite the Charter of Fundamental Rights of the European Union, which at the time was a document of political value, binding only on the Community institutions). ·

To illustrate the different attitudes shown by the Court, I consider it necessary to distinguish four phases in constitutional jurisprudence: in the first, the Court's attention is focused on examining the ECHR and the other Charters of Rights exclusively from the standpoint of the system of sources; in the second and third, the relationship of integration through interpretation of the Constitution and Charter of Rights is instead the predominant point of consideration;[14] however, in the fourth and final phase, which is not the subject of this paper, the Court re-uses reference to the system of sources – that is,

---

12   See the conclusion made by the Constitutional Court in case no. 113 of 2011. See D. TEGA, 'L'ordinamento costituzionale italiano e il "sistema" CEDU: accordi e disaccordi' and M. CAIANIELLO, 'Profili critici e ipotesi di sviluppo nell'adeguamento del sistema interno alle sentenze della Corte europea dei diritti dell'uomo', both published in V. MANES and V. ZAGREBELSKY (eds.), La Convenzione europea dei diritti dell'uomo nell'ordinamento penale italiano, Giuffrè, Milano 2011, pp. 193–239 and pp. 547–572.

13   The reference is to the ample analysis made by A. RUGGERI, 'Carte internazionali dei diritti, Costituzione europea, Costituzione nazionale: prospettive di ricomposizione delle fonti in sistema' (2008) Forum dei Quaderni Costituzionali (www.forumcostituzionale.it); A. RUGGERI, 'Sovranità dello Stato e sovranità sovranazionale, attraverso i diritti umani, e prospettive di un diritto europeo "intercostituzionale"' (2001) Diritto pubblico comparato ed europeo 544; A. RUGGERI, Fonti, norme, criteri ordinatori. Lezioni, Giappichelli, Torino 2001, pp. 146 ff.; A. RUGGERI, '"Nuovi diritti" fondamentali e tecniche di positivizzazione' (1983) Politica del diritto 183, 194.

14   For a more articulate examination, D. TEGA, 'Le Carte dei diritti nella giurisprudenza della Corte costituzionale (e oltre)', in A. PACE (ed.), Corte costituzionale e processo costituzionale. Nell'esperienza della Rivista "Giurisprudenza costituzionale" per il cinquantesimo anniversario, Giuffrè, Milano 2006, pp. 953–986.

Article 117, paragraph 1 – to undertake a more explicit and extended reflection on the ECHR as a sub-constitutional source.[15]

2.1. THE FIRST PHASE: A TRADITIONAL DUALISM

In this initial phase, which refers to the judgments between 1960 and 1993, the Court developed an interpretation of Article 10, paragraph 1, of the Constitution, which was to remain valid until 2007: a) the customary rules of international law do not cover the international agreements made by the State through international treaties, as shown by constitutional provisions and the preparatory works; b) effect within the legal system is given to international treaties solely by acts of law that make them enforceable in the national legal system; c) any conflict between these rules falls outside the judgment of constitutionality, resulting in a conflict between ordinary laws.

With case no. 104 of 1969, concerning freedom of residence, the Court dealt with the obligation to report the arrival, departure and destination of foreign citizens or stateless persons by those giving them accommodation for any reason, or work. The Constitutional Court showed some hesitation: on the one hand the judges denied constitutional value for the ECHR, according to the reading already seen of Article 10, paragraph 1; on the other hand, the Court claimed that the limitations imposed by Article 8(2) ECHR showed 'against correlative provisions of the Constitution some shades of better clarification of the right to privacy,' concluding that it is the basic difference between citizen and foreigner, consisting of the former's original and permanent relationship with the State, as opposed to the latter's acquired and generally temporary relationship, that prevents even a possible recognition of the ECHR's special force of resistance in the Italian system.

In these decisions, the position in the system of the ECHR is intertwined with the history and the scandals that the country faces: case no. 188 of 1980 in which the Constitutional Court, speaking once again about the boundaries and content of the so called right of self-defence,[16] affirms that both the ECHR and the International Covenant on Civil and Political Rights relied on by the applicants as a parameter, along with Article 24 of the Constitution, of the constitutionality of Articles 125 and 128 of the Code of Civil Procedure (insofar as they require the appointment of a public defender's office also for the accused who refuses any assistance), in the absence of a specific constitutional provision, have only the value of ordinary law. In particular, for the judges, international

---

[15]   See the essay by G. Repetto, in this *Volume*, and D. Tega, *I diritti in crisi tra Corti nazionali e Corte europea di Strasburgo*, Giuffrè, Milano 2012.

[16]   With regard the violent decision of not using public defence made by the *brigatisti* (members of the Red Brigades), which led to the 28 April 1977 murder of Fulvio Croce, President of the Turin order of lawyers.

treaty rules are excluded not only from the scope of Article 10, paragraph 1, but also from Article 11 of the Constitution, as these international rules do not provide for any limitation of national sovereignty.

In the same decision, the judges demonstrated great knowledge of the Strasbourg jurisprudence since they included, for the first time, two decisions of the then Commission, in order not only to highlight the erroneous interpretation made by lower courts of Article 6(3)(c) of the ECHR, but also to demonstrate, perhaps with some ambiguity, that article 24 of the Constitution is otherwise consistent with this interpretation.

In case no. 17 of 1981 on holding open-door trials for minors, the Court used Article 6(1) ECHR and Article 14(4) of the Covenant on Civil and Political Rights in support of the reasoning followed in considering the proposed question of constitutionality unfounded. In this case, the reference to Charters of Rights is made with a view merely to confirm reasoning based on the constitutional parameter – after having stated from a formal standpoint that the ECHR, implemented by means of an ordinary law, cannot be used to argue that the balance between the need to have an open-door process and the need for the protection of youth is constitutionally reserved for the judge, so as to totally exclude any legislative discretion.

The following year the Court, in case no. 15 of 1982, ruling on the reasonableness of the length of preventive detention between the filing of the order for committal for trial and the judgment of first instance, states that it is impossible to connect the principle of reasonableness to Article 5.3 ECHR due to the fact that 'the said provision of the Convention [...] is not at the same level as the constitution [...]'.[17] But the Court in this case also highlights the lack of sufficient specification of the wording of the ECHR, concluding that '[...] an assessment of reasonableness that is not connected with a specific criterion, but only to a vague and elastic statement, can become questionable in the absence of a more detailed analysis.'

In case no. 10 of 1993, the Constitutional Court uses a reference both to the ECHR and the International Covenant on Civil and Political Rights to interpret article 143 of the Code of Criminal Procedure in order to ensure the accused foreigner's right to hear the pleadings in his own language. In doing this, the Constitutional Court, in an *obiter dictum*, stated that article 143 Code of Criminal Procedure, which contains a standard apparently stricter than international ones, far from repealing them on the basis of the *lex posterior* criterion, provides in practice the same assurance of the effectiveness and applicability because '[...] these are provisions arising from a source with atypical competence, and, as such, they are insusceptible to being repealed or

---

[17]   Along the same line, cases nos. 153 of 1987 and 323 of 1989, commented upon by A. D'ATENA, 'Gerarchia delle fonti e adattamento ai trattati internazionali' (1989) *Giurisprudenza costituzionale* 1482, and case no. 73 of 2001.

modified by ordinary laws.' The judges concluded by according particular expansive force to Article 143 C.C.P. arising from the relationship with the principles contained in the Charter of Rights and fed by the necessary link with the constitutional values relating to the rights of defence, pursuant to Article 24 of the Constitution, considered as fundamental principles in accordance with Article 2 of the Constitution. Therefore, in this case, the Constitutional Court grants, on the one hand, a passive resistance to the repeal arising from a source coming from atypical competence and, on the other hand, recognizes in the principles of international treaty law a unique integration within the constitutional parameter.

The *obiter dictum* is highly innovative with respect to the established orientation which, as we have seen, has always denied both to the ECHR and to the International Covenant a place in the hierarchy of sources that was not that of ordinary law. The Court would have had to devote to this approach – innovative and a break with the past – a place and a boundary that was less apodictic, as such an *obiter* is obscure and thus ambiguous.

Conversely, the Court, in subsequent rulings, although touching on the theme of the Charters of Rights, neither took on this statement any further, nor developed it in an articulate way. This clearly shows that the *obiter dictum* cannot be considered as an overruling of the previous case law. Rather, the position contained in case no. 10 of 1993 could be interpreted as an attempt to draw a distinction between international treaty law *tout court* and international documents on human rights. If it is true that the atypical character mentioned by the judges can be traced back not to the formal terms, but to the material ones, it may be concluded that the Court felt the need to enhance precisely the matter of rights as an element capable of influencing the passive force of the national law incorporating the treaties.[18]

2.2. THE SECOND PHASE: A MORE 'MODERN' DUALISM

What I consider the second phase, which does not directly involve the ECHR but whose conclusions are reflected upon the Convention above all, may be identified starting from judgment no. 404 of 1988 on the so-called right to housing. On this occasion, in fact, the Court, in recognizing that the failure to provide for succession in leaseholding by a cohabiting partner conflicts with the values proclaimed in the Constitution and, in particular, with a 'social right to housing that can be placed among the fundamental human rights in Article 2 of the

---

[18]   E. LUPO, 'Il diritto dell'imputato straniero all'assistenza dell'interprete tra codice e convenzioni internazionali' (1993) *Giurisprudenza costituzionale* 66; E. CANNIZZARO, 'Gerarchia e competenza nei rapporti tra trattati e leggi interne' (1993) *Rivista diritto internazionale* 351.

Constitution,' adopted a new use of the Charters of Rights. What it meant is that the same rulings made by the Court earlier in cases involving access by people's savings to home ownership (cases nos. 252 of 1983, 49 of 1987 and 217 of 1988) 'have a more general scope connected with the fundamental human right to housing established by Article 25 of the Universal Declaration of Human Rights and Article 11 of the International Covenant on Economic, Social and Cultural Rights [...]'.

The use is new in comparison with the attitude shown by the first block of decisions that were seen, because in this case, while not serving as a basis for comparison, the formal aspect of the placement within the system of sources is left aside. Rather, it cites the UN Declaration, never formally implemented in Italy, and the Charters of Rights are used as a tool to recognize the existence of such a social right. But there is more: as just pointed out, the Court previously recognized that a State cannot abdicate its responsibility to contribute and ensure for the greatest number of citizens the right to housing pursuant to Article 47, paragraph 2, of the Constitution, but in its case no. 404 grounds the assertion of the inviolability of the right to housing, on the one hand, upon the provisions of Article 2 of the Constitution, as interpreted by the reading of the standard agreement understood as an 'open clause',[19] and on the other hand, precisely upon the Charter of Rights which, in earlier decisions on the same subject, were not used.

This trend is also confirmed in case no. 125 of 1992, in which it is stated that the recovery of deviant minors, descending from the principles laid down by the Constitution, is to be considered as also imposed by the International Covenant on Civil and Political Rights. However, it is in proclaiming the so-called right of expatriation, in case no. 278 of 1992, that the Court appears to render explicit the tendency to convey through the 'open reading' of Article 2 of the Constitution, the real value of the Universal Declaration of Human Rights: '[...] Article 13 of the Universal Declaration of Human Rights of 1948 has laid down for each individual the right to leave any country, including his own, as well as to return. Whatever the value accorded to the international Declaration, there is no doubt that the fundamental human rights provided by Article 2 of the Constitution of the Republic also include the right to leave one's own country. So legislation that would impede the exercise of this fundamental right would be inconsistent with the current context of international and constitutional values'.

More recently, the Constitutional Court, in its case no. 494 of 2002, in according the children born of incestuous relationships the right to their biological identity, reconstructed precisely this case law as 'a constitutive element of personal identity, protected not only by the Articles 7 and 8 of the Convention on the Rights of the Child but also by Article 2 of the Constitution'.

---

[19] A. BARBERA, *supra* n. 7, p. 107; *contra* A. PACE, 'Problematica delle libertà costituzionali, Parte generale', CEDAM, Padova 1983, pp. 3–41.

To conclude, in this phase the Constitutional Court no longer feels the need to point out the position of the Charters of Rights in the system of sources, perhaps because the version adopted since 1960 is well-established, perhaps because the way the reference to these Charters is used appears to be (in contrast to the past) instrumental to the recognition of subjective situations worthy of protection. The provisions of Article 2 of the Italian Constitution, in its interpretation as open clause,[20] offers a natural enlargement of the parameter, as demonstrated by the Court's decisions. Moreover, president Saja's press conference on the Court's activity in 1987 officially consecrated the reading of Article 2 as an 'open list', so that constitutional jurisprudence, through the means of interpreting historical evolution, can identify any additional subjective inviolable positions. The natural step made one year later by the Constitutional Court was to include, amongst the tools of interpretation, the Charters of Rights.

2.3. THE THIRD PHASE: A DUALITY 'IN TRANSFORMATION'

The third phase, at least for a large portion of legal scholarship, consists of a broader openness to the Charters of Rights. Case law provides a number of insights on the interpretation of the constitutional principle in light of the ECHR, highlighting the difficulty of determining a single attitude on the part of the Court towards using the Charters from the standpoint of interpretation. In case no. 324 of 1998, the judges, in holding that the detention in judicial hospitalization of mentally ill minors is unconstitutional, used the reference to international standards (in particular the Convention on the Rights of the Child of 1989) as a simple way to strengthen the principles established in the Constitution.

In case no. 349 of 1998, on the other hand, the Constitutional Court, in admonishing the regulation of the minimum age gap that must exist between adoptive spouses and adopted minors, insofar as it does not provide that the court may order the adoption in the exclusive interest of the child when the age of one of the adoptive spouses does not exceed the minimum gap of eighteen years, used not only a reference to its case law (see cases nos. 183 of 1988, 44 of 1990, 148 of 1992, 303 of 1996), oriented towards overcoming the absolute rigidity of the requirements related to the age difference between adopters and

---

[20] By the expression 'open clause', the Italian scholarship means that Article 2 is intended to ensure a constitutional status also for those rights not explicitly enumerated in the Constitution but recognized by courts. For an initial analysis of the Constitutional Court's case law regarding Article 2 and the rights established at international level see A. LA PERGOLA, 'L'adeguamento dell'ordinamento interno alle norme del diritto internazionale dei diritti umani', in *I diritti umani a 40 anni dalla Dichiarazione universale*, CEDAM, Padova 1989, pp. 46–51.

adoptees, but also the principles underlying both the Constitution and the Charters of Rights that guarantee the rights of children or establish their protection in the event of adoption. This last statement takes on quite a significant weight when one considers that the unconstitutionality of the provision was then declared without indicating the breach of any constitutional parameters.

In its case no. 399 of 1998, the Court considered unfounded the question of constitutionality raised with regard to regulating notification to the accused in the event of unavailability, as provided by the Code of Criminal Procedure. The case is interesting because it highlights, albeit within a new trend, the lack of homogeneity in evaluations in the Court's opinions of the rules under the Charters of Rights: in other words the ECHR (as well as a judgment of 12 February 1985 by the Strasbourg Court), relied upon by the national court on the basis of integrating the parameter, is brought, by the Court's reasoning, entirely within the provisions of Article 24 of the Constitution. One need only consider point 6 of the decision: 'The innovations introduced by the new code denote that the legislature has sought to adapt the legislation concerning unavailable accused parties to international conventions and to Article 24 of the Constitution, which, in proclaiming the defence inviolable at every stage and level of the proceedings, assure a kind of protection which certainly includes the right, explicitly stated by the European Convention, to take notice of the proceedings concerned, and to have the opportunity and the time to prepare one's defence'.

In this regard, taking a step back, it should however be noted that the Court, some years earlier, in case no. 62 of 1992 on the protection of linguistic minorities and the use of their language in civilian pleadings, had explicitly stated that, due to the fact that the International Covenant on Civil and Political Rights of 1966 recognized the guarantee of the right to use the mother tongue as an essential part of the protection of ethnic minorities, even if not ratified by enough states to make it operative as a multilateral treaty, '[...] the Covenant must at least be accorded the value of criterion of interpretation of the existing provisions in international law and of the national rules of the UN member states, as it establishes objectives considered by the states to be worth pursuing and fulfilling'.

This tendency to use the Charter of Rights as rules of interpretation of constitutional principles, invoked from time to time, was also confirmed in 1994 by case no. 168 in which the court, affirming the constitutionality of the Criminal Code, insofar as it does not exclude the applicability of imprisonment for the child, in light of the wording of Article 27, paragraph 3, and 31 of the Constitution, states it is '[...] appropriate, in order to clarify the meaning of the other constitutional parameters, to analyze and verify our legislation's compliance with international-level commitments.' The Court reviewed the wording of the ECHR, the Declaration of the Rights of the Child of the League of

Nations of 1924, the Universal Declaration of Human Rights of 1948, the Declaration of the Rights of the Child of 1959, the Standard Minimum Rules for the Administration of Juvenile Justice 1985 (the so-called Beijing Rules) and the New York Convention on the Rights of the Child of 1989, which evince, alongside the more general protection of the child, a more specific inapplicability of the death penalty for crimes committed by minors as well as the prohibition of life imprisonment. The Court concluded by stating that such statements are entrusted to the legislative implementation of the member states, and that in the Italian system the main point of contact is Article 31 of the Constitution.

Its case no. 388 of 1999, again on trial guarantees (the object of the judgment was in fact Article 696 Code of Civil Procedure, in the part that does not allow full valuation of the damage during preventive technical assessment or judicial inspection, in contrast with Articles 24 and 11 of the Constitution, with regard to Article 6(1) of the Convention), repeated, albeit in different words, a position that appears to have become definitively established: standards conventions, beyond the value to be attributed, are not on a par with the Constitution; however, human rights, 'also guaranteed by universal or regional agreements signed by Italy, find expression, and no less intense guarantee, in the Constitution [...] not only for the value to be attributed to the general acknowledgment of the inviolable rights of man made by art. 2 of the Constitution, increasingly felt by the contemporary consciousness as co-essential to the dignity of the person [...], but also because, beyond coinciding with catalogues of these rights, the different formulas that express them integrate each other, complementing one other in their interpretation'.[21] Here, then, the Court reiterated what in this period was its main focus: the relationship of integration, through interpretation, between the Constitution and Charters of Rights, beyond the fact that the latter, not being a constitutional source, cannot, taken alone, be a parameter of constitutionality.[22] The solution adopted in its case no. 388 – in many ways brilliant, yet inconclusive – appears to reflect the goals upon which the Court has run around.

The Court shows it is uninterested in looking at the past, retreating to that purely formalistic attitude established in 1960 and never denied; it shows it does not deem it necessary to bring the *obiter dictum* stated in case no. 10 of 1993 to clearer and more mature consequences; it decides, without providing either theoretical or practical justification, to place itself on a different level of reasoning, and harking back to the attitude emerging from case no. 404 of 1988,

---

[21]   C. PINELLI, 'La durata ragionevole del processo fra Costituzione e Convenzione europea dei diritti dell'uomo' (1999) *Giurisprudenza costituzionale* 2997; L. MONTANARI, 'Dalla Corte una conferma sul rango primario della Convenzione europea dei diritti dell'uomo: ma forse con un'inedita apertura' (1999) *Giurisprudenza costituzionale* 3001.

[22]   A. CORASANITI, 'Protezione costituzionale e protezione internazionale dei diritti dell'uomo' (1993) *Diritto e società* 607; M. LUCIANI, 'La hiérarchie des normes constitutionnelles et sa fonction dans la protection des droits fondamentaux' (1990) VI *Annuaire international de justice constitutionnelle* 175–176.

to advocate an interpretation of rights 'enriched' by reference to the Charters of Rights which, in this way, rise to recognition of the emerging trends in the field of the so-called new rights.

Indicative of the emerging evolution is, among others,[23] case no. 413 of 2004 in which the court, referring to the ECHR and the International Covenant on Civil and Political Rights, states that 'the interpretation in conformity with the Constitution is supported by significant regulatory instructions, including those with supranational origins'.

A similar approach is adopted in case no. 154 of 2004, where the judges declared eligible for intervention third parties claiming to have been defamed, as denial of their participation would contradict 'the constitutional guarantee of the right to justice and full adversarial hearing, established by Articles 24 and 111 of the Constitution, and also protected by Article 6 of the Convention for the Protection of Human Rights and Fundamental Freedoms, as applied by the Strasbourg Court (see most recently the judgment of 30 January 2003, *Cordova v. Italy No. 1 and No. 2*).' It is interesting to note that in this case, the Constitutional Court refers to the ECHR as it is understood by the case law of the Strasbourg Court – namely, an understanding of the law in a dynamic and evolutionary way, like a living instrument to be interpreted in light of the conditions of modern life.[24] A statement of this kind, which extends the reference to Strasbourg's jurisprudence as well, is symptomatic of an approach shown to have totally overcome an interest in the systematics of the sources of law and, at the same time, an approach, as stated at the outset, that considers the ECHR and the other Charters of Rights as important criteria for interpretation in the activity of cobbling together different models of safeguards characterizing the Italian system of protection of rights.

---

[23]   Cases nos. 235 of 1993, 28 and 108 of 1995, 109 of 1997, and 231 of 2004.
[24]   Cases nos. 299 of 2005 and 61 of 2006.

RETHINKING A CONSTITUTIONAL ROLE FOR THE ECHR

The Dilemmas of Incorporation into Italian Domestic Law

Giorgio Repetto

1. THE NEW RANKING OF THE ECHR AND THE SHIFT TO 'CONSTITUTIONAL DUALISM'

The recent transformations concerning the impact of the ECHR in the Italian legal system can be best understood if closely linked to some basic features of the internal constitutional background, far beyond its dualistic approach *vis-à-vis* international law. Along with the increasing role played by the ECHR and its judicial machinery, these transformations show that European human-rights law calls today for a wider consideration of the mutual influence between systems of protection of fundamental rights, which are difficult to grasp with general, universally valid theories, and seem rather to be driven by 'porous' forms of interaction.[1]

Although dualism has traditionally played a significant role in shaping the relationships of internal law with international law, and with the ECHR in particular, it must be stressed that in the last twenty years Italian judges and scholars have progressively challenged the *Grundnorm* of this approach, i.e. the opinion according to which the rank of international treaties (like the ECHR) is that of the statutory law that ratified them. Or better still, the increasing relevance of the ECHR has fostered a judicial and scientific trend, aimed at rethinking its role beginning from the substantial intertwinement between guarantees under the constitution and those under the ECHR.

Until the 90s, with rare exceptions, the dualistic tenets have been substantially unchallenged, also because the prevailing opinion was that the constitutional catalogue of fundamental rights had to be considered *in general*

---

[1] H. Keller and A. Stone Sweet, 'Assessing the Impact of the ECHR on National Legal Systems' in IID. (eds.), *A Europe of Rights. The Impact of the ECHR on National Legal Systems*, Oxford University Press, Oxford 2008, 677.

far more progressive and complete than the ECHR. For most civil rights such as those enshrined in Articles 8–11 of the Convention, the Constitution provided narrower limits to their enjoyment and therefore a more intensive protection, whereas in other areas, like property, the greater breadth of the limits established by the Constitution to the enjoyment of the right in comparison with the ECHR was justified by the protection of some basic constitutional values, such as the 'social function' of rights or 'dignity'. Only the right to a fair criminal proceeding, enshrined in Article 6 of the ECHR, was deemed to ensure a higher protection than that afforded by constitutional norms (Article 25 of the Constitution).[2]

Even if within such a narrow framework, the Court of Cassation during and after the 90s began to sketch out a new role for the ECHR: on several occasions, it disregarded internal statutory law in order to apply for the most part some procedural guarantees enshrined in Article 6 of the ECHR,[3] by invoking their para-constitutional status and grounding their effect, according to the different circumstances, on Articles 2, 10 or 11 of the Constitution.[4] On the contrary, the Constitutional Court has always been much more reluctant to accord to the ECHR a similar primacy over statutes. It has indeed steadily reasserted the merely legislative status of the ECHR, even by confirming that conventional guarantees are not equated in principle with international customary law, and the only exception to this trend, as in case no. 10 of 1993, remained quite isolated. On that occasion, the Constitutional Court argued that the statute ratifying the Convention (Law 4.8.1955, no. 848) had to be assigned special force, in that it could not be derogated by a statute passed later in time. In a likewise minoritarian trend, aimed at partially undermining the centrality of formal aspects, the Constitutional Court stressed that the final outcomes of the judicial enforcement of fundamental rights at the national level, even when they stem from international law, have to be grasped through a fully-fledged interpretation (cases nos. 388 of 1999, 376 of 2000 and 445 of 2002). The basic assumption of this case law was therefore that the formal status of the ECHR was that of

---

2   A. Pace, 'La limitata incidenza della C.e.d.u. sulle libertà politiche e civili in Italia' (2001) 7 *Diritto pubblico* 1, 10–16.

3   The leading case is to be considered Court of Cassation, case no. 2194 of 1993 but see also, among others, cases no. 6672 of 1998 and no. 28507 of 2005. For a general overview and further references on this trend see E. Cannizzaro, 'The Effect of the ECHR on the Italian Legal Order: Direct Effect and Supremacy' (2009) XIX *Italian Yearbook of International Law* 173, 175–177.

4   Article 2 states that 'The Republic recognises and guarantees the inviolable rights of the person, both as an individual and in the social groups where human personality is expressed. The Republic expects that the fundamental duties of political, economic and social solidarity be fulfilled'; Article 10 that 'The Italian legal system conforms to the generally recognised principles of international law' and Article 11 that 'Italy agrees, on conditions of equality with other States, to the limitations of sovereignty that may be necessary to a world order ensuring peace and justice among the Nations. Italy promotes and encourages international organisations furthering such ends' (official translation).

statutory law and its only effect could be, if at all, to further an interpretation of the internal law consistent with the principles set out in the Convention and in the case law of the European Court of Human Rights.

This assumption remained valid even after the entry into force in 2001 of the new Article 117, para. 1 of the Constitution, according to which '[l]egislative powers shall be vested in the State and the Regions in compliance with the Constitution and with the constraints deriving from EU legislation and international obligations.'

After a long debate, the Constitutional Court departed from its assumptions only in 2007, with the so-called 'twin cases' no. 348 and no. 349, by acknowledging for the first time that, pursuant to the new Article 117, the ECHR should no longer be ranked at the level of statutory law, nor at the level of the Constitution (like EU law), but rather at an intermediate ranking between them (in accordance with the model of the so-called 'interposed rules'). This means that if a statute infringes the ECHR or a decision of the Court of Strasbourg, it must be quashed through a decision of annulment by the same Constitutional Court, without the ordinary judges being enabled to ensure the primacy of the Convention over statutory law by disregarding it. At the same time, the ECHR as well as the rulings of the ECtHR must respect the Constitution.[5]

What should be highlighted are the implications of this judicial arrangement and, moreover, the transformations that the following judgments have introduced, more or less 'covertly,' in order to provide for an interaction between national and conventional rights and liberties going beyond this formal assessment.

In the judgments of 2007, the attribution to the ECHR of a *supra*-legislative status should not in any case be associated with a complete overcoming of dualism, since some methodological features of this approach remain substantially undisputed, for the following reasons: (a) due to its sub-constitutional status, the primacy of the ECHR over statutory law is not guaranteed as such, but only thanks to the formal shield of Article 117, para. 1 of the Constitution; (b) as a consequence of this, the incorporation of the ECHR is not limitless, for it must be arrested whenever it collides with a constitutional norm, be it a right or basic principle, or a 'simple' operative norm; (c) like the rights and liberties of the ECHR, the decisions of the ECtHR must also be considered as 'external facts' that must be taken into account as such, and not

---

5   The basic elements of this 'judicial revolution' have been carefully reported in several comments, also accessible to non-Italian speakers, and therefore it is not necessary to take them into account in detail: for further insights see, among others, O. POLLICINO, 'Constitutional Court at the crossroads between parochialism and co-operative constitutionalism' (2008) 4 *European Constitutional Law Review* 363 and F. BIONDI DAL MONTE and F. FONTANELLI, 'The Decisions No. 348 and 349 of 2007 of the Italian Constitutional Court: The Efficacy of the European Convention in the Italian Legal System' (2008) 9 *German Law Journal* 889, as well as the contribution of D. TEGA in this *Volume*.

Giorgio Repetto

adapted or interpreted in light of internal law; and (d) in any case, only the Constitutional Court, through its formal scrutiny over legislation, is entitled to quash statutory law conflicting with the ECHR or with ECtHR case law.

For all these reasons, the Constitutional Court has proposed a sort of 'constitutional dualism', in that the separation between systems of protection is no longer outlined across the legal orders considered as a whole (which are currently far more connected than in the past, by virtue of the increased legal status of the ECHR), but rather across the different formal sphere of action of the two catalogues of rights (under the Constitution and the ECHR), as interpreted by the two supreme Courts (Constitutional Court and ECtHR), each within its own constitutional domain. The '2007 turn' therefore paved the way for opening up the internal legal system, since statutory law is now forced to give way to the ECHR in case of a conflict, but, at the same time, it has correspondingly strengthened the impermeability of the Constitution – and of the fundamental rights enshrined therein – vis-à-vis the Convention.[6]

The persistence of such constitutional dualism can be explained with some basic assumptions made in the 'twin cases', as well as by bearing in mind their ultimate institutional consequence. As regards the first aspect, crucial is the emphasis placed by the Constitutional Court on the fact that the incorporation of the ECHR does not exclude the scrutiny of the potential violation of a constitutional norm caused by the Convention, 'in order to avoid falling into the paradox of a legislative provision being declared unconstitutional on the basis of another interposed provision, which in turn breaches the Constitution'.[7] The ECHR is therefore an international treaty which remains external to domestic legal order, but unlike EU law it must abide by every single constitutional norm in the same way every other statute does. If not, 'this court has a duty to declare the inability of the Constitution to supplement that principle, providing, according to established procedures, for its removal from the Italian legal order'.[8]

For this reason, the Constitution is depicted like a sort of 'stronghold under siege', whose rights and principles cannot in any case be modified, even when the level of protection of a given constitutional right is elevated by the ECHR.[9] Consequently, the two catalogues concur in identifying the higher level of protection, but each for its own sphere of influence: they should not influence each other, since this would mean, on the one hand, altering the external nature of the ECHR and, on the other hand, imperilling the unity of the Constitution

---

6   For further critical elements on this approach see my own work, G. REPETTO, 'Diritti fondamentali e sovranità nello stato costituzionale chiuso' (2008) *Giurisprudenza italiana*, 309, 313–314.
7   Case no. 348 of 2007, para 4.7 (hereinafter, cases will be cited according to their official translation).
8   Case no. 348 of 2007, para 4.7.
9   This assumption was already made by A. PACE, 'Metodi interpretativi e costituzionalismo' (2001) *Quaderni costituzionali* 35, 48 in relation to Article 6 of the ECHR.

(as would happen if the meaning and the scope of a constitutional rule changed as a consequence of the incorporation of the ECHR). This approach implies moreover that the judgment over the level of protection of a given right is the result of an asymmetric balancing, because the ECHR, due to its external nature, is not *per se* a term of balancing: according to the Court, its control over the compliance with the Constitution 'must always aim to establish a reasonable balance between the duties flowing from international law obligations, as imposed by Article 117 para. 1 of the Constitution, and the safeguarding of the constitutionally protected interests contained in other articles of the Constitution.'[10]

With reference to the institutional outlook of the 'twin cases', the strong commitment to a formal point of view and the connected 'constitutional dualism' can be fully grasped if we consider that the complex machinery established by the Constitutional Court has the function of reserving to itself the monopoly over the solution of conflicts between the ECHR and domestic law. If the European Convention had been accorded a constitutional status like that of EU law, the ordinary judges would not have been deprived of the capacity to apply it directly, which would have called into question the Court's centrality in the process of constitutional adjudication.

2. THE CONSTITUTIONAL BACKGROUND OF THE 2007 REVOLUTION

To put it succinctly, the new ranking accorded to the ECHR in 2007 thus originated from the effort made by the Constitutional Court to take the new Article 117 of the Constitution seriously, while seeking to prevent the new doctrines from being able to modify the traditional structure of constitutional adjudication. The underlying strategy aims at strengthening a complex and multi-faceted balance of powers, which affects the relationships of the Constitutional Court with ordinary judges as well as its role within the constitutional system *vis-à-vis* political actors and, at a still deeper level, the outlook and the sustainability of a judge-made constitutional law in the field of fundamental rights.

2.1. 'ABSTRACTNESS' AND 'EMBEDDEDNESS' IN CONSTITUTIONAL ADJUDICATION

Behind the arrangement set out in the 'twin cases', as formalistic as it may appear at first sight, it is necessary to identify the flow of contrasting options

---

[10]   Case no. 348 of 2007, para 4.7.

about some major issues of constitutional law and theory: is the Constitutional Court a judicial or a *sui generis* body? Does it provide individual or constitutional justice? How far can it substitute its decisions for those of political actors? And those of ordinary judges?

First of all, the solutions concerning the incorporation of the ECHR require considering the hallmarks of the role and of the tasks of the Constitutional Court, which may be summarized with the essential tension between the *abstract* nature of its control over legislation, on the one hand, and the *embeddedness* of its action in legal dynamics, on the other. Apart from its functions of dispute resolution between State and Regions and in the absence of a procedure of direct complaint, the Italian *Corte costituzionale* is normally called upon to control the legitimacy of a statute as referred to by an ordinary judge through a preliminary ruling. While the latter is entitled to raise doubts about the constitutionality of a statutory rule that he or she must apply in order to settle a dispute pending before him or her, the former is bound to verify the *abstract* compliance of that rule with the Constitution, i.e. it must not take expressly into account the facts of the case. Technically the Court is only a judge of the law.[11] In this sense, the basic model of Italian constitutional justice has been set out as if it aimed directly at providing an objective safeguard of the Constitution and, only as an indirect outcome, a subjective protection of individual rights and liberties.[12]

Nonetheless, the abstractness of the review should not be stressed so much as to forget that, in reality, a casuistic trend has progressively penetrated the Court's reasoning from the outset, since the outlines of the review are inevitably also shaped by the facts of the case. The Kelsenian model of an abstract subsuming of the lower norm into the higher one proved itself from the outset inadequate, essentially because in the end the decision must be applied in the case and, due to its *erga omnes* effect, in all similar cases. For this reason, the grounds of illegitimacy are inevitably linked with a wider range of issues, primarily those stemming from the facts of the case and, secondarily, those concerning the coherence of the decision within the framework of legal system, with reference to all similar cases in which it must be applied. More precisely, the quite peculiar casuistry of Italian constitutional adjudication (not unlike other systems) is

---

[11]   P. PASQUINO and J. FEREJOHN, 'Constitutional Adjudication: Lessons from Europe' (2004) 82 *Texas Law Review* 1671, 1689.

[12]   The most prominent supporter of this thesis in Italian constitutional law scholarship is F. MODUGNO, *Riflessioni interlocutorie sull'autonomia del giudizio costituzionale*, Morano, Napoli 1966. The abstractness of the control is, among others, drawn by the internal rule of the Constitutional Court according to which the interruption of the main proceeding does not inhibit the prosecution of constitutional review (Article 18 of the *Norme integrative per i giudizi davanti alla Corte costituzionale*). The weakness of this model *vis-à-vis* European legal integration has been recently highlighted by F. RUBIO LLORENTE, 'Divide et obtempera? Una reflexión desde España sobre el modelo europeo de convergencia de jurisdicciones en la protección de los Derechos' (2003) 23 *Revista Española de Derecho Constitucional* 49, 54.

characterized by the guiding relevance of such a way of conceiving facts and interests, which play a significant role in constitutional litigation depending on their qualification by the legal system's different branches. In other words, concrete issues and claims, like those arising from the violation of a fundamental right, do not stand before the Constitutional Court as such, but rather as interests qualified in a certain way by the overall legal system. In order to assess whether a statutory rule conferring rights or duties has infringed a constitutional right, it must for example be ascertained which is the prevailing interpretation of that rule by the judges and the underlying assessment of the facts at stake (the so-called *diritto vivente*, i.e. 'living law'), if and to what extent it is consistent with the Constitution, or what the Parliament has decided in similar cases, and so on.[13]

All these elements contribute to extending the meaning and scope of the Constitution, whose content is derived not only from textual, historical and consequentialist reasoning, but also from the systemic encroachment of these means of interpretation upon the most relevant decisions of the ordinary judges and upon the basic parliamentary choices. In this circuit, the supremacy of the Constitution is obviously also preserved *against* Parliament and the judiciary, but only in exceptional cases, since in ordinary life their decisions are supposed to enact the Constitution. They both are deemed to be, each within its own agency, constitution-makers for everyday life. The Constitutional Court consequently takes their decisions into account and comes properly into play, with a ruling of annulment, whenever this everyday life is interrupted by a proper constitutional violation, because they have simply trespassed on the borders of what must be considered, in the last resort, a breach of the Constitution.[14]

In this way, a two-fold separation of powers in the field of constitutional interpretation is reinforced. The Constitutional Court does not claim to exhaust the power to interpret the Constitution, both by leaving the Parliament the power to enact constitutional provisions in all those matters that involve a political discretion, and by ensuring for the judiciary that its prerogatives as to the resolution of controversies are intact even in those cases that require a direct application of the Constitution. In setting these boundaries, the Constitutional Court fosters a quite sensitive institutional balance, for it checks constitutional infringements while safeguarding the contribution given by political and judicial actors to encompassing the meaning of the Constitution within political and judicial practice.

---

[13]   For general remarks on this point see L. PALADIN, *Diritto costituzionale*, CEDAM, Padova 1996, pp. 156 and 239–241.

[14]   A similar reading has been proposed, albeit on a more general level, by R. BIN, *Diritti e argomenti. Il bilanciamento degli interessi nella giurisprudenza costituzionale*, Giuffrè, Milano 1992, pp. 154–169.

2.2. THE MODEL OF THE ECHR AS 'INTERPOSED RULE' AND ITS INSTITUTIONAL UNDERPINNINGS

It should now be clear that the solution forged in 2007 as to the internal treatment of the ECHR is largely drawn from this background. The ranking of the ECHR as an 'interposed rule', placed at an ideal median between the statutory law and the Constitution, is among other things aimed at striking a balance between the openness of the domestic catalogue of fundamental rights and its encompassment within the boundaries of constitutional adjudication.

According to the above-mentioned model of 'constitutional dualism', ordinary judges are vested with the right to seek interpretations of domestic law that are consistent with the ECHR, but they do not have the right to overcome statutes, which is reserved for the Constitutional Court. The contribution made by the judiciary is indeed no different from their usual task of providing an interpretation of the law consistent with the Constitution, and in so doing they supply an initial embedment of the Convention into domestic law, simply by expanding the content of legislative measures, insofar as this does not clash with their text or their systemic function.[15] If this is not the case, they must refer the question to the Constitutional Court as if they were dealing with a breach of the Constitution. The doubts they raise are formally abstract, because there seems to be no logical difference from an ordinary constitutional complaint, but the supporting reasons are even more deeply embedded in the legal system, since an even wider range of issues must be taken into consideration: the trend in case law both at the internal and at the European level, the factual features of the claim at stake as compared with other similar cases, the legislative enactment of a given principle, the precedents of the Constitutional Court, and so on.

On the other hand, because the judicial approach cannot also remove every conflict of domestic law with the ECHR – for example in those cases that require a legislative implementation in order to fulfil a ruling of the ECtHR – the 2007 model accorded a peculiar centrality to parliamentary law as the main instrument called upon to comply with the obligations arising from the ECHR. In principle, conventional rights are not intended to be judicially enacted because Parliament remains the preferential actor upon which is conferred the function of 'letting' conventional rights and liberties 'into' domestic law.[16]

The model of the 'interposed rules' looks indeed like the most appropriate way for the Constitutional Court to promote the highest ranking of the ECHR

---

[15]   For an insightful approach to the embeddedness of international treaties in domestic law, and of the ECHR in particular, see L.R. HELFER, 'Redesigning the European Court of Human Rights: Embeddedness as a Deep Structural Principles of the European Human Rights Regime' (2008) 19 *EJIL (European Journal of International Law)* 125, 138–141.

[16]   The centrality of parliamentary legislation in the enactment of the ECHR is purported in case no. 348 of 2007, para. 4.6: a critical reassessment of this passage can be found in E. CANNIZZARO, *supra* n. 2, p. 181.

and the strongest influence of its principles in the judicial and legislative practice and, at the same time, to safeguard the same institutional balance that underlies its ordinary review of legislation. However, this model has been traditionally used by the Court whenever the content of a certain constitutional norm can be concretely ascertained only through the reference to its statutory implementation: for example in the scrutiny over delegation of legislative powers to the Government (that must respect the law of delegation provided by Parliament in accordance with Article 76 Const.) or over the compliance with basic state laws by regional statutes. Traditional scholarship has emphasized that the Constitutional Court, with the instrument of interposed rules, has for the most part pursued the concurring objectives of preserving the centrality of parliamentary legislation and of strengthening its own monopoly over judicial review of legislation.[17]

In other words, this approach reinforces in general,[18] and with reference to the incorporation of the ECHR in particular, the model of the Constitutional Court as a *sui generis* (and not strictly judicial) institution, which provides mainly constitutional (and not individual) justice and therefore quite limited chances for judge-made law in the field of fundamental rights.

3. THE QUEST FOR SUBSTANTIAL INTERACTION BETWEEN CONSTITUTIONAL AND CONVENTIONAL GUARANTEES

Despite all of this, several commentators have raised many doubts as to the viability of an approach of this kind, mainly suggesting that the deeper incorporation of the ECHR poses unprecedented problems that cannot be faced with the instruments conceived for the ordinary review of legislation, and above all the formal neutralization purported by the model of interposed rules. Once the ECHR has been assigned a *supra*-legislative status – according to the main argument of this critical reading – it appears quite difficult to ignore the substantial transformations involving constitutional rights and liberties, whose significance and extent are inevitably influenced by the growing quest for their coherent protection in the light of the ECHR's incorporation.[19]

---

[17] M. SICLARI, *Le 'norme interposte' nel giudizio di costituzionalità*, CEDAM, Padova 1992.

[18] A representative stance on the 'exceptional' role of the Constitutional Court is held by A. BALDASSARRE, 'Structure and Organization of the Constitutional Court of Italy' (1996) 40 *St. Louis University Law Journal* 649, 652 according to which 'while the Judiciary is the key authority under the 'rule of law,' the Constitutional Court is the key authority under the 'rule of the Constitution.''

[19] P. RIDOLA, 'La Corte costituzionale e la Convenzione europea dei diritti dell'uomo: tra gerarchia delle fonti nazionali e armonizzazione in via interpretativa', in ID., *Diritto comparato e diritto comune europeo*, Giappichelli, Torino 2010, pp. 193 ff., A. RUGGERI, 'Corte

Even the Constitutional Court, although never expressly setting aside the basic features of the 2007 turn, has shown on several occasions a certain reluctance towards a strict enforcement of the most formalistic key points of the two leading cases.

The most relevant effort to take this substantial dimension into account comes from two important rulings of 2009, in which the incorporation model of the ECHR was partially reshaped thanks to a more integrated model of reasoning. On this occasion, the emphasis was placed far more upon the final interpretive outcomes of the intertwining guarantees than upon the formal hierarchy between these. First, the Court conceded that the Convention is not a monolith, whose relevance in domestic law depends exclusively on its formal status, since several guarantees enshrined therein (like Articles 2 and 3) should be considered international customary law and, consequently, could be applied directly by judges pursuant to Article 10 of the Constitution.[20]

Moreover, the encapsulation of the ECHR within a restricted conception of 'interposed rules' is to a certain degree left in the background, especially when the Court states that the Convention cannot be assigned a fixed ranking, because its status in the domestic legal order remains on the one hand that of an ordinary statute (with which it has been formally incorporated), but nevertheless, on the other hand, has a constitutional status (at least in substance):

> '[s]ince an ECHR provision effectively supplements Article 117(1) of the Constitution, it receives from the latter its status within the system of sources, with all implications in terms of interpretation and balancing, which are the ordinary operations that this Court is required to carry out in proceedings falling within its jurisdiction.'[21]

This passage should be highlighted as a first step toward a detachment of form and substance in the domestic constitutional adjudication involving the ECHR. More generally, this partial devaluation of formalism looks like the consequence of a new attitude toward the ECHR dictated by the quest for a more structured interaction between the different levels of protection of fundamental rights concurring before domestic jurisdictions. Whereas in 2007 this interaction was widely limited by the emphasis placed on the external nature of the ECHR, which risked threatening the form and substance of constitutional rules, in these judgments it is acknowledged that the duty of compliance with international obligations can occasionally overcome the established interpretation of a constitutional right and lead to its further expansion with the support of the ECHR.

---

costituzionale e Corti europee: il modello, le esperienze, le prospettive' in F. DAL CANTO and E. ROSSI (eds.), *Corte costituzionale e sistema istituzionale*, Giappichelli, Torino 2011, pp. 168–173 and O. POLLICINO, *supra* n. 5, pp. 378–382.

[20]   Case no. 311 of 2009, para. 6.

[21]   Case no. 317 of 2009, para. 7.

'It is evident that this Court not only cannot permit Article 117(1) of the Constitution applying to determine a lower level of protection compared to that already existing under internal law, but neither can it be accepted that a higher level of protection which it is possible to introduce through the same mechanism should be denied to the holders of a fundamental right. The consequence of this reasoning is that the comparison between the Convention protection and constitutional protection of fundamental rights must be carried out seeking to obtain the greatest expansion of guarantees, including through the development of the potential inherent in the constitutional norms which concern the same rights.'[22]

By virtue of this, even the asymmetric balancing that the 'twin cases' had proposed in order to safeguard the external nature of the ECHR seems to lose its edge, given that the Constitution and the ECHR are jointly called upon to foster the greatest expansion of fundamental rights common to both catalogues. The risk that a constitutional rule could in some way be altered by the ECHR is replaced by the necessity that, in some cases, the higher protection afforded by the latter prevails over a consolidated interpretation of the former, insofar as this further protection is potentially contained in the constitutional provision.

However, it must be stressed that this reasoning does not bring with it a drift towards a straight casuistry, as would probably be the case if the choice between constitutional and conventional guarantees were driven only by the aim to enhance this greatest protection. In fact, it is not clear with respect to what factors the breadth of the protection should be evaluated. One might answer: with respect to the enjoyment by the individual of the claimed right, of course. This is obviously true but, on the other hand, it is not the definitive answer, since the Constitutional Court emphasizes that:

'The concept of the greatest expansion of protection must include, as already clarified in judgments Nos. 348 and 349 of 2007, a requirement to weigh up the right against other constitutionally protected interests, that is with other constitutional rules which in turn guarantee the fundamental rights which may be affected by the expansion of one individual protection. This balancing is to be carried out primarily by the legislature, but it is also a matter for this Court when interpreting constitutional law. [...] The overall result of the supplementation of the guarantees under national law must be positive, in the sense that the impact of individual ECHR rules on Italian law must result in an increase in protection for the entire system of fundamental rights.'[23]

Individual and systemic dimensions of fundamental rights are therefore strongly connected, since the incorporation of the ECHR is not grounded alternatively either upon the broadest enjoyment by individuals or upon the abstract higher

---

[22]   *Ibid.*
[23]   *Ibid.*

protection of a certain right. From these rulings on, constitutional adjudication over fundamental rights indeed implies a steady comparison between levels of protection, which appear now substantially equated and whose interactions appear driven not only by grounds of formal legitimacy, but rather by canons of coherence and adequacy with respect to the enmeshment of both subjective (individual) and objective (constitutional) profiles.[24]

4. 'ITALIAN STYLE' AND THE ECHR: THE CURRENT SITUATION

The response given in 2009 by the Constitutional Court is symptomatic of the dilemmas raised by the incorporation of the ECHR in a system of law originally marked by a strong dualistic tenet; however, in its final results, it cannot be understood if one ignores the specific features of a constitutional culture strongly indebted to a systematic vision of fundamental rights.

As regards the first aspect, it should be remarked that the evolution triggered by the Constitutional Court aims at expanding the internal status of the ECHR, but in a manner limited to the role played by the ECHR in constitutional adjudication, since the power of the judiciary to directly enforce the ECHR by disregarding internal law was denied without question in 2009 as well as in 2007. Unlike Germany, where the *Bundesverfassungsgericht* reserved to itself a merely monitoring function over the judicial enactment of the Convention even with respect to statutes passed later in time,[25] the 'Italian way' is post-dualistic since the conflict between domestic law and the Convention, in the last resort, is transposed to a constitutional conflict carried out before the Constitutional Court, which is the only institution entitled to strike the correct balance between national and supranational guarantees.

---

[24] A clear example of this new trend is to be found in the case no. 187 of 2010, concerning the legitimacy of the restriction in the enjoyment of incapacity benefits to aliens with a residence card. On that occasion, the Constitutional Court declared the restriction unconstitutional under Article 117, para. 1, Const. in connection with Article 14 and Article 1, First Protocol, ECHR because, on the one hand, the benefit amounted to a remedy aimed at enabling the effective satisfaction of 'primary needs' pertaining to the sphere of protection of individuals which, on the other hand, according to the case law of the ECtHR (decision on admissibility of 6 July 2005 in *Stec and others v. United Kingdom*), should not be denied to lawfully resident foreigners for grounds other than their individual circumstances. The interplay between national and conventional guarantees aimed at ensuring the highest standard has been so tight in this case, that doubts have been raised on the effective necessity to refer to the ECHR, given that a similar outcome could potentially be provided for by invoking the equality principle enshrined in Article 3 of the Constitution (S. NINATTI and M.E. GENNUSA, 'Italy and the ECHR – Report 2011' (2011) 4 *Ius Publicum Network Review* 1, 11 (www.ius-publicum.com)).

[25] H. KELLER and A. STONE SWEET, *supra* n. 1, p. 685, but see the contribution of A. DI MARTINO in this *Volume*.

As regards the second aspect, this outcome is also linked to the peculiar role played by fundamental rights, which in the absence of both a direct complaint promoted by individuals (as in Germany and Spain) and a scrutiny over legislation entrusted to the judiciary (as in common law countries), have traditionally promoted a 'constitutionally-ordered' legislation rather than ensuring a fully-fledged system of protection of individual guarantees.[26] Except for the field of procedural guarantees, constitutional rights had great difficulty directly penetrating the legal system through the judiciary, since their functioning depended largely upon their legislative enactment, so that their protection was for the most part entrusted to the Constitutional Court. They have consequently inherited the traditional structure that the review of legislation conferred upon every constitutional rule, which is deeply biased by the tension between abstractness and embeddedness sketched out above. By seeking a steady enmeshment of their content within the legal order, while not simply imposing upon it, fundamental rights ended up acting, in Dworkinian terms, far more like constitutional 'interests' than like straight 'trumps.'[27]

Nevertheless, the evolution summarized above in para. 3. is significant in that it leaves the most conservative aspects of constitutional dualism behind. By detaching the ECHR from the formal ranking of the statute that incorporated it, on the one hand, and by opening the Constitution to the mutual influence of the values and principles enshrined in the Convention, on the other, the relationships between the two catalogues have been partially shifted toward a substantial equalization.[28] The Constitution is no longer represented as a 'stronghold under siege', since it is in principle open to a refashioning of its basic contents, and the ECHR is consequently no longer called upon to comply formally with every constitutional rule but, more reasonably, to respect a sort of constitutional hard-core in the field of fundamental rights which is identified with respect for the constitutional 'system'.

It must however be remarked that this approach has not meant a total turning point from the precedents of 2007. Beyond the substantial equalization with the ECHR, and the consequences thereof with regard to balancing and interpretation, the other hallmarks of the model set out in 2007 have been challenged only in a limited way.

---

[26] P. RIDOLA, 'La Corte costituzionale: giudice delle libertà o dei conflitti?' (2012) 5 *Federalismi* 1, 2 (www.federalismi.it).

[27] R. DWORKIN, 'Rights as Trumps', in J. WALDRON (ed.), *Theories of Rights*, Oxford University Press, Oxford 1984, pp. 155–157. It must however be remarked that the greater enmeshment of principles and policies is to be considered as a consequence of the importance given by the Italian Constitution, as well as by several European constitutions, to social rights and policies: O. CHESSA, *Libertà fondamentali e teoria costituzionale*, Giuffrè, Milano 2002, pp. 332 and 354.

[28] E. CANNIZZARO, 'Il bilanciamento tra diritti fondamentali e l'art. 117, 1° comma, Cost.' (2010) *Rivista di diritto internazionale* 128, 130.

Firstly, the interpretive entrenchment between constitutional and conventional rights, as well as the role played by the judgments of the Strasbourg Court in ascertaining the concrete content of a given right, have led the Constitutional Court to take more extensively into account the elements of 'individual justice' provided for by its adjudication, albeit without dethroning the centrality of the 'objective protection'. This has been the case, among others, for the question concerning the prohibition against invoking an ECtHR judgment declaring a violation of Article 6 ECHR committed on the occasion of a criminal proceeding, in order to reopen it after a final judgment. In 2008, with case no. 129, the Court stated that this prohibition was consistent with the principle of legal certainty enshrined in several constitutional norms. Moreover, the prohibition was deemed to be in line with the basic assumptions of Italian criminal procedure, which ensures the reopening only in the event of new 'facts' emerging after final judgment, whilst a judgment by the Strasbourg Court cannot in any event be considered as a mere fact, but rather as a legal novelty. With case no. 113 of 2011, the Constitutional Court has completely reversed its own precedent, by stating that a prohibition of this kind is unconstitutional since it clashes with the duty to ensure the fulfilment of ECtHR's judgments arising from Article 46 of the Convention, which must be vested with a primacy over conflicting constitutional principles. The strong commitment to the individual nature of the claim, as shown by the withdrawal of the constitutional principles that prevailed only three years earlier, should however not be overestimated if one considers that the issue was not grounded upon Article 6 ECHR, but upon the different parameter of Article 46 ECHR, which emphasizes the general and 'objective' duty of the member States to execute the judgments of the ECtHR.

Secondly, the Constitutional Court seems therefore to have accepted that the incorporation of the ECHR at a constitutional level points out, more than in the past, the judicial (and not merely *sui generis*) nature of its particular review. Nonetheless, one should rather say that the evolution after 2009 has not altered the institutional balance that underlies constitutional adjudication in the field of human rights. Although the Court has progressively dismissed the more blatant aspects of its 'exceptionalism', several cases show that its special role in the constitutional domain has been safeguarded due to its function of a systematic reading of the Constitution in order to set limits to the ECHR. It has repeatedly been stated that the ECHR and the case law of the Strasbourg Court must be substantially respected, with a margin of appreciation which is necessary to preserve the special features of the national constitutional order.[29] This reasoning, be it similar to the distinguishing technique or not,[30] ends up strengthening the Court's monopoly, since no other institution is entitled to

---

[29]   Among others, see the most recent cases nos. 236 of 2011, 303 of 2011 and 230 of 2012.
[30]   See on this aspect the contribution of A. GUAZZAROTTI, in this *Volume*.

assess whether the ECHR or a judgment of the ECtHR is purported to respect the 'substance' of the constitutional order.

Lastly, the greatest reluctance to dismiss the traditional approach must be individuated in the narrow space left to a judge-made law for the fulfilment and adapting of the ECHR into domestic law. Whereas a greater consideration for a substantial interaction has marked out the post-2009 case law, as regards this aspect the Constitutional Court has been largely conservative, limiting the role of the judiciary to purport an interpretation of the law consistent with the ECHR and, therefore, to act as a preliminary filter for the constitutional review in the light of the Convention. Nothing less, but nothing more, either.

5. THE INCORPORATION OF THE ECHR: A MATTER OF CONSTITUTIONAL THEORY?

To conclude, the model of incorporation of the ECHR into Italian legal order appears to be a work in progress, since some basic tenets of the 'twin cases' of 2007 have been abandoned – in particular those concerning the 'constitutional dualism' – while others are going to be slightly reshaped.

I have sought to demonstrate that this transitional situation is not surprising, because the difficulties linked to the arrangement of a stable model, if possible at all, arise from an in-depth rethinking of some basic problems of constitutional theory, such as those concerning the emerging enmeshment of formal and value-based reasoning in the field of fundamental rights and, more generally, the chances to introduce new rights and principles in a Constitution which is traditionally deemed to be interpreted with a strong systematic bias.

For all these reasons, the most recent scholarship points out that the comprehension of the new guidelines for this evolution calls for a special focus on the legal reasoning used by the Constitutional Court and the ordinary judges, in order to set new interpretive paradigms beside the traditional criteria centred upon the sources of law (which had an undisputed centrality until now).[31] What is at stake in the handling of the ECHR is therefore a sort of hybridization, since the traditional methods of interpretation of the Constitution seem to evolve from the inside, i.e. by hosting emerging paradigms while seeking a compatibility with the traditional hallmarks of constitutional adjudication.

Among these paradigms, the turn to casuistry and the notion of 'greatest expansion of a right' seem undoubtedly to be the ones that have triggered the deepest transformation in constitutional theory, since their introduction – albeit still at an early and uncertain stage – has raised questions that highlight the constitutional potential of the ECHR.

---

[31]   See the representative contributions of P. RIDOLA and A. RUGGERI, *supra* n. 19.

As already observed, the peculiar embeddedness that marked Italian constitutional review must be seen as a quest for the general consistency of the Constitutional Court's rulings with the legal system, rather than as their properly casuistic allure (at least in the sense of the common law tradition). In this way, the function of the judiciary was preserved, in that the decisions of the judges were limited by general rulings of the Constitutional Court, in which the *erga omnes* effect prevailed and a principled reasoning was fostered. Actually, the introduction of the rulings of the ECtHR as elements able to drive constitutional interpretation, due to its status as 'preferential interpreter' of the ECHR, will probably alter this balance since the scrutiny of the Constitutional Court will have to take into account the specific factual features of the case resolved by the Strasbourg Court in order to eventually quash the internal law conflicting with it. In so doing, a comparison shall be made between the relevant circumstances of the claims before the two Courts, which also involves the consideration of factual matters that until now have remained largely outside the realm of constitutional review, since they were dealt with exclusively by the judges. The recent saga of the so-called 'statutory retroactive interpretations' has highlighted this problem in a quite considerable way, because the Constitutional Court has chosen to incorporate the substance of the ECtHR's case law on this matter by suggesting a reading of it which differed greatly from the one prevailing in the judiciary. It seems therefore certain that this trend risks excluding the judiciary from the ongoing dialogue between the two major Courts, by depriving it of the task of evaluating factual matters which, among others, is on the contrary a key element for a necessary legal and judicial pluralism in domestic as well as in European law.[32]

The other emerging paradigm, that of the 'greatest expansion of a right', poses different but even harder problems. By invoking this principle since case no. 317 of 2009, the Constitutional Court has implicitly taken a stance on a complex and highly debated question of constitutional theory, i.e. the openness of the catalogue of fundamental rights enshrined in the Constitution and, consequently, the interpretive patterns leading to the introduction of 'unprecedented' rights. This final question reflects a major issue in the topic dealt with in these pages, since this principle provoked a rethinking of a leading constitutional paradigm, according to which the system of written constitutional rights sets the boundaries of what has been deemed to have a constitutional relevance.[33] From this perspective, values and rights lying outside the textual

---

[32]   The increased role of the fact-finding powers of the ECtHR in recent years, according to L.R. HELFER, *supra* n. 15, pp. 142–144, calls for an even more structured dialogue between national and European judges. The problems affecting the excessive separation between constitutional courts and the judiciary in this field is emphasized by F. RUBIO LLORENTE, *supra* n. 12, pp. 58 ff., while the risks facing the post-2009 case law of the Constitutional Court are highlighted by E. CANNIZZARO, *supra* n. 28, pp. 130–132.

[33]   The current debate is overviewed by P. RIDOLA, *Diritti fondamentali. Un'introduzione*, Giappichelli, Torino 2006, pp. 172–174, and, with reference to German constitutional law, see R. ALEXY, *Theorie der Grundrechte*, Suhrkamp, Frankfurt a.M. 1994, pp. 338–342.

perimeter of the Constitution may play a very limited role, since their introduction risks narrowing the spheres of liberty conferred by the 'true' constitutional rights and, consequently, threatening the unity of the Constitution conceived as a set of given and untouchable principles.[34] By introducing a model of interaction centred upon the 'greatest expansion of a right,' be it constitutional or conventional, the Constitutional Court has on the contrary endorsed a prospective constitutional theory that emphasizes the balancing between single guarantees and between systems of protection as an interpretive technique called upon to foster, among other things, the basic evolution of the internal constitutional order as well as a prospective influence on the interpretive action of the ECtHR.[35] In this light, it will be crucial to critically evaluate how constitutional identities embodied in the different catalogues of fundamental rights will interact through interpretive practices and, consequently, in which directions some basic ideals and concepts underlying the constitutional protection of rights will be led: first of all the interaction between individual freedom and its social constraints.[36] It is hard to foresee the contours of this interaction, for much will depend on the capacity of the Constitutional Court, as well as of the Italian legal system in its entirety, to deal with the conflicts and the inconsistencies arising from the ECHR's machinery. What should lastly be emphasized is that the growing awareness of the principled interaction between domestic and European law calls for a 'new grammar' of fundamental rights that could involve in the future, albeit along different lines, every European legal scholar.

---

[34] The most representative position, in this field, is held by A. PACE, *supra* n. 9, 43–46, whereas the Constitutional Court since case no. 404 of 1988 is more inclined to hold moderately the 'openness' thesis. For further insights on this judicial trend see D. TEGA, in this *Volume*, p. 33.

[35] According to E. CANNIZZARO, *supra* n. 3, p. 183, 'the impact between national and international systems of protection of fundamental rights is bidirectional, thus feeding the international system of protection with emerging needs coming from the States' legal order'.

[36] Which has traditionally played a highly significant role in European continental constitutionalism of the last sixty years. Theoretical insights, from an Italian standpoint, on the interpretive interactions between the notions of 'negative' and 'positive' freedom can be found in O. CHESSA, *supra* n. 27, pp. 309 ff., whereas an inquiry over the model of property enshrined in the ECHR as an example of 'neoliberal' threat to constitutional values (from a British perspective) is that of D. NICOL, *The Constitutional Protection of Capitalism*, Hart, Oxford-Portland, 2010, pp. 128 ff.

STRASBOURG JURISPRUDENCE AS AN INPUT FOR 'CULTURAL EVOLUTION' IN ITALIAN JUDICIAL PRACTICE

Andrea GUAZZAROTTI

1. STRASBOURG JURISPRUDENCE AND 'CULTURE' OF JUDICIAL PRECEDENT IN ITALY

Fundamental rights in Italy represent one of the 'core missions' of the Constitutional Court: the Italian Constitution has quite a rich catalogue of such rights, whose guarantee is assured by constitutional adjudication. In contrast with the paradigm of the Supreme Court of the United States (or other common law Supreme Courts), constitutional adjudication in Italy is mostly a matter of 'norms' and not of 'facts', in accordance with an abstract model. The Italian Constitutional Court has to compare the meaning of a statute law against the meaning of one or more articles of the Constitution, even if the potential conflict between the two sources of law must arise from a concrete matter of application (preliminary questions by ordinary courts). Contrary to this model of adjudication is the practice of the ECtHR, which is increasingly eroding the Constitutional Court's mission as to the protection of human rights at the internal level. The way Strasbourg decides its cases is, mostly, a matter of facts, and the attention the ECtHR gives to the factual dimension of the cases has a seminal influence over the final judgment. Even if there are powerful objections to the assimilability of the ECtHR to a common law Supreme Court,[1] Strasbourg's jurisprudence can be compared to a 'system of precedents' as perceived in the common law culture; this cannot be valid for the jurisprudence of the Italian Constitutional Court. What Strasbourg and, for instance, the US Supreme Court have in common is precisely the importance they give to the factual dimension of the case. From that dimension, one can derive the 'inductive, incremental, and empirical' process typical of the doctrine of

---

[1] See, among others, S. GREER, *The European Convention on Human Rights: Achievements, Problems and Prospects*, Cambridge University Press, Cambridge 2006, p. 231.

precedent, as opposed to the 'paradigmatic model of adjudication issuing from the civil law tradition.'[2]

Within this framework, the question is the following: how can the jurisprudence of the ECtHR have an impact on the Italian system in terms of injecting a 'culture of precedent' as perceived in the common law systems? The usual way relationships between ECtHR and national judges are conceived is the question about the constraints deriving from the condemnation of a State, according to Article 46 of the Convention. Considering the growing importance Strasbourg jurisprudence has in Italian judicial practice, can its influence be differently conceived from this usual way? The most common approach to the effects of the Strasbourg case law on the national systems is now aimed at clarifying the hierarchical role of the Convention's provisions or their potential for 'direct effect,' following the scheme offered by the evolution of the relationships between Community (now EU) law and national law.[3] My contribution tries to look beyond this conceptual horizon and to suggest another way to see how things are going on in the daily tensions between national judges of a particular civil law tradition and the judges sitting at Strasbourg. The focus rests on the main object of both the national and European adjudication processes: the protection of fundamental rights. The suggestion is that the method of 'precedent' injected by the ECtHR into Italian judicial practice can well integrate the internal tools for the protection of human rights, filling the gaps in the Italian abstract method of constitutional adjudication.[4]

2. COMPARING THE REPORTING SYSTEM OF THE STRASBOURG AND ITALIAN JURISPRUDENCE

It may seem quite a difficult task to speak about 'precedent' at Strasbourg, while the ECtHR itself has clearly rejected the binding force of its previous decisions (so-called 'horizontal precedent'), while stressing the opportunity of maintaining a certain degree of predictability.[5] However, looking at what

---

2   M. Rosenfeld, 'Comparing constitutional review by the European Court of Justice and the U.S. Supreme Court' (2006) 4 *Int'l J. of Const. Law* 618, 628.

3   See H. Keller and A. Stone Sweet (eds.), *A Europe of Rights: The Impact of the ECHR on National Legal Systems*, Oxford University Press, Oxford 2009; G. Martinico and O. Pollicino (eds.), *The National Judicial Treatment of the ECHR and EU Laws. A Comparative Constitutional Perspective*, Europa Law Publishing, Groningen 2010.

4   Comparing the Italian Constitutional Court's case law and that of the US Supreme Court on freedom of expression, Bin stated that the 'clear and present danger test' created by the latter is not workable for the former, because it consists of the qualification of actions that already occurred, while the Italian Constitutional Court has no power to evaluate any concrete action: R. Bin, *Diritti e argomenti. Il bilanciamento degli interessi nella giurisprudenza costituzionale*, Giuffrè, Milano 1992, pp. 123 and 126.

5   '[T]he Court is not bound by its previous judgments; indeed, this is borne out by Rule 51 para. 1 of the Rules of Court. However, it usually follows and applies its own precedents, such

prominent former judges of the Court wrote about precedent as a working method of the Court (if not 'the' working method),[6] we must take seriously the hypothesis of drawing a parallel between the Strasbourg jurisprudence and precedent in common law. On the other hand, a few elements of comparison between the Italian judicial system and that of the ECHR will provide some idea of the different approach to the method of precedent. Italy has a very weak culture of 'precedent.' This is due to several factors, but one of these is surely the practice of the *Corte di Cassazione*, the Italian judge of last resort, which is supposed to ensure a uniformity of the interpretation of the law among all Italian courts[7] by virtue of its precedents. This task is not shared with the Constitutional Court, which theoretically has only to tackle questions of (suspected) unconstitutionality of statute laws and to declare them void (but see below). Even if the force of the precedents of the *Cassazione* is just *persuasive* and not *binding*, surely the jurisprudence of that Court is far more important in the daily practice of lawyers and judges than the jurisprudence of other Courts. But those precedents and their use in daily practice are quite different from precedents of *common law*. In Italy, the ordinary use of precedent is not based upon the reading of the whole judgment and the reconstruction of the *ratio decidendi*, but consists of a very short and abstract statement representing the core of the meaning of a legal rule, as interpreted by each individual judgment. It is the so-called *massima*, which includes a legal assertion concerning the interpretation of the rule applied in that case without any reference to the facts of the case. 'Therefore the *massima* is stated as if it were a statutory norm.'[8] Those precedents are reported by an official organ of the *Cassazione* itself, the *Ufficio del Massimario*, whose function is to extract from the judgments of the Court one or more *massime*. In doing so, however, the *Massimario* often mixes *ratio decidendi* with *obiter dicta*, and therefore reading a *massima* is not enough to

---

a course being in the interests of legal certainty and the orderly development of the Convention's case law. Nevertheless, this would not prevent the Court from departing from an earlier decision if it was persuaded that there were cogent reasons for doing so' (*Cossey v. UK*, judgment of 27 September 1990, para. 35); 'While it is in the interests of legal certainty, foreseeability and equality before the law that the Court should not depart, without good reason, from precedents established in previous cases, a failure by the Court to maintain a dynamic and evolutive approach would risk rendering it a bar to reform or improvement' (*Demir and Baykara v. Turkey*, judgment of 12 November 2008, para. 138).

6   See L. Wildhaber, 'Precedent in the European Court of Human Rights', in *Mélanges Rolv Ryssdal. Protecting Human Rights: The European Perspective*, Carl Heymanns, Köln 2000, pp. 1529 ff.; V. Zagrebelsky, 'La giurisprudenza casistica della Corte europea dei diritti dell'uomo; fatto e diritto alla luce dei precedenti', in *La fabbrica delle interpretazioni*, (*Convegno annuale della Facoltà di Giurisprudenza dell'Università di Milano-Bicocca, 19–20 November 2009*), Giuffrè, Milano 2012, pp. 61-71, which reports the way Strasbourg judges discuss their cases, stressing that only in the absence of consistent precedents they would start investigating the meaning of one provision of the Convention.

7   Royal Decree of 30 January 1941 n. 12 (article 65).

8   M. Taruffo, 'Precedents in Italy', in E. Hondius (ed.), *Precedent and the Law*, Bruylant, Bruxelles 2007, pp. 181 ff.

understand if it actually corresponds to the *ratio decidendi* of the case and what kind of connection exists between the *massima* and the facts of the case.[9]

In the well known ECtHR database (HUDOC), one cannot find anything similar to the Italian *Massimario*. The only way to grasp the scope of the decisions of the ECtHR without reading their whole content is to read their (official) *Press Release* which, however, contains the summary of the case in its factual and normative dimension: nothing to do with the Italian *massime*. Moreover, the database contains another source of information: the *Notice*, setting out not only the names of the parties, the Section of the Court, the article of the Convention relevant for the judgment, etc., but, more importantly, the list of 'precedents' cited in the decision. Significantly, the English version does not use the term 'precedent' but the less specific term 'jurisprudence', and the number of previous decisions listed is often very high, but represents a clear sign of the importance Strasbourg gives to the method of precedent. Other inputs are the degree of authority of the decision – if ruled by the Grand Chamber or by a Section – together with the unanimity of the judges: these are all important tools capable of helping the national judge in discerning the 'authority' of the Strasbourg precedent.[10] The only analogy with the Italian judicial system is the possibility to distinguish the simple Section decisions of the Court of Cassation from those of the United Sections (*Sezioni Unite*), while the Constitutional Court (as every court in Italy) has no separate or concurring opinion.

3. THE ECHR AND THE '*AD HOC* BALANCING DELEGATED TO COURTS'

It seems no more questionable that the ECHR system of individual claims to an international body of *judicial* character has injected a great deal of judicial discretion into the national legal systems. This phenomenon can be conceived as a 'delegation of powers' from the Strasbourg authorities to the national ordinary courts. A good example is the *Medrano* case of the Italian Court of Cassation, one of the first cases in Italy where the Convention received a direct application by an ordinary judge.[11] Here, the Court of Cassation held that the criminal statute law providing for the mandatory deportation of aliens convicted of drug-related crimes must be interpreted compatibly with the right to respect for family life, according to Article 8 of the ECHR as interpreted by the ECtHR. The latter having affirmed that where the alien has real family ties in the territory of the

---

9   M. TARUFFO, *supra* n. 8, p. 182.
10 Referring to the authority of a judgment of the Grand Chamber, the UK Supreme Court has recently affirmed that it 'will not without good reason depart from the principles laid down in a carefully considered judgment of the European Court sitting as a Grand Chamber': *Cadder (Peter) v. HM Advocate* [2010] UKSC 43, [2010] WLR 268, para. 45.
11 Judgment of the Court of Cassation, 1st Criminal Sect., of 12 May 1993.

State in which he is resident, the deportation is justified with regard to Article 8 only if it is proportionate to the legitimate aim pursued, the Court of Cassation held that the public security issues under the criminal provision in question must be evaluated in light of the right to maintain one's own family ties.[12] That is to say that the seriousness of the crime committed must be balanced with the importance of the family ties in question.

We are faced with a sort of reservation to the judiciary of the power to test the proportionality of a legal measure – a power not originally present in the letter of the (statute) law; it is the national judge (the Court of Cassation, in the Italian case) which derives such power directly from the scope of one article of the Convention, by virtue of the interpretation given by the ECtHR on similar cases. Indeed, this was not unknown to the Italian judges: such an interpretative device was already familiar under the name of 'ad hoc balancing delegated to courts.'[13] It was the Constitutional Court that created this device: instead of rendering void the provision of a statute law because of its excessive rigidity in terms of the prevalence of one constitutional interest over another, the Constitutional Court used to declare the partial unconstitutionality of the provision as long as it did not leave enough discretion to the judge in balancing the two competing interests in each case.

But there is an important difference between the two phenomena at issue: the Constitutional Court performs a centralized scrutiny on the constitutionality of statute laws, which is abstract in nature. The balancing tests created by the Court in its constitutional adjudication are delivered entirely to ordinary courts, without the possibility for the Constitutional Court to revise their correct application in the material case. Currently, in Italy there is no room for an individual complaint to the Constitutional Court, as there is in Spain (*recurso de amparo*) or in Germany (*Verfassungsbeschwerde*). Also, the fact that those balancing tests are often formulated by the Constitutional Court in judgments of 'rebuttal of the question of unconstitutionality' is important; by means of these decisions the Court states that a norm is not in conflict with the Constitution provided it is interpreted in a given way (*sentenze interpretative di rigetto*). But the force of such decisions is merely persuasive and not binding on the ordinary courts.

Quite different is the case where the balancing test is delivered by the ECtHR. First of all, it opens a certain degree of direct application of the Convention by ordinary courts, which can exercise the power to render a statute law more 'flexible' (as the *Medrano* case showed) without passing through the centralized scrutiny of the Constitutional Court. The risk of uncertainty in the judicial

---

12   The ECtHR judgments quoted in the *Medrano* case are: *Beldjoudi v. France*, judgment of 26 March 1992; *Moustaquim v. Belgium*, judgment of 18 February 1991; *Berrehab v. the Netherlands*, judgment of 21 June 1988; *Abdulaziz, Cabales and Balkandali v. UK*, judgment of 28 May 1985.

13   R. BIN, *supra* n. 4, pp. 91 and 127.

application of national laws is mitigated by the guiding role assigned to the Strasbourg system of precedents.[14] Second, the correctness of the application of a balancing test delivered by Strasbourg to national judges may be tested each time by the same Court that created the test: the ECtHR. By virtue of the individual application to the European Court, each person who finds his or her rights violated by an improper application of the Strasbourg tests at the internal level may have recourse to the European Court. A clear example of such scheme is the Italian statute law on the excessive length of the judicial proceedings,[15] which states that the award of just satisfaction by national courts must not differ from the standards of Strasbourg.[16]

It is worth noting that, in some cases, it is the Convention itself which requires that the admissible limits to the right in question are balanced by the judiciary and not by the legislature, thus creating a genuine 'reservation of judicial power' at the national level. A paradigmatic example is the right to a public hearing.[17] The Italian Constitutional Court decided on several occasions that the public nature of the proceedings could have been limited according to the admissible limits listed in the second sentence of the first paragraph of Article 6. The prevalence of one of those limits on the public nature of the hearings was the result of a balance decided by the legislature: no scope for '*ad hoc* balancing delegated to courts'.[18] Quite the contrary seems to be the Strasbourg approach to the publicity issue and, after three condemnations of Italy on this point,[19] the Constitutional Court changed its interpretation. Accordingly, ordinary Courts were empowered with the task of balancing, *in each case*, the competing interests of publicity, on the one hand, and of morals, public order, etc., on the other; this was carried out by the Constitutional Court by partially declaring the unconstitutionality of the internal rules on proceedings.[20]

Another interesting example is the matter of expropriations in Italy: after having been condemned by Strasbourg several times for, among other reasons, the inadequacy of compensation for expropriation, the Constitutional Court

---

14   See M. CAPPELLETTI, 'Giustizia costituzionale soprannazionale' (1978) 54 *Rivista di diritto processuale* 1, 6 ff.
15   Law no. 89 of 24 March 2001 (the 'Pinto Act').
16   See, among many others, *Scordino v. Italy (no. 1)*, judgment of 29 March 2006 and *Simaldone v. Italy*, judgment of 31 March 2009.
17   Article 6, para. 1: 'Judgment shall be pronounced publicly but the press and public may be excluded from all or part of the trial in the interests of morals, public order or national security in a democratic society, where the interests of juveniles or the protection of the private life of the parties so require, or to the extent strictly necessary in the opinion of the court in special circumstances where publicity would prejudice the interests of justice.'
18   Cases nos. 12 of 1971; 16 and 17 of 1981; 373 of 1992; 235 of 1993.
19   *Bocellari and Rizza v. Italy*, judgment of 13 November 2007; *Perre and others v. Italy*, judgment of 8 July 2008; *Bongiorno and others v. Italy*, judgment of 5 January 2010.
20   Case no. 93 of 2010.

declared the norm of the statute law on expropriation void.[21] Its decision, however, established that the legislature must act on that matter so that the right of the owners to full compensation, as established by the ECtHR, could not render the expropriation's cost exorbitant and thus prevent the fulfillment of other constitutional interests superior to those of the owners, such as the building of hospitals and schools. According to this decision, the legislature enhanced a general rule of full compensation coupled with a derogation permitting the 25% reduction of the market value on the expropriated private property. This derogation takes place when the purpose of the expropriation is a 'socio-economical reform.'[22] Apart from the vagueness of the derogatory rule, it is evident that such a norm leaves a margin of appreciation for public authorities and hence for Courts, corresponding to a balancing test between the interest of the owners and that of society as a whole. The performance of such a balance was already admitted by the Strasbourg judges themselves, who referred to 'economic reform or measures designed to achieve greater social justice,' but in a sort of 'casuistic' way. The ECtHR actually listed a few 'paradigmatic' cases which clearly intended to play the role of 'precedents' that national judges have to follow if they do not want to cause the condemnation of their country.[23] Here again, national judges are placed under the (indirect) control of the ECtHR and even if the original intent of the Italian Constitutional Court was to mitigate the European rule of 'full compensation' of the expropriation, Strasbourg jurisprudence assumes a more active role than before.

4. THE 'CONCRETENESS' OF THE TESTS PROVIDED BY THE EUROPEAN COURT OF HUMAN RIGHTS

Another important factor of influence exercised by Strasbourg on national judicial practice is the 'concreteness' of the tests supplied by the ECtHR. A good example is the decision of the Court of Cassation on the legality of deportations to Tunisia of people charged with terrorism. Because of the high risk of torture and inhuman treatment (Article 3 of the Convention) run by deported people charged with terrorism in Tunisia, Italy was, in more than one case of deportation, condemned by Strasbourg. As a consequence, the Court of Cassation formulated the principle that each judge, on the merit testing the legality of a deportation to Tunisia, must ensure whether the conditions asserted

---

[21]   Case no. 348 of 2007.
[22]   Law no. 244 of 28 December 2007 (budgetary law), Article 2, para. 89.
[23]   Leasehold-reform legislation; nationalization of companies; fundamental changes of a country's constitutional system (*Scordino* case, *supra* n. 16, para. 97).

by Strasbourg persist, and, if so, refuse the execution of the measure.[24] On this occasion, Italian and European judges had to face the following problem: the Italian Government too easily believed the guarantees given by Tunisia about the treatment the deported persons would receive, while not giving enough weight to the widespread sources of information on the actual practice of torture and inhuman treatment committed by the local authorities on persons suspected of being terrorists. We are confronted with a humanitarian issue linked with an administrative practice, not with the normative content of a statute law, and therefore an issue that the Italian Constitutional Court could not tackle. We are also confronted with issues of a highly political nature, such as immigration and terrorism. In these circumstances, the importance of having a supranational Court empowering the national judge with effective tools to face the political branch is crucial.

In the case law on deportations already mentioned, we also find a circulation of tests which are quite concrete in nature, such as the duty of the (administrative and judicial) authorities to trust the reports of Amnesty International about the seriousness of the risk that deported people are tortured or subjected to inhuman treatments in some countries.[25] Here again, we are confronted with an interpretative device of a high 'operational nature' delivered by Strasbourg to national courts – a device that cannot be easily created and spread by the abstract adjudication process of the Italian Constitutional Court.

5. DISTINGUISHING AND DECISIONS NO. 348 AND NO. 349 OF 2007 OF THE ITALIAN CONSTITUTIONAL COURT

According to the Italian constitutional reform of 2001, the national and regional legislatures are required to abide by the EU law and the international obligations (Article 117, para. 1, of the Constitution). In the seminal decisions nos. 348 and 349 of 2007, the Italian Constitutional Court affirmed that this reform has given the ECHR a higher status than domestic ordinary law. That means that, in the event of conflict, the judges hearing the case must request the intervention of the Constitutional Court, by way of preliminary ruling. In its turn, the Constitutional Court may declare the domestic law void on the ground of the indirect violation of Article 117, para. 1, of the Constitution. This process is quite different from the case of conflict between EU law and ordinary domestic law, where ordinary courts

---

[24]   *Corte di Cassazione*, judgment of 28 April 2010, n. 20514, which expressly refers to ECtHR decisions *Saadi v. Italy*, judgment of 23 January 2008; *Ben Khemais v. Italy*, judgment of 24 February 2009; *Sellem v. Italy*, judgment of 5 May 2009; *Trabelsi v. Italy*, judgment of 13 April 2010.

[25]   See *Corte di Cassazione*, judgment of 8 July 2010, no. 32685, quoting ECtHR decision on *Saadi v. Italy, supra* n. 24.

are enabled to give prevalence to the EU norm at issue, if provided with direct effect, simply by deciding the non-application of the domestic norm. What is important here is that the Constitutional Court specifies that the exact meaning of the ECHR can be ascertained only as it is interpreted by the ECtHR (the rights enshrined in the Convention must be interpreted as 'living in the case law of the European Court of Human Rights'). In so doing, the Constitutional Court did not distinguish between the force Strasbourg jurisprudence has in decisions pronounced against Italy on the unconventionality of the specific domestic rule at issue (according to Article 46 of the Convention) and the force Strasbourg jurisprudence has in general. Given the casuistic nature of some if not most of the case law of the ECtHR, the risk is declaring void a domestic rule contrary to an interpretation of the Convention given in a different context (a decision issued against another country or relating to a similar but not coincident domestic norm). The lack of the preliminary ruling mechanism in the ECHR system makes it difficult for both the ordinary and the constitutional courts to apply the Convention at the domestic level in the 'living meaning' of the Strasbourg case law.

The risk of being 'more papist than the Pope' can be (and has been) avoided by the common law technique of distinguishing. It was the Italian Court of Cassation which initiated such a strategy of confrontation with the authority of the precedents ruled at Strasbourg. In the unlawful expropriations saga, after being condemned by the ECtHR for the lack of certainty in the rules on expropriation (so called 'indirect expropriation'), the Court of Cassation tried to distinguish the current case from the case decided at Strasbourg, but the effort was quite 'desperate' and it failed.[26] The Constitutional Court, however, has often asked the ordinary Courts to distinguish their cases from the relevant precedents of Strasbourg. The way the Constitutional Court itself performs the technique of distinguishing is, however, very revealing.

Before analyzing an exemplary case of distinguishing by the Italian Constitutional Court, it bears mentioning that the 'culture of precedent' showed by the Constitutional Court with regard to its own precedents is very weak[27] – nothing like the authority of the 'horizontal precedent' in the common law tradition.

---

[26]   See *Corte di Cassazione*, S.U., dec. no. 5902 of 14 April 2003 and no. 6853 of 6 May 2003 (in *Foro italiano* 2003, I, 2368), where the plenary Section of the Court of Cassation tried to distinguish their cases from those decided by the ECtHR (*Belvedere Alberghiera* and *Carbonara e Ventura v. Italy*, judgments of 30 May 2000), noting that the facts of the Strasbourg precedents happened before the seminal decision no. 1464 of 1983, by the same plenary Section of the Court of Cassation, in which the judge-made law on 'indirect expropriation' was clarified and made sound. It followed that the indirect expropriations occurring after that decision could not be considered as lacking in legal certainty. It was quite a rosy picture of the uncertain domestic case law on this issue which the ECtHR did not share in the dozens of condemnations ruled against Italy afterwards (see, among others, *Binotti v. Italy (no. 1)*, judgment of 17 November 2005).

[27]   See A. ANZON, *Il valore del precedente nel giudizio sulle leggi*, Giuffrè, Milano 1995.

For a schematic but clear picture of the attitude towards the jurisprudence of the ECtHR shown by the Italian Constitutional Court, we may start from the dichotomist definition on precedent given by Frederick Schauer. Precedents are what 'impede an otherwise preferred current decision, rather than [the method through which] some previous decision is selected in order to support an argument now.'[28] 'Precedential constraint in law is precisely this obligation to follow previous decisions just because of their existence and not because of their perceived (by the current decision maker) correctness, and this counter-intuitive form of reasoning [...] is importantly different from the typical form of analogical reasoning.'[29] 'Whereas analogical reasoners are widely understood to have a choice among various candidate source analogs [...], such freedom is ordinarily absent with respect to constraint by precedent'.[30]

If we turn to the Italian scenario and to the relationships between Strasbourg and the domestic courts, we can assume that the latter usually made reference to the case law of the ECtHR according to the 'analogical reasoning' method. This is to say, Italian courts did not follow the true meaning of precedent, but its 'apocryphal' version, thus making reference to Strasbourg precedents only when those could support their reasoning in a given decision. This was true before the turning point of the Constitutional Court's decisions nos. 348 and 349 of 2007, cited above. After this watershed, things changed, at least formally. By virtue of the obligation imposed on domestic legislation by the new Article 117, para. 1, of the Constitution, constitutional judges have told themselves and ordinary courts that the ECHR is binding for what the ECtHR says to be its correct interpretation and not for what each individual domestic court says. Domestic courts, even the Constitutional Court, are no longer free to choose the Strasbourg precedents that most fit their choice in the case at issue.[31]

Moreover, the constitutional change in 2007 has determined not only the introduction of the authority of precedent relating to Strasbourg jurisprudence in Italy, but also the common law technique of distinguishing, a technique whose features are intrinsic to the 'factual dimension' of precedent. A good example is the recent decision no. 236 of 2011 by the Constitutional Court, where the former was called upon to assess the constitutionality of a domestic norm mitigating the criminal law only for the future and not for the past. This could possibly counter the precedent of the ECtHR in the case *Scoppola v. Italy (no. 2)*, where another domestic norm was declared not to comply with the principle of the retrospective

---

28   F. SCHAUER, 'Why Precedent in Law (and Elsewhere) is Not Totally (or Even Substantially) About Analogy' (2007) Research Working Paper RWP07-036, p. 8.
29   F. SCHAUER, *supra* n. 28, p. 9.
30   F. SCHAUER, *supra* n. 28, p. 3.
31   See E. LAMARQUE, 'Il vincolo alle leggi statali e regionali derivante dagli obblighi internazionali nella giurisprudenza comune', in *Corte costituzionale, giudici comuni e interpretazioni adeguatrici*, Giuffrè, Milano 2010, p. 153.

application of the more lenient criminal law.[32] For the Constitutional Court, this precedent of Strasbourg, 'although aimed at establishing a general principle [...], remains nonetheless linked to the concreteness of the case in which it was ruled: the fact that the European Court is called to assess upon a material case and, most of all, the specificity of the single case issued, are factors to be carefully weighed and taken into account by the Constitutional Court, when applying the principle ascertained by the Strasbourg Court at the domestic level, in order to review the constitutionality of one norm allegedly at odds with that principle.'[33]

6. THE *AGRATI* CASE, OR THE FAILURE OF THE ITALIAN WAY TO MANIPULATE PRECEDENTS

The 'apocryphal' version of precedent is however still present in the practice of the Italian Constitutional Court. In other words, Italian constitutional judges still prefer the 'analogical' way of reasoning: the fact of relying on a previous decision of Strasbourg seems just 'a choice among various candidate source analogs.'[34] The *Agrati* case is a typical example. The Constitutional Court had to tackle the question of constitutionality of a retrospective provision aimed at interpreting another previous provision so as to restrict the rights of the applicants, as consistently applied by ordinary courts (and the Court of Cassation itself). In similar cases, Strasbourg had repeatedly ruled that 'although the legislature is not prevented from regulating, through new retrospective provisions, rights derived from the laws in force, the principle of the rule of law and the notion of a fair trial enshrined in Article 6 preclude, except for compelling public-interest reasons, interference by the legislature with the administration of justice designed to influence the judicial determination of a dispute.'[35] What was (and is) the 'compelling public-interest reason' which could justify the retrospective legislation is a matter of precedent – i.e. it can be ascertained by the domestic court only by virtue of a careful analysis of Strasbourg case law. The way the Italian Constitutional Court carried out this analysis is quite revealing. Among the different precedents of the ECtHR, the Italian constitutional judges decided to rely heavily on one case against Germany; in that case, Strasbourg 'absolved' the contested interpretative provision with retrospective force because, among other things, it did not prevent the applicant from presenting her case before the domestic courts and, most of all, before the German Constitutional Court which assessed the

---

[32] Grand Chamber, judgment of 17 September 2009.
[33] Constitutional Court, case no. 236 of 2011, para. 12.
[34] F. SCHAUER, *supra* n. 28.
[35] Grand Chamber, *Zielinski, Pradal and Gonzalez and others v. France*, judgment of 28 October 1999, para. 57.

constitutionality of the retrospective nature of the provision in question.[36] That was, according to the Italian Constitutional Court, exactly what happened in Italy with the interpretative provision under scrutiny: its constitutionality was already assessed in a previous decision of the Constitutional Court itself (case no. 234 of 2007).

The choice of the *Forrer-Niedenthal* case as relevant precedent of the ECtHR is highly questionable for several reasons. First of all, the Italian Constitutional Court neglected to consider that in that case the Strasbourg Court clearly pointed out the *very* exceptional nature of the circumstances of the case, because they were strictly bound to the reunification of Germany: nothing to do with the subject-matter of the Italian question (the 'reunification' of the legal status of the caretakers in the public schools). Secondly, the German provision was enacted in a situation of legal uncertainty where the applicant could not rely on any previous clearly established judicial precedent related to the right claimed: quite the contrary to the Italian question, where the legislature enacted the retrospective provision just in order to overcome the steady interpretation given by ordinary courts and confirmed twice by the Court of Cassation itself. While the German provision gave the domestic courts some interpretive criteria about how to check the validity of the expropriations enacted under the former Democratic Republic of Germany, without preventing the applicant from disputing the validity of the expropriation of her property, the Italian provision clearly prevented the applicants from having their salary rights recognized. The fact that in both cases the question on the constitutional validity of the prospective nature of the provision reached the Constitutional Courts, which both ruled on the merit, is merely a coincidence which had nothing to do with the heart of the legal questions at issue. What is more, the Italian Constitutional Court failed to take into account the deepest difference between the *ratio decidendi* of Strasbourg's case law on the admissibility of prospective provisions enacted by the legislature in order to give an authoritative interpretation for a previous provision and the *ratio decidendi* of the Italian Constitutional Court's case law on the same subject. According to Strasbourg, actually, such a legislative interpretation may be enacted, among other things, in order to re-establish the original and *unequivocal* intent of the legislature, when the *interpreted* provision is enacted.[37] At the same time, according to the case law of the Italian Constitutional Court, the legislature may re-establish *one of the possible versions* of the original intent of the past legislature.[38]

Not surprisingly, the Court of Strasbourg declared, with brief reasoning, the Italian provision in question as contrary to the right to a fair trial (Article 6 of the ECHR). No weight is given to the previous decisions by the Italian

---

[36]   *Forrer-Niedenthal v. Germany*, judgment of 20 February 2003, para. 65.
[37]   *Zielinski, Pradal and Gonzalez and others v. France, supra* n. 35, paras. 54 and 59.
[38]   Cases no. 234 of 2007, para. 9; nos. 39, 135 and 274 of 2006.

Constitutional Court on the case above, which Strasbourg hardly mentioned.[39] It was virtually a sort of humiliation for the Italian constitutional judges and their effort to apply the technique of distinguishing to the Strasbourg precedents on prospective legislative provisions.

7.   CONCLUSION

In Italian judicial practice, two roads lead to the same place, i.e. to the method of precedent as a way to approach the Strasbourg jurisprudence. Those are the two ways by which the Italian ordinary courts and the Constitutional Court are driven to acknowledge the external influence coming from the Strasbourg practice and to initiate a sort of 'cultural change' in the way they perform human rights protection. On the one hand, we find the strengthening of the judicial techniques aimed at balancing one or more fundamental rights with the competing public interests in each case at issue. This strengthening is partly to the structure of the Convention itself, and partly to the approach shown by Strasbourg towards the domestic legislation, which is often less deferential than the one shown by the Constitutional Court. As already noted, the technique is more or less the same one as has been long experimented with in the Italian judicial system ('*ad hoc* balancing' delegated by the Constitutional Court to ordinary courts): the difference is that such delegation of judicial power, when made by Strasbourg, is more effective than the one made by the Constitutional Court (ordinary courts' rulings can be always 'checked' by the ECtHR).

However, Strasbourg represents not only a strict supranational supervisor of domestic courts but also their 'assistant.' As a judgment on the facts of the case and not only on the abstract norms applied, Strasbourg's decisions usually provide the domestic ordinary courts with more powerful tools than those provided by the Constitutional Court to test whether the domestic measure restricting the fundamental right at issue is legal. The cases on deportations of aliens referred to above are quite revealing, but mention must also be made of a recent case on overcrowding in the Italian prisons, in which the prison judge of Lecce condemned the State to pay a pecuniary indemnity to a prisoner for the very first time; in fact, it was the first case of a prisoner suffering a period of detention in an overcrowded cell being awarded an indemnity.[40] In so doing, the judge made more than one reference to the ECtHR *Sulejmanovic* decision, where the detention in a cell with less than 3 square meters of personal space was recognized as amounting to degrading treatment under Article 3 of the

---

[39]   *Agrati v. Italy*, judgment of 7 June 2011, para. 62. The Italian Government asked unsuccessfully for the referral of the case to the Grand Chamber.

[40]   Magistrato di sorveglianza di Lecce (judge Tarantino), order of 9 June 2011, available at www.penalecontemporaneo.it.

Convention.[41] Such a 'dimensional' threshold of gravity, for its discretion, could have been established by a court other than the Strasbourg Court, which also provided the Italian prison judge with the monetary parameter for the indemnity.

The second road leading to the method of precedent is the technique of distinguishing, which the Italian Constitutional Court and ordinary courts started practicing in order to avoid an excessively deep and generalized impact of the Strasbourg jurisprudence on the Italian legal system. Even if this second road seems to have an intent at odds with the first (the limitation and not the exaltation of Strasbourg's influence at the domestic level), it contributes to the injection of a 'culture of precedent' in Italy. As a matter of fact, if the domestic courts want to persuade Strasbourg that their cases differ from the relevant precedents ruled by the ECtHR on the same subject, they have to manage adequately the common law technique of distinguishing. This is to say that Italian judges, and most of all the Constitutional Court, have to familiarize themselves with a new way to use precedents which is not the way they have followed thus far. In other words, they must start to pay attention to the factual dimension of each Strasbourg precedent, comparing similarities and differences with their own cases, and thus avoiding handling the European precedent as a '*massima*' – the domestic way by which precedent is often perceived, and a very generic legal assertion concerning the interpretation of the rule applied in the previous case without any reference to the facts of the case. Such a change could represent a small 'revolution' in Italian judicial practice.

---

[41]   *Sulejmanovic v. Italy*, judgment of 16 July 2009.

PART I.B

THE MOST DANGEROUS BREACH? THE RIGHT TO A FAIR TRIAL AND THE QUEST FOR EFFECTIVENESS

THE STRASBOURG COURT'S INFLUENCE ON THE ITALIAN CRIMINAL TRIAL

Mariangela MONTAGNA

1. THE DIALOGUE BETWEEN COURTS AND THE PROTECTION OF FUNDAMENTAL RIGHTS, BETWEEN CHANGING ROLES AND NEW OUTLOOKS OF INTERPRETATION

Over the past decade, the Italian criminal trial has been positively influenced by the decisions of the European Court of Human Rights. The strengthened protection of the fundamental human rights enshrined in the European Convention on Human Rights is the result of a rich and fruitful dialogue that has been established between the Strasbourg Court, the Constitutional Court, and the Court of Cassation. In particular, the two domestic Courts, through their interventions, have played a decisive role, responding readily and sensitively to the indications originating from the European Court of Human Rights, and thus offsetting the lawmakers' persistent inertia.

Of decisive importance on this path were the changes that took place within the European Court of Human Rights, as it went from being the judge called upon to verify whether, in the specific case, the holding of the trial violated one of the rights enshrined in the Convention, into being an oversight body that is also qualified to indicate the internal regulatory 'gaps' underlying the violation. This different formulation, expressed in the so-called 'pilot judgments', has also been developing with the purpose of finding appropriate solutions to guarantee greater effectiveness for the Strasbourg Court's rulings, and to prevent the repetition of violations and the consequent activation of complaints before that Court.

Along with these changes in the Strasbourg judge, alterations have also been seen at the level of the domestic legal system. In Italy, these alterations have been to the jurisprudence of the Constitutional Court. Reference is made to the outlook of interpretation to the relationship between domestic and supranational sources, initiated with the well-known constitutional rulings nos. 348 and 349 of

2007. The ECHR's articles were qualified as 'interposed rules' in the meaning attributed to them by the ECtHR's own jurisprudence, and such as to supplement the constitutional parameter pursuant to Article 117, paragraph 1, Const., in the part where it requires domestic legislation to comply with the constraints deriving from international obligations. This arrangement was kept in place by the Court in later judgments as well,[1] albeit with gradual adaptations aimed, among other things, at tempering the European Court's potential excessive creativity.[2]

The circulation of knowledge that thus developed generated adaptations at the domestic level to ensure compliance with international obligations and, in the setting of the Italian criminal trial, led to some changes. The sectors where this communication has produced concrete results, achieved above all through jurisprudence, are the trial *in absentia* and the public hearing.

2. TRIAL *IN ABSENTIA* AND REMEDIES

The 'dialogue' between Courts has produced important results in the sector of *in absentia* proceedings and the pertinent remedies aimed at ensuring, to defendants tried *in absentia* who have not been informed directly of the proceedings against them and have not unequivocally waived their right to appear at their trial, the right to full participation in the trial. On this issue, the supranational judges have underscored how the defendant's right to be present at the trial, although not expressly provided for in para. 1 of Article 6 ECHR, may still be surmised from the norm taken as a whole. This norm actually fails to explicitly mention the right to attend the trial, as is done in Article 14, para. 3(d) of the International Covenant on Civil and Political Rights signed in New York on 16 December 1966. However, para. 3 of Article 6 ECHR, under (c), (d) and (e), attributes to the defendant rights that he or she can enjoy only by attending the trial in person.

In principle, a trial held in the defendant's absence does not conflict with the guarantee established in Article 6 ECHR. However, for the purposes of holding a fair trial in compliance with the fundamental human rights guaranteed by the Convention, the party convicted *in absentia* must 'be able to obtain that a jurisdiction will rule again, after having heard him, on the grounds of the charge in fact and in law, when it is not unequivocally ascertained that he has waived his right to appear and defend himself'.[3] Therefore, there is a conflict with Article 6 ECHR whenever a person convicted *in absentia* then finds himself

---

[1] Constitutional Court, cases nos. 317, 311 and 239 of 2009, no. 38 of 2008; and, more recently, cases nos. 80 and 113 of 2011.
[2] Constitutional Court, case no. 236 of 2011 and no. 317 of 2009.
[3] ECtHR, *Somogyi v. Italy*, judgment of 18 May 2004.

unable to obtain a new assessment as to the charges brought against him, and at the same time it is established that he has not been effectively informed of the existence of proceedings against him and has not unequivocally waived his right to be present in court.[4]

2.1. PRESSURES FROM THE EUROPEAN COURT OF HUMAN RIGHTS

Based on the principles just set out,[5] Italy has been ruled against by the supranational judge on a number of occasions. In particular, the regulations of the Code of Criminal Procedure (Article 175) aimed at guaranteeing a 'fresh' trial for defendants tried *in absentia* who have not been informed directly of the proceedings against them and have not unequivocally waived their right to appear at their trial, and consequently at safeguarding their right to personally attend the trial, were censured. Two aspects of the regulation appeared particularly critical to the Strasbourg judges: the difficulties borne by the interested party in demonstrating non-voluntary absence of knowledge of trial documents; and the short deadline granted to the party convicted *in absentia* within which to make a reinstatement claim.[6]

This specific censure from the European Court was made possible by those changes to the type of control exercised by it, as referred to above. In the *Sejdovic v. Italy* judgment of 2004 regarding trial *in absentia* and made in accordance with the scheme of the so-called 'pilot judgments', it was stressed how the violation of the fundamental rights suffered by the applicant did not represent an isolated case, and could not be attributed to events occurring in the individual proceedings, but rather was to be ascribed to a structural gap in the domestic legal system as regards *in absentia* proceedings. On that occasion, the Strasbourg judges called upon Italy to fulfil its international obligations by taking individual and general measures: the former aimed at removing the prejudice suffered by the individual, and the latter at preventing the violation from being repeated against other defendants.

Following this censure, a sort of virtuous circle was created, which first saw the legislature's immediate action to reform Article 175 of the Code of Criminal Procedure by adapting it to the indications originating from supranational

---

[4]   ECtHR, *Sejdovic v. Italy*, judgment of 10 November 2004; and ECtHR, Grand Chamber, *Sejdovic v. Italy*, judgment of 1 March 2006; ECtHR, Grand Chamber, *Zuic v. Italy*, judgment of 21 December 2006.

[5]   See ECtHR, *R.R. v. Italy*, judgment of 9 June 2005; ECtHR, *Sejdovic v. Italy*, judgment of 10 November 2004; ECtHR, *Somogyi v. Italy*, judgment of 18 May 2004; ECtHR, *Belziuk v. Poland*, judgment of 26 March 1998; ECtHR, *F.C.B. v. Italy*, judgment of 28 August 1991; ECtHR, *Colozza v. Italy*, judgment of 12 February 1985.

[6]   ECtHR, *Sejdovic v. Italy*, judgment of 10 November 2004; ECtHR, *Somogyi v. Italy*, judgment of 18 May 2004.

jurisprudence, and then found further realization in the interventions by the Court of Cassation and the Constitutional Court.

2.2. 'INTERNAL' SOLUTIONS: THE LEGISLATURE'S ACTION

Specifically, after pressure from the supranational judge, the Italian legislature took action with decree law no. 17 of 21 February 2005, converted into law no. 60 of 22 April 2005, and introduced modifications to Article 175 of the Code of Criminal Procedure, interpolating paragraph 2 and adding paragraph 2-*bis*. The first of these two paragraphs established that, in the case of a trial *in absentia* or a conviction, the defendant, upon request, is reinstated in the time limit to appeal or bring opposition 'unless he has had actual knowledge of the proceedings or of the measure, and has voluntarily waived his right to appear or to appeal or bring opposition.' For these situations, again in accordance with the reformed Article 175, paragraph 2, of the Code of Criminal Procedure, the judicial authority will bear the burden of making the necessary verifications. On the other hand, paragraph 2-*bis* of Article 175 of the Code of Criminal Procedure has established that the aforementioned application for reinstatement in the time limit must be submitted by no later than thirty days (no longer ten days) after actual knowledge of the measure has been gained.[7]

In this way, the intention was to remedy the censures against the system made by the ECtHR: on the one hand the burden of proof borne by the defendant was affected, and on the other the deadline by which to activate the remedy was extended.

Although this set of modifications improves the mechanism of the remedies for the *in absentia* defendant, it cannot be said to have fully met the requirements for a complete reopening of the case for persons convicted *in absentia* that have not been informed effectively of the proceedings against them and have not unequivocally waived their right to appear at their trial. Actually, despite the aforementioned changes in the domestic regulation, for these defendants there continues to be only the possibility of resorting – once reinstated in the time limit to appeal – to the trial on appeal, in which, among other things, new oral argument for the defendant *in absentia* (Article 603, paragraph 4, of the Code of Criminal Procedure) is connected with the existence of prerequisites coinciding with those originally provided for by Article 175, paragraph 2, of the Code of Criminal Procedure. This is without considering, then, that in the appeal trial, faculties and rights that find broad realization only in the first-level tribunal (think of the choice of alternative procedure or the right to evidence) cannot be exercised.

---

[7]   Also specifying that, in the case of extradition abroad, the deadline for submitting the application is counted starting from the convict's delivery.

It follows that, while it is indeed true that the legislature's intervention in 2005 with regard to Article 175 of the Code of Criminal Procedure acquires significance as the Italian legal system's 'response' to supranational demands, it is just as true that the remedies prepared on that occasion continue not to fully meet the supranational parameters inherent to the defendant's right to be present at the trial in person.

In this regard, it should be pointed out that the 'structural' gaps that continue to persist appear ascribable to a sort of 'original flaw.' In the Italian legal system, remedy in the case of an *in absentia* trial has always been calibrated upon reinstatement of the time limit to activate an appeal. No solutions have ever been worked out that, in the presence of circumstances legitimating the declaration of the defendant's absence, would lead to suspending the trial with suspension of the statutes of limitations or to the the the so-called 'expurgation', which is to say the possibility of holding a fresh trial.[8] These are solutions provided for in other legal systems, and certainly more in line with a trial that wishes to calibrate itself upon the adversarial model as well as the canons of the fair trial.

After the first *Sejdovic v. Italy* ruling,[9] the Italian government presented an appeal pursuant to Article 43 ECHR. Pending the judgment, the legislative modification of Article 175 of the Code of Criminal Procedure took place, and the Grand Chamber, taking note of the lawmaker's intervention, did not express itself on the compatibility of the change with the norms of the Convention, holding that this was premature, and preferring to await the jurisprudential interpretation that the new norm would then receive. Also significant from this standpoint was the Strasbourg Court's judgment of 25 November 2008, *Cat Berro v. Italy*, which underscored how the legislature, through the modifications introduced to Article 175 of the Code of Criminal Procedure, offset some of the regulatory shortcomings censured by that Court in the past, and how, however, it was necessary to await the interpretation that jurisprudence would give the changed norm.

2.3. ACTION BY THE CONSTITUTIONAL COURT

Given that the aforementioned Article 175 of the Code of Criminal Procedure in the matter of remedies against the *in absentia* judgment always and only poses the possibility of being reinstated in the time limit to appeal, an additional interpretative question arose internally, as to whether the defendant's right to appeal was 'consummated' when the appeal was presented by counsel. It is clear that, depending on the various ways to understand this circumstance, the

---

[8]   A solution in this sense had been outlined in Article 475 of the Code of Criminal Procedure, 1913.

[9]   ECtHR, *Sejdovic v. Italy*, judgment of 10 November 2004.

operative space of the remedy for the defendant tried *in absentia* changes, and consequently the degree of internal norms' consistency or conflict with supranational ones makes no difference, due to how they, among other things, are destined to 'live' in the context of the judgments adopted by the European Court.

In this regard, it must be kept in mind that the modifications made in 2005 to Article 175 of the Code of Criminal Procedure have also had an impact in annulling from this regulation the part that contemplated the preclusion, for the defendant tried *in absentia*, from being reinstated in the time limit to appeal if the appeal had already been brought by counsel. On the other hand, another norm in the Code of Criminal Procedure, Article 571, paragraph 3, is connected with the aforementioned Article 175 on this specific issue. It has also undergone changes over time, with specific regard to the circumstance now under discussion. To put it extremely briefly, in the original formulation of the code launched in 1988, Article 175 of the Code of Criminal Procedure prevented reinstatement in the time limit to appeal for the absent party if the appeal had already been brought by counsel. This counsel acted, pursuant to Article 571 of the Code of Criminal Procedure, at the absent party's specific mandate issued at the time of appointment, or thereafter. The requirement of a specific mandate corresponded to the need to ensure the defendant's full awareness of the activation of controls that, if begun at the exclusive initiative of the defence, would have prejudiced his subsequent trial choices.

In fact, at a certain point, the legislature suppressed (Article 46 of law no. 479 of 16 December 1999) that part of paragraph 3, Article 571 of the Code of Criminal Procedure that prescribed the presence of a specific mandate to appeal for the absent party's counsel. Consequently, the absent party's counsel, whether or not court-appointed, found himself unconstrained in the choice of whether to appeal the judgment adopted following *in absentia* proceedings.[10] However, the absence of *ad hoc* mandates to appeal the judgment rendered *in absentia*, resulting from the 1999 development, continued until 2005 to coexist with a version of Article 175, paragraph 2, of the Code of Criminal Procedure that established that reinstatement in the time limit to appeal for the defendant *in absentia* was precluded in the presence of appeal by counsel. This resulted in considerable applicative problems for defendants tried *in absentia* who have not been informed directly of the proceedings against them and have not unequivocally waived their right to appear at their trial, especially where there was court-appointed counsel that, with no specific mandate, by appealing exhausted the client's right to appeal the decision. As already discussed, in 2005, the obstacle – prefigured by Article 175, paragraph 2, of the Code of Criminal

---

[10]   This is at any rate without prejudice to the possibility for the defendant to remove effectiveness of the appeal brought by counsel in the manner established for the waiver, in accordance with the provisions of Article 571, paragraph 4, of the Code of Criminal Procedure.

Procedure – to reinstatement in the time limit to appeal, derived from appeal by counsel, lapsed.

On this issue – of decisive importance for formulating the question of *in absentia* judgments and possible remedies – the Court of Cassation developed a jurisprudential interpretation, confirmed by a Joint Sections intervention of 2008, according to which, giving prevalence to the principle of the single appeal, the absent party's right to appeal was spent in the event that counsel (court-appointed or otherwise) had already used the corresponding choice that the legal system entrusts to him through Article 571, paragraph 3, of the Code of Criminal Procedure. Consequently, according to this outlook, the *in absentia* defendant cannot be reinstated in the time limit pursuant to Article 175, comma 2 of the Code of Criminal Procedure.[11]

In the face of this interpretation of the norms, considered as 'living law,' it was the First Criminal Section of the Court of Cassation,[12] as judge *a quo*, that brought the interpretative question before the Constitutional Court. The single section of the Court of Cassation, called upon to act in cases similar to those that had generated the aforementioned prevailing interpretative orientation, found itself in the unique situation of not being able to distance itself, but of fully realizing the dissonance between the outcome of this interpretative operation and the fundamental rights of the ECHR as interpreted by the Strasbourg Court. Also aware of this was the Court of Cassation, gathering in Joint Sections, in adopting the aforementioned pronouncement of 2008. However, on that occasion, the Supreme Court opted for an interpretation of the norms aimed mainly at safeguarding the reasonable duration of the trial having as its constitutional reference Article 111 Const.

This formulation was disavowed by the Constitutional Court which, in consideration of the international obligations deriving from Article 117, paragraph 1, Const. and of the consequent multi-level safeguarding of fundamental human rights, declared Article 175, paragraph 2, of the Code of Criminal Procedure constitutionally illegitimate in the part where it does not allow reinstatement in the time limit of the defendant that has not had effective knowledge of the proceedings or of the measure, in order to bring an appeal against the *in absentia* judgment, in the concurrence of additional conditions indicated by law, when a similar appeal has been brought earlier by the same defendant's counsel.[13] In other words, constitutional judgment no. 317 of 2009 made it possible to bring the domestic norm on remedies for the defendant tried *in absentia* back into harmony with the supranational framework, even while retaining the systemic aporias mentioned above, which would require

---

[11]   Court of Cassation, Sez. Un., 31 January 2008, Huzunenau, in *Diritto penale e processo* (2008) p. 428.
[12]   Court of Cassation, Sez. I, 17 September 2008, V.F., in *Gazz. Uff.*, 1° Serie speciale, 2009, n. 1, 86.
[13]   Constitutional Court, case no. 317 of 2009.

lawmakers' more incisive structural intervention: operating not only in terms of reinstatement in the time limit to appeal, but reasoning over suspending the trial or 'fully' reopening the case.

3.   RIGHT TO A PUBLIC HEARING

Among the fundamental rights of the accused enshrined in the European Convention that have found broader realization in the Italian criminal trial system thanks to the influence of supranational jurisprudence is the accused's right to a public hearing. The European Court has had the opportunity to discuss this issue on a number of occasions with critical tones towards Italy. In particular, the area over which the Strasbourg judges have been called upon to exercise their control regarded, initially, Italian prevention proceedings, and then, more recently, the reparation procedure for unfair detention. In both cases, these are procedures collateral to the criminal trial regarding merit.

The second case is a matter of the reparation procedure for unfair detention suffered by someone who was later acquitted by irrevocable judgment. In this area, the ECtHR recently ruled against Italy[14] on the grounds of violation of Article 6 para. 1 ECHR, in the part where it enshrines every person's right to a fair and public hearing, covering the same steps already marked in the supranational jurisprudence that has developed on the issue. No response in terms of 'general' interventions has arrived for the moment from the domestic legal system. On this point, it will be necessary to see what subsequent developments will be suited to bringing domestic law into harmony with the supranational landscape, in order to avoid more rulings against Italy in this area.

On the other hand, the sector in which 'corrective' domestic interventions have been encountered, to be understood as general measures suitable for preventing the repetition of violations of the fair trial, is that of public hearing in prevention proceedings.

These proceedings do not decide the individual's criminal liability with regard to one or more unlawful facts, but, rather, their aims and purpose turn out to be entirely distinctive, and their compliance with constitutional principles has always been very much in doubt, even though unshakable interpretations in 'domestic' jurisprudence have prevented any evolutionary reading of the matter: the consideration – which cannot be shared – according to which these proceedings do not pertain to the 'criminal' sector in the strict sense, and therefore do not enjoy the guarantees established for that area in the Constitution, has made it possible for proceedings dealing with unlawful acts to be created in which, through recourse to mere presumptions and in the absence of proof, penalizing measures that may be likened in scope and dimension to

---

14   ECtHR, *Lorenzetti v. Italy*, judgment of 10 April 2012.

penalties in the strict sense of the word are taken. Thus, some subjects considered habitually dedicated to criminal trafficking or 'users' of unlawful proceeds and deemed dangerous for public safety, are subjected to personal prevention measures, such as special surveillance, the prohibition against staying, or the obligation to stay. Then, if there are subjects 'named' as belonging to criminal associations of particular importance, or as having committed certain particularly serious crimes, that have at their direct or indirect disposal assets whose value is out of proportion to the income capacities of the individuals or to the economic activities performed by them, or if there is sufficient grounds to believe that this is the result of unlawful activities and the subject in question does not demonstrate the assets' legitimate provenance, through this procedure measures against property, such as attachment and confiscation, can be adopted.

Now, the proceedings through which to adopt these measures, before the censure from the ECtHR and the consequent re-adaptation by the Italian Constitutional Court and then by the legislature, were held with no public hearing at any judicial level: the *in camera* hearing was the sole possibility,[15] with no provision for exceptions or alternatives in favour of the subject of the prevention measure. This was an entirely critical element in prevention proceedings, above all for the cases in which these proceedings led to the adoption of prevention measures, and especially for measures against property (attachment and confiscation), which are particularly important for the interests involved.

As is known, the right to a public hearing is enshrined by Article 6 para. 1 ECHR as among the fundamental rights for holding a fair trial, and is explicitly mentioned in other international charters. Although this right has no express reference in the Italian Constitution, it has always held constitutional importance thanks to the link that exists between popular sovereignty (Article 101 Const.) and a system of public hearing.[16]

However, it may be said that the 'dimension' of being a fundamental human right and a parameter whose presence is indispensable for holding a fair trial has been assumed by virtue of its establishment in the supranational Charters that, among other things, also identify the exceptional circumstances for derogation.[17]

The Strasbourg Court, called upon to assess compliance with the aforementioned principle by certain prevention proceedings developed in Italy, stressed the impact on individual rights derived from prevention proceedings

---

[15] Expressing itself in this sense was Article 4, paras. 6, 10, and 11, of law no. 1423 of 1956 with reference, respectively, to first instance and appeal.

[16] Constitutional Court, cases no. 373 of 1992 and no. 12 of 1971.

[17] Cf. G. Di Chiara, 'Against the administration of justice in secret: la pubblicità delle procedure giudiziarie tra Corte europea e assetti del sistema italiano', in A. Balsamo and R.E. Kostoris (eds.), *Giurisprudenza europea e processo penale italiano*, Giappichelli, Torino 2008, pp. 293 ff.

and from the consequent enforcement measures. Therefore, the public's control over the exercise of jurisdiction appeared to be an indispensable requisite for respecting the rights of the subjects involved, to the point of having to offer these subjects 'at least the possibility of urging a public hearing before the specialized sections of the tribunals and appeals courts' with jurisdiction.[18]

According to the European Court, publicly heard court procedures protect the accused from the dangers of secret justice beyond the public's control, and is an instrument for preserving the individual's faith in jurisdictional bodies. It is a fundamental human right necessary for achieving a fair trial, and must find realization in all democratic societies.

In the outlook adopted by the Strasbourg judges, there may be reasons that permit legitimately derogating from this right, but these are situations connected to the particular nature of the case being tried, the kinds of questions to be discussed, as in the case of the 'highly technical' nature of the dispute, or situations that, for precautionary reasons, must be dealt with at particular speed.

Quite different, according to the supranational judge, is the situation of prevention proceedings where, both in the court of first instance and on appeal, a procedure is established on the merits, in the total absence of public hearing, by virtue of an internal regulation with no possibility of being derogated.

As concerns prevention proceedings, the Strasbourg Court stressed that the interests 'in play', quite often of a considerable economic scope when dealing with confiscation and attachment, are of such dimensions as to hold that the public's control over the exercise of jurisdiction, at least at the urging of the person involved, is an indispensable condition for considering the interest party's right to a public hearing to be guaranteed.

Among the European Court's decisions that took place on the issue, with a critical view of Italy, there is one in particular, the *Bongiorno v. Italy* judgment of 5 January 2010, that acquires special importance, because in addition to reaffirming principles already broadly established in the Strasbourg Court's jurisprudence, it was followed a few months later by a judgment by the Constitutional Court on the Constitution's compliance with the regulations regarding prevention proceedings, in the part in which no public hearing is provided for among the procedures to be followed for the application of prevention measures, whether personal or against property: judgment no. 93 of 2010, with reference to the profile discussed, declared the constitutional illegitimacy of the domestic regulation of reference, referring to the interpretation that emerged at the ECtHR. In particular, relying on the interpretative relationship between domestic regulations, supranational

---

[18]   ECtHR, *Bongiorno v. Italy*, judgment of 5 January 2010; *Perre v. Italy*, judgment of 8 July 2008; *Bocellari and Rizza v. Italy*, judgment of 13 November 2007; and, more generally, on the scope and meaning enshrined by Article 6, para. 1 ECHR with regard to the public hearing, ECtHR, *Riepan v. Austria*, judgment of 14 November 2000, and *Tierce v. San Marino*, judgment of 25 July 2000.

principles, and interpretation made of it by the Strasbourg Court, following the model outlined by constitutional judgments nos. 348 and 349 of 2007, the constitutional judges declared the constitutional illegitimacy of Article 4 of law no. 1423 of 1956 and Article 2-*ter* of law no. 575 of 1965, in the part where they do not permit, at the petition of the interested parties, the proceedings for applying prevention measures, both personal and against property, to be held in a public hearing, on the grounds of conflict with Article 117, paragraph 1, Const.

The Constitutional Court's intervention with judgment no. 93 of 2010 heralded, at the level of the domestic legal system, that 'general measure' aimed at preventing the repetition of the violation of the right enshrined in the ECHR, which the Member States are held to for the purpose of carrying out the judgments of the ECtHR. In fact, the Committee of Ministers, in the Resolution (2011) 123 102[19] adopted on 13 September 2011 as part of the oversight powers that this body wields for the purpose of verifying the state of execution of the ECtHR's judgments, upon noting the Constitutional Court's action with the aforementioned judgment, held that Italy had complied with the obligations derived from Article 46 ECHR for the aforementioned cases, and considered the examination closed.

It must then be pointed out that the dialogue between Courts that developed on the issue of the public hearing in prevention proceedings was also followed, as already pointed out, by the lawmakers' intervention. Actually, on the occasion of the complete reordering of the existing regulations in the matter of prevention measures (legislative decree no. 159 of 6 September 2011), among other things some modifications to the public hearing rules were introduced, thus giving concrete implementation to the constitutional and supranational censures. Article 7 of legislative decree no. 159 of 2011, for the trial ordering the measure, and Article 10 of legislative decree no. 159 of 2011,[20] for the appeal trial, provide that the hearing may be held without the public present, but may proceed in a public hearing if the interested party so requests.[21]

---

19   *Bocellari and Rizza; Bongiorno and others; Leone; Perre and others v. Italy.*
20   For the proceedings for applying prevention measures against property, see Article 23, legislative decree no. 159 of 2011, and the reference contained therein.
21   This is without prejudice to the original formulation (proceedings in the council chamber) for holding the trial before the Court of Cassation. On this point, see Constitutional Court, case no. 80 of 2011.

THE ECHR'S INFLUENCE ON THE ITALIAN REGULATION OF THE ADMINISTRATIVE TRIAL

The Right to an Independent and Impartial Tribunal

Marta MENGOZZI

1. INTRODUCTION: THE RIGHT TO A FAIR TRIAL IN THE CONVENTION SYSTEM

Article 6 of the ECHR, which recognizes the right to a fair trial, indicating all the guarantees in which this right takes substance, is the provision of the Convention that, historically, gave rise to the greatest number of judgments in the half-century between 1959 and 2010:[1] the norms contained in this article have been invoked in more than one half of the trials held before the Strasbourg Court (8,019 out of a total of 13,697); and not merely with reference to the problem of reasonable time – which also figures greatly in the number, with judgments corresponding to a little more than one half (4,469) – but also as regards the other guarantees, the claimed violation of which has resulted in more than 3,500 trials (a number decisively higher than any other norm in the Convention).[2]

This fact points to a high rate of problems arising in identifying and applying these guarantees in many countries that signed the Convention. At any rate, on a more general level, it must be recognized that trial guarantees occupy a central role in all legal systems, in that they are crucial to the actual protection of all the other rights, and legitimate the very performance of jurisdictional function.

---

[1]   Reference is made to the statistical data on the years from 1959 through 2010, published on the institutional website of the European Court of Human Rights (www.echr.coe.int).

[2]   For an idea of the proportion, it is sufficient to consider that, of the other norms, the one that has given rise to the highest number of questions before the ECtHR is that pursuant to Article 1 of Protocol No. 1 protecting property, with 2,414 trials; then, the right to liberty and security (Article 5) with 1,944 trials.

Hence the particular intensity that dialogue between the Convention system and the domestic system has taken on with regard precisely to those issues, producing, from time to time, outcomes that differ, but that are always (or almost always) on a constitutional level: either because they are able to directly influence the same domestic norms on a formally constitutional level, leading the constitutional lawmaker to modify their text; or because they are of importance for the purpose of reading the guarantees contained in the constitutional clauses, conditioning their interpretation and helping to define the actual range of their provisions.

With reference to the Italian system, both these possible models of influence find concrete correspondence.

In fact, in the first place, the formulation of Article 6 of the ECHR was the main source of inspiration for a major constitutional reform, implemented with constitutional law no. 2 of 1999, which modified Article 111 of the Italian Constitution, introducing guarantees that mostly retraced the corresponding ECHR norm[3] and that earlier had not been formulated in such explicit terms in the 1948 Constitution (although largely already surmisable through interpretation from other constitutional norms).[4]

This is a case in which the influence of the ECHR system is evident – albeit while not being the only reasons for reform – and emerges explicitly from the same parliamentary debate during which numerous references may be traced to the perceived need to insert the guarantees under Article 6 ECHR into the Constitution. In fact, it should be kept in mind that at the time of the reform – before constitution law no. 3 of 2001 inserted into Article 117, para. 1, Const., the reference to lawmakers' necessary respect for international obligations – the legislative norms for carrying out international treaties were held in the Italian system as operating at a level equivalent to that of ordinary legislation.

However, it is more complicated – and more interesting – to investigate the other type of constitutional influence by the ECHR system on the national legal system: that which operates on the level of interpreting, and thus defining, the actual meaning of constitutional guarantees in their concrete applications. It is a setting in which the interaction between national systems and the convention system operates in accordance with more complex and articulated means.

---

[3] The very expression 'due process,' now introduced into the first paragraph of Article 111 of Italian Constitution, in addition to evoking the *due process of law clause* in the American tradition, refers to and even models itself after the title of Article 6 ECHR ('right to a fair trial'). On the identical value of the expressions 'due process' and 'fair trial,' see the considerations by S. Fois, 'Il modello costituzionale del giusto processo' (2000) *Rassegna Parlamentare* 572.

[4] For a more complete analysis both of the genesis of the Italian constitutional reform cited in the text and of its innovative scope – topics that cannot be discussed here in any depth – reference may be made to M. Mengozzi, *Giusto processo e processo amministrativo*, Giuffrè, Milano 2009, pp. 24 ff.

In effect, it is precisely how constitutional provisions are understood and exist in the legal system that defines their actual configuration; it is therefore precisely the analysis of this type of influence that allows the outcomes of the domestic legal system's relationship with the ECHR system to be truly and fully grasped.

This work thus proposes to re-examine the various occasions for dialogue and mutual influence between the Italian legal system and the convention system, precisely with respect to the reading of trial guarantees, analyzed in relation to the concrete problems posed by the national regulation of the administrative trial.

2. THE GUARANTEE OF THE JUDGE'S IMPARTIALITY AND THE VARIOUS OUTCOMES OF THE DIALOGUE BETWEEN LEGAL SYSTEMS

For the purposes of the analysis to be made, more particular account will be taken of one of the aspects of the guarantees under the Convention that has given rise to the most significant opportunities for exchange between the systems: that regarding the judge's impartiality – a guarantee that the Strasbourg Court has qualified, even recently in the *Udorovic* judgment of 2010, as 'inalienable' and not susceptible to appeal, exception or offsetting.[5]

It is thus a requirement that is present both in Article 6 of the ECHR and in the aforementioned text of Article 111 of the Italian Constitution (which speaks of 'an impartial judge in third party position').[6]

Its concrete applications have raised considerable problems, especially with reference to the regulation of the administrative trial, and, as already pointed out, have given rise to a lively interaction between the ECtHR and domestic legal systems, leading from time to time to different outcomes.

---

[5] *Udorovic v. Italy*, judgment of 18 May 2010; see in particular para. 47, for the definition of the judge's independence and impartiality as guarantees that are unalienable. In other words, Strasbourg's jurisprudence has indicated a sort of ranking of guarantees, stressing that the need for the trial to be held before an independent and impartial judge is an essential rule not susceptible to exceptions, on any occasion, unlike other guarantees, such as for example that of a public hearing, which do not find necessary application in all cases, thus permitting exceptions.

[6] The terms 'impartial' and 'third party,' in fact, are mostly used interchangeably, as a hendiadys, in Italian constitutional jurisprudence (see, for example, judgment no. 131 of 1996, in which the Court defines the judge's 'impartiality' as an aspect of his 'third party position' characterizing the exercise of his functions, distinguishing it from that of all the other public subjects). Some attempts to attribute to each of these terms its own autonomous meaning have actually been advanced by Italian doctrine (see, among others, N. ZANON-F. BIONDI, *Diritto costituzionale dell'ordine giudiziario*, Giuffrè, Milano 2002, p. 111), but they are always formulated in quite problematic terms, and often lead to the conclusion that 'the two profiles absolutely cannot be separated' (M. CECCHETTI, *Giusto processo (dir. cost.)*, in *Enciclopedia del diritto*, V aggiornamento, Giuffrè, Milano 2001, p. 610).

In particular, three problems will be considered; although distinct from one another, they are all connected with the theme of the judge's impartiality, with regard to which the dialogue between national and supranational judges in fact appears to have yielded divergent results.

On the first issue, that of the so-called force of prevention, one may note a considerable influence by ECHR jurisprudence on the orientations of domestic jurisprudence – an influence in fact that although mostly not explicitly recognized, is evident all the same.

However, on the second issue (the relationship between jurisdictional and consultative functions), we are dealing with a more complex dialogue. In fact, on the one hand, the ECHR system's conditioning of the national systems cannot be denied: however, this conditioning, while quite strong in some countries, has not been as strong with regard to Italy, where the deep historical roots of certain institutions created staunch resistance to the more extreme outcomes. On the other hand, it must be noted in this case that certain positions by the European Court have, over time, been formulated so as to also take into account the organizational needs of the Member States (among which, of course, Italy): that is, in certain respects, the influence between the two systems has worked 'backwards', from down up, causing the arrangements widespread in many member states to end up guiding how the same guarantee is understood in the ECHR legal system as well.

Lastly, on the third issue, that of non-judicial positions, a 'missed' dialogue must be recorded, as indications from European jurisprudence have met with no response in Italy.

3. A CASE OF CLEAR ECHR INFLUENCE: THE SO-CALLED FORCE OF PREVENTION

The first point, as just discussed, thus regards the so-called force of prevention.

For years, Strasbourg's jurisprudence has pointed, as an element objectively capable of raising doubts as to the judge's impartiality[7] pursuant to Article 6 of the ECHR, to the *cumul des fonctions judiciares* that occurs when a judge, also in

---

[7] It should also be kept in mind that the Strasbourg Court, in applying the principle of the judge's impartiality, developed the so-called doctrine of appearances: for the requirement of impartiality to be met, it is extremely important not only for the judge to be effectively equidistant from the interests at play, but also for him or her to appear as such to the parties, and to inspire trust in those subjected to his or her judgment. Therefore, for the decision-making body to be deemed impartial, it is enough that the circumstances create the appearance of a prevention, at least when this suspicion is founded upon elements that have objective consistency (and therefore, it cannot merely be the personal opinion of those subjected to judgment that comes into relief, but objective justifications for a fear of this kind are needed): see the judgments *Piersack v. Belgium* of 1 October 1982, and *Castillo Algar v. Spain* of 28 October 1998.

the context of the same level of proceedings, is entrusted with different decision-making stages: after having expressed a judgment in a given phase, the magistrate will appear biased when having to return to the same choices at another point in the trial.[8]

This interpretation of the impartiality requirement is more far-reaching than that adopted in the Italian legal system, in which the judge's incompatibility was affirmed only between different levels of jurisdiction.

However, the Italian Constitutional Court long ago adopted the indications originating from Strasbourg, at least with respect to the criminal trial, stressing the existence of a 'natural tendency [of the judge] to maintain a judgment already expressed or an attitude already taken in other decision-making points in the same proceedings',[9] that may compromise his or her impartiality; it thus referred the incompatibility provided for by the Italian Code of Criminal Procedure[10] not only to the various levels of jurisdiction, but also to the distinct phases in a given trial.

In civil and administrative trials, on the other hand, although developments were far more cautious, they have not been lacking in more recent years: these developments have not gone so far as to touch the relationship between pre-trial proceedings and decision on the merits (a point to be returned to shortly), but regarded other particular cases which, until a few years ago, ruled out application of the abstention obligation in the event of a judge coming to the case 'as a magistrate in another level of the trial' (according to the provisions of Article 51, no. 4, of the Italian Code of Civil Procedure,[11] to which the regulation of the administrative trial makes express reference; see Article 17 of the Administrative Trial Code).

Thus, with the decision of the Plenary Assembly no. 2 of 2009, the Council of State expressly modified its prior jurisprudence, declaring the aforementioned case of obligatory abstention applicable to rehearing as well, and affirming the incompatibility of the judge/physical person that has taken part in the decision later nullified by review.

Actually, on this point, national jurisprudence has gone even further than what was required by the orientations of the ECtHR, which considers incompatible, in rehearings, judges that have already taken part in the first decision in cases where nullification is determined on procedural grounds

---

8   Among the earliest decisions taken in this regard by the European Court, see the *Piersack* judgment of 1 October 1982 and the *De Cubber* judgment of 26 October 1984.

9   Starting from the case no. 432 of 1995, which innovated prior constitutional jurisprudence on the point; see also, among the most significant judgments, cases nos. 155 of 1996 and 131 of 1996.

10 See Article 34, para. 2, of the Code of Criminal Procedure.

11 According to this measure, the judge must abstain 'if he has given counsel or lent advocacy in the case, or has deposed in it as a witness, or has come to the case as a magistrate at another level of the trial, or as arbitrator, or has lent assistance as technical consultant.'

(*Vaillant* judgment).[12] At any rate, the Council of State's *revirement* appears absolutely guided, or at least highly conditioned, by the indications originating from the European setting. In truth, it bears noting that ECHR jurisprudence is in no way cited in the Council of State's decision, which, rather, justifies the change in orientation on the basis of a series of other factors: the constitutional need for an impartial judge in third party position, the doctrine of the so-called force of prevention, and some other precedents in the jurisprudence of the Italian Constitutional Court and the Court of Cassation. However, it is precisely these elements that are in turn in some way ascribable – as already discussed – to the stimuli originating from the Convention system.

On the occasion of the same important decision, the Plenary Assembly declared the aforementioned case of obligatory abstention applicable in repeal as well[13] – not only, as was already accepted, in the case in which the judge's malice is claimed (Article 395, no. 6, of the Code of Civil Procedure), but also when the petition is based upon an error of fact (Article 395, no. 4, of the Code of Civil Procedure), even when it is a matter of 'blunder of senses' and not of erroneous appreciation;[14] here, in this case as well, was an innovation from prior positions.

However, this case is not considered applicable in third-party opposition proceedings,[15] given that, in this case, the Code of Civil Procedure (Article 405) establishes that the decision belongs to the judge that made the judgment.

There was no change, however, as regards the relationship between the various phases of the same level of jurisdiction, and in particular that between pre-trial proceedings and decision on the merits. On this point, national administrative jurisprudence is firm in holding that Article 51, no. 4, of the Code of Civil Procedure does not apply.

---

[12]   *Vaillant v. France*, judgment of 18 December 2008: '*Il y a lieu en effet de distinguer le renvoi en cas de vice de fond affectant de manière irrémédiable la décision attaquée de celui où, comme en l'espèce, ce n'est qu'un problème de procédure qui est en cause. Si l'on peut concevoir, dans la première hypothèse, des appréhensions du justiciable à l'égard de l'impartialité des magistrats appelés à rejuger l'affaire, tel est difficilement le cas dans la seconde hypothèse*'.

[13]   This is the special means of appeal provided for by Articles 106 and 107 of the Administrative Trial Code and regulated in the administrative trial through broad reference to Articles 395 and 396 of the Code of Civil Procedure as regards the cases and modes of appeal.

[14]   The type of error that may justify recourse to the repeal instrument, based on Article 395, no. 4, of the Code of Civil Procedure, is in fact: 'merely perceptive error that in no way involves the judge's assessment of trial situations exactly perceived in their objectivity, and is not apparent in principle when a presumed erroneous assessment of the trial records and results, or an anomaly in the logical proceedings of interpretation of evidentiary material is complained of, as, in this case, everything comes down to in an error of judgment' (Consiglio di Stato, sect. V, 19 June 2009, no. 4040; Consiglio di Stato, Ad. Plen., 17 May 2010, no. 2).

[15]   This is another means of extraordinary appeal, regulated by the Administrative Trial Code under Articles 108–109, following the pattern of the configuration this institution has in the civil trial.

The Italian Constitution Court has justified this choice by stating that the relationship between pre-trial proceedings and decision of merit differs in civil and administrative proceedings from what occurs in criminal ones.[16] That is to say, in the former, the two points would be treated as sequential phases within the same trial, in which the ruling must be based on different elements. There is no identity of the *res judicanda*, because the ruling on the *fumus* typical of the pre-trial phase would be qualitatively different from that on the merits, it being a matter of a summary ruling. In the criminal trial, however, the pre-trial proceedings have to take into account all the possible elements of the final decision and, although not based upon actual proof but merely on clues, could not be treated as a ruling of a summary nature, and would not have an object substantially different from that on the merits, expressing a 'positive prognostic ruling'.

Although this now well-established arrangement has received various criticisms from doctrine, especially trial/civil-law doctrine,[17] it does not appear to have been cast into doubt by the Strasbourg Court which, although not having ruled precisely on the point, at times seems to attribute an importance, in evaluating questions that are in some way similar, to the circumstance that the trial puts rights of a civil nature rather than criminal charges into play. In the *Sacilor Lormines* judgment,[18] for example, in assessing the importance of decisions taken by the judge prior to the trial for the purposes of meeting the impartiality requirement, it expressly states that '*En "matière civile", le simple fait, pour un juge, d'avoir déjà pris des décisions avant le procès ne peut passer pour justifier en soi des appréhensions relativement à son impartialité*', holding, rather, that the judgment is rendered based on the evidence produced and the arguments made in the hearing. Although the cases in point, both in the judgment just mentioned and in the precedents it cites, differ and do not regard the relationship between pre-trial proceedings and decision on the merits, the specification made by the Court appears in some way to follow the logic of a possible different approach to the problem of the force of prevention in the various types of proceedings.

---

[16]   See case no. 326 of 1997; this arrangement was then adopted and used in various subsequent orders by the Constitutional Court, which makes reference to it in its cases no. 359 of 1998; no. 168 of 2000 and no. 497 of 2002.

[17]   B. Capponi, 'Brevi osservazioni sull'articolo 111 della Costituzione (procedimento monitorio, processo contumaciale, Article 186 quater c.p.c.)' and N. Scripelliti, 'L'imparzialità del giudice ed il nuovo articolo 111 della Costituzione', both in M.G. Civinini and C.M. Verardi (eds.), *Il nuovo articolo 111 della Costituzione e il giusto processo civile*, Giuffrè, Milano 2001, respectively pp. 105 and 108.

[18]   *Sacilor Lormines v. France*, judgment of 9 November 2006.

4. A CASE OF EXTREMELY COMPLEX DIALOGUE: THE SIMULTANEOUS PRESENCE OF CONSULTATIVE AND JURISDICTIONAL FUNCTIONS IN THE BODIES OF ADMINISTRATIVE JUSTICE

An additional issue that allows us to reflect upon the mutual influence between the domestic legal system and that of the ECHR is, with reference to the guarantee of the judge's impartiality in the administrative trial, that of the simultaneous presence of consultative and jurisdictional functions in certain bodies of administrative justice. This issue is a highly delicate one, in that it regards arrangements deriving from long-standing traditions, and involves the systems of administrative justice in various member states (including Italy).

European jurisprudence has dealt with this aspect on a number of occasions and, over time, has gradually diminished its action, settling upon a 'minimal' reading of the requirement of impartiality.

Probably, as already discussed, in this case it may be said that the 'dialogue' between legal systems has worked in the other direction, and the Strasbourg Court has ended up being influenced by how the guarantee in question is understood by many of the national legal systems it addresses.

The first ruling on the issue, 1995's *Procola* judgment[19] rendered against Luxembourg, in fact provided a glimpse of potentially high-impact developments which, however, were allowed to lapse in later decisions. Indeed, even though the judgment is based exclusively upon the fact that the physical persons of the magistrates that had dealt with the same issue in two different guises materially coincided (four out of five members of the panel of judges had already dealt with the same issue in consultation), the Court had also gone so far as to add – albeit only incidentally – that the very fact that the members of Luxembourg's Council of State could exercise both functions with regard to the same act was enough to raise doubts as to the institution's 'structural impartiality.'

The finding opened scenarios of considerable scope. It is no accident that the content of this decision led Luxembourg to a constitutional reform[20] that profoundly modified the arrangement of the Council of State, separating the two functions: this body retained only the consultative function, which was further reinforced,[21] while jurisdictional duties were given to an administrative court created *ad hoc*.

---

[19]   *Procola v. Luxembourg*, judgment of 28 September 1995.

[20]   Through the constitutional revision of 12 July 1996, which entered force on 1 January 1997.

[21]   The Council of State was, in fact, also vested with the mission of preventatively checking that bills and regulations complied with higher-level legal norms. See www.conseil-etat.public.lu/fr/historique/index.html. On the issue, cf. also V. PARISIO, 'Il Consiglio di Stato in Italia tra consulenza e giurisdizione alla luce della Convenzione europea dei diritti dell'uomo', in EAD.

Thereafter, however, the Court never developed these points, settling on the now well-established position inaugurated in 2000 by the *McGonnell* judgment[22] and then adopted in the *Kleyn* judgment of 2003[23] and the *Sacilor Lormines* judgment of 2006:[24] the Convention does not require the States to adopt a given conception of the relations between powers, and the Court must limit itself to assessing the circumstances of the individual case; the 'dual' structure of certain bodies of administrative justice (in Italy, the issue involves, above all, the Council of State) is thus considered acceptable and compatible with Article 6 ECHR, provided that the differentness of the physical persons dealing with the same questions in the two venues is guaranteed.

Therefore, as already discussed, the Court – after the first, more courageous pronouncement – then opted for a reading of the impartiality requirement that did not radically upset the organizational arrangements present in many of the member states, going no further than demanding the minimum guarantee that the subjects that, on the various occasions, decide the same issues, do not coincide.

The problem of course remains of establishing when it is a matter of the 'same issue,' especially in the case of acts connected with one another.[25]

(ed.), *Diritti interni, diritto comunitario e principi sovranazionali. Profili amministrativistici*, Giuffrè, Milano 2009, p. 245, and, *ibid.*, J. MORAND-DEVILLER, *La Cour Européenne des droits de l'homme et le droit admistratif français*, p. 216.

22   *McGonnell v. United Kingdom*, judgment of 8 February 2000.

23   Grand Chamber, *Kleyn and others v. the Netherlands*, judgment of 6 May 2003. This is probably the judgment in which the Court expressed its clearest refusal to abstractly assess the compatibility of the institution's structure with Article 6 ECHR, while adopting and emphasizing some considerations that had remained only hinted at in the *McGonnell* decision.

24   *Sacilor Lormines v. France*, judgment of 9 November 2006. This decision actually marks a decided convergence towards the orientation indicated in the text, because it was taken unanimously. In *Kleyn*, on the other hand, the decision was made by a majority with 12 votes in favour and 5 votes against (this was a Grand Chamber decision). In particular, the dissenting judges' opinions (see above all the opinion of the judges Thomassen and Zagrebelsky) stressed that where there is no clear separation of functions within a given body, there must be particularly rigorous scrutiny as to the deciding panel's objective impartiality. Another dissenting opinion (by three other judges), went even further, stigmatizing in more general terms the mingling of jurisdictional and government functions in the same bodies, and urging, as the absolutely most effective solution for removing any doubt as to the impartiality of these bodies, the clear separation between the two functions. In *Sacilor Lormines*, on the other hand, none of the judges expressed doubt any longer as to the correctness of the arrangement that had been adopted. The only dissenting opinions, in fact, regarded a different aspect of the issue. On the latter decision, in Italian doctrine, see V. PARISIO, *Il Consiglio di Stato in Italia*, supra n. 21, p. 247; and P. DE LISE, *Corte europea dei diritti dell'uomo e giudice amministrativo*, Report to the Congress *Le giurisdizioni a contatto con la giurisprudenza della Corte europea dei diritti dell'uomo* held in Rome on 20 April 2009, and published at www.giustizia-amministrativa.it.

25   The Court initially (in the *McGonnell* judgment) provided a broader interpretation of the reference to the 'same issue,' and then adopted a far more restrictive reading in the *Kleyn* and *Sacilor Lormines* judgments; in the latter decisions, it ended up providing, from this standpoint as well, a less rigorous assessment of the impartiality guarantee.

One might at any rate expect that Italy may be thought to be in line with the 'minimal' reading of the impartiality requirement adopted by the Court with reference to this issue.

In reality, however, a number of problems remain open, for which the influence of the ECHR legal system does not yet appear to have completely fulfilled its potential.

In the first place, the new Administrative Trial Code[26] abrogated the long-standing regulation (until that time still in force in the Italian legal system) contained in Article 43, para. 2, of the consolidation act of laws of the *Consiglio di Stato*,[27] which expressly established the prohibition against taking part in decisions in the jurisdictional setting for magistrates that had, in the consultative section of the Council of State, contributed to providing an opinion on the issue that was the object of the petition ('Council members that have, in the consultative section, contributed to providing an opinion on the issue that is the object of the petition cannot take part in the decisions').

Today, these special grounds for abstention might be considered to come under the case of obligatory abstention pursuant to Article 51, no. 4, of the Code of Civil Procedure (to which Article 17 of the Administrative Trial Code refers for determining the grounds for abstention and recusal), in the part in which it states that the judge who has 'given counsel' in the case must abstain. In fact, beyond any possible doubt as to the two possibilities coinciding, this formulation now appears based upon the need to interpret the corresponding norms in a manner that complies constitutionally (and '*conventionally*'), as per Article 117, para. 1, and Article 111 of the Constitution. Any other interpretation, at any rate, would expose Italy to international liability before the European Court.

In any event, given the delicacy of the issue, it would perhaps be preferable to leave the already existing specific case of abstention in force. The inappropriateness of this abrogation appears quite clear when considering that, exactly following the positions taken on that point by the European Court, a similar case of incompatibility was in fact recently introduced in France, with decree no. 225 of 6 March 2008.[28]

An additional problem is linked to the innovation introduced by decree law no. 112 of 25 June 2008, under Article 54, which appears to run counter to the indications coming from Strasbourg's jurisprudence, thereby increasing the confusion between the two functions held by the Council of State. The rigid

---

[26] A code approved in Italy in more recent years, with legislative decree no. 104 of 2 July 2010.

[27] Royal decree no. 1054 of 1924. Moreover, the norm was already present in consolidation act no. 638 of 1907, under Article 35.

[28] The decree 2008-225 introduced the rule according to which '*les membres du Conseil d'Etat ne peuvent participer au jugement des recours dirigés contre les actes pris après avis du Conseil d'Etat, s'ils ont pris part à la délibération de cet avis*'. On the point, see J. MORAND-DEVILLER, *La Cour Européenne des droits de l'homme*, supra n. 21, p. 216, and V. PARISIO, *Il Consiglio di Stato in Italia*, supra n. 21, p. 248.

breakdown of consultative and jurisdictional functions between the various sections of the Council of State (the first three with consultative functions, the others with jurisdictional functions) was thus eliminated, in favour of a 'flexible' division that was to change every year at the determination of the President of the Council of State who, upon hearing the Council of Presidency, by his own measure, identifies which sections are to perform one type of function, and which ones the other. This system appears to multiply rather than reduce the occasions for possible 'prevention' by the judges.

Lastly, certain special cases might pose an additional problem, where the General Assembly of the Council of State, composed of all the magistrates in service at the Council of State, is called upon to render an opinion on an act (as may occur at the request of the consultative section for regulatory acts, or of the President, based on the regulations provided for by Article 17, para. 28, of law no. 127 of 1997). In this case, the minimal guarantee required by the European Court could not be met, in the case of subsequent jurisdictional appeal of the same act (consider, for example, a regulation by the executive, which may well be the object of a petition before the bodies of administrative justice).

5.   A CASE OF MISSED DIALOGUE: NON-JUDICIAL POSITIONS HELD BY ADMINISTRATIVE MAGISTRATES

Lastly, moving on to the third point, some observations need to be made regarding an additional opportunity for dialogue that, for now, has been missed. We are referring to the issue of non-judicial positions held by administrative magistrates, *vis-à-vis* the guarantee of impartiality.

In this regard, the European Court, in the aforementioned *Sacilor Lormines v. France* decision – despite having deemed admissible the government's appointment of State Councillors by virtue of the guarantee of non-removability that characterizes their position[29] – declared the violation of Article 6 ECHR for the circumstance that one of the administrative judges that had decided the jurisdictional petition had, a few days prior to the publication of the ruling, been

---

[29]   From this perspective, the French regulation is similar to Italy's. In this regard, Strasbourg Court's position actually appears difficult to share. It is, however, entirely similar to the one that, in Italy, the Italian Constitutional Court had already taken long ago (judgments no. 1 of 1967 and no. 177 of 1973) with respect to this system of investiture, which in Italy is regarded as a component both of the magistrates of the Council of State and of those of the Court of Auditors. This puzzling arrangement leaves room for perplexity, and appears to confuse the two guarantees of independence and impartiality. At any rate, on this point, domestic constitutional jurisprudence and supranational jurisprudence have shown themselves in perfect alignment and consistency; it thus does not appear necessary to dwell on the subject in this work.

appointed Secretary General of the Ministry that had been a party to the proceedings. According to the Court, the magistrate had to have already been 'in the running' for this appointment for some time. And this amounts to an objective prejudice to the judge's appearance of impartiality.[30]

On this front, the introduction into the Italian legal system, in more recent times (legislative decree no. 35 of 2006), of the obligation to publicize non-judicial positions given to administrative judges is undoubtedly to be hailed favourably. Nevertheless it still remains to be established how, in the Italian system, the need for a substantial containment of said positions – a need that, given a practice of broad reliance on them that has always been quite widespread in the Italian system, has been urged not only by doctrine[31] but also by the Constitutional Court, which already expressed itself in this sense many years ago[32] – has gone absolutely unanswered.

In fact, the regulation in force in Italy, contained in DPR no. 418 of 6 October 1993, is anything but restrictive. At any rate, the fact that such regulatory provisions are completely insufficient for the purpose of effectively containing the phenomenon is demonstrated, empirically but significantly, by the data on the number and importance of the positions assigned to administrative magistrates every year.[33]

On this issue, therefore, the Italian national system and the European system do not yet appear to have entered a real conflict; it is a conflict, however, that appears unavoidable in the future.

6. CONCLUSION

Many other aspects of the Italian regulation of the administrative trial might offer an opportunity for considerations similar to those made here, and also with reference to requirements other than that of impartiality. All the guarantees provided for in Article 6 ECHR, in their concrete application, have in fact opened possibilities for dialogue and mutual influence between the systems, in

---

[30] Actually, on this point, the decision was taken by majority; three judges in fact expressed a dissenting opinion, holding that the so-called doctrine of appearances could lead to excessive outcomes, as in the case in point, in which there was no objective proof of the lack of impartiality.

[31] Among others, cf. F. SORRENTINO, 'Profili costituzionali della giurisdizione amministrativa' (1990) *Diritto Processuale Amministrativo* 71; U. ALLEGRETTI, 'Giustizia amministrativa e principi costituzionali' (2001) *Amministrare* 200; S. PANUNZIO, 'Il ruolo della giustizia amministrativa in uno stato democratico. Osservazioni sul caso italiano', in V. PARISIO (ed.), *Il ruolo della giustizia amministrativa*, supra n. 21, pp. 89 ff.; A TRAVI, 'Per l'unità della giurisdizione' (1998) 3 *Diritto Pubblico* 371 ff.

[32] See case no. 177 of 1973.

[33] Today these are easily retrievable, as they are published every six months by the Council of Presidency of Administrative Justice, as well as on its institutional website.

some cases showing a strong influence of the Convention's legal system, and in other cases a more difficult and disputed relationship.

For example, of great importance is certainly the issue of reasonable time, and of the compensation obligations that descend from violating this right – which, however, cannot be discussed here.[34]

The domestic system and the ECHR one may now be said to have been placed in stable communication with one another, and this relationship now makes comparison inevitable.

Moreover, awareness of this appears to have been demonstrated by the drafters of the recent Italian Administrative Trial Code which, in Article 1, expressly indicated the intention to ensure a jurisdictional protection 'in accordance with the principles of the Constitution and of European law' – which inevitably includes the ECHR system.

---

[34] Here we merely point out that the ECHR's regulations have had, among other things, the effect of necessitating the introduction in Italy of an internal remedy for violation of the right to the reasonable time for the trial: an instrument, that is, that would afford the individual 'effective recourse in the presence of a national claim' in order to invoke the injury, as required by Article 13 ECHR. This remedy is the one instituted by the so-called Pinto law, no. 89 of 24 March 2001.

PART I.C

ECHR IN NATIONAL CONSTITUTIONS: COMPARATIVE PERSPECTIVES

TOWARD A CONVERGENCE BETWEEN THE EU AND ECHR LEGAL SYSTEMS?

A Comparative Perspective

Oreste Pollicino

1. THE POST-ENLARGEMENT AGGRESSIVE PHASE OF THE EUROPEAN COURT OF HUMAN RIGHTS

The process of enlargement of Europe to the east has presented different challenges for the European Union (EU) on the one hand and for the European Convention of Human Rights (ECHR) system on the other hand, provoking different, if not conflicting, reactions in the two European Courts.

Elsewhere[1] it has been argued that, because of those reactions, the two European Courts seem to have involuntarily started to converge in terms of their 'idea' of the domestic effects of EU law and the ECHR in the legal orders of the Member States of the two supranational organizations.

More precisely, the above-mentioned trend of convergence has its roots in the two opposite ways in which the two European Courts have reacted to the challenges emerging from the enlargement of the European Union and of the Council of Europe towards Eastern Europe. In fact, on the one hand, the ECtHR has opted for an acceleration of judicial activism according to which the Strasbourg judges have started to amplify the direct and indirect effect of their case law on the domestic legal orders; on the other hand, the ECJ seems to have privileged, since the great enlargement of 2004, the appraisal of national constitutional values even of single Member States.

As regard the ECHR dimension, since the end of the Cold War, the Council of Europe has experienced a dramatic increase in the number of members. In 1989, the Council of Europe was an exclusively Western European organization with 23 Member States. By 2007, its membership had grown to 47 countries,

---

1   O. Pollicino, *Allargamento dell'Europa ad est e rapporti tra Corti costituzionali e corti europee. Verso una teoria generale dell'impatto interordinamentale del diritto sovranazionale?*, Giuffrè, Milano 2012.

including almost all the former Communist states of Central and Eastern Europe.

Our assumption is that the ECtHR has reacted to the Council of Europe's enlargement to the east with a more explicit understanding of itself as a pan-European constitutional court, as a result of both the exponential growth of its case load and the realistic possibility for it to examine systemic human rights violations in Central and Eastern European (CEE) countries. This has implied a shift away from an exclusively subsidiary role as 'secondary guarantor of human rights' to a more central and crucial position as a constitutional adjudicator.

It is arguable that this change in the judicial attitude of the ECtHR emerged for the first time in 1993, in Judge Martens' concurring opinion in the *Branningan* case.[2] On that occasion, the majority of the Court, recalling a judgment from 1978,[3] stated that the determination of whether the life of the nation may be threatened by a 'public emergency' has to be left to the wider margin of appreciation of the Member States. By reason of their direct and constant contact with the current, pressing needs of the moment, in fact, it was observed, the national authorities are in a better position than international judges to decide both on the actual occurrence of such an emergency, and on the nature and scope of the necessary derogations to avert it. Conversely, in his concurring opinion, Judge Martens argued that 'since 1978 present day conditions' have considerably changed. Apart from the developments to which the arguments of Amnesty refer, the situation within the Council of Europe has changed dramatically. It is therefore by no means self-evident that standards which may have been acceptable in 1978 are still so. The 1978 view of the Court as regards the margin of appreciation under Article 15 was, presumably, influenced by the view that the majority of the then Member States of the Council of Europe might be assumed to be societies which had been democracies for a long time and, as such, were fully aware both of the importance of the individual right to liberty and of the inherent danger of giving too wide a power of detention to the executive. Since the accession of CEE States that assumption has lost its pertinence.

Another call for a more proactive role for the ECtHR as a reaction to the Council of Europe's enlargement came from the same Judge Martens' separate opinion in the Court's 1995 decision in *Fisher v. Austria*.[4] To the then typical self-restraint of the Strasbourg Court, according to which 'the European Court should confine itself as far as possible to examining the question raised by the Court before it',[5] Judge Martens objected that 'no provision of the Convention compels the Court to decide in this way on a strict case by case basis. This self-

---

2   ECtHR, *Branningan and McBride v. United Kingdom*, judgment of 26 May 1993, para. 43.
3   ECtHR, *Ireland v. United Kingdom*, judgment of 18 January 1978, para. 207.
4   ECtHR, *Fisher v. Austria*, judgment of 26 April 1995.
5   *Ibid.*, para. 44.

imposed restriction may have been a wise policy when the Court began its career, but it is no longer appropriate. A case law that is developed on a strict case by case basis necessarily leads to uncertainty as to both the exact purport of the Court's judgment and the precise content of the Court's doctrine.'[6]

The message was indeed quite clear: an explicit invitation addressed to the Court to assume a more general constitutional and centralized role, by drawing the necessary conclusions from its then recent proclamation that the Convention was a 'constitutional instrument of European public order'[7] and, consequently, by going beyond the original aim of ensuring (only) individual justice. The Strasbourg Court gradually got the message by applying a more innovative and intrusive judicial approach with respect to its consolidated case law, and more precisely by moving in two distinct directions.[8] The first tendency was to amplify the 'direct effect' of its judgments, that is, their effectiveness *vis-à-vis* the state that was party to the case. The second, known as indirect effect, seems to lead to an interpretative primacy of ECtHR jurisprudence with regard to other contracting States not involved in the case in which the particular judgment is delivered. What emerges from the summation of these two tendencies seems to cast doubt on some characteristic traits of ECtHR jurisprudence, in particular its asserted effectiveness *inter partes*, exclusively addressed to the parties involved in a specific judgment, and its foundations on the principle of individual justice.[9]

2. THE OPPOSITE POST-ENLARGEMENT REACTION OF THE COURT OF JUSTICE OF THE EUROPEAN UNION

The further centralization of the ECtHR's adjudication powers, which has been analyzed in the previous paragraph, along with the reduction of the margin of appreciation of the contracting States, need not be regarded as a foolish leap into activism by the Strasbourg judges. This is because, in the words of Wojciech Sadurski: 'if there is a domain in which concern over national identity and

---

[6] *Ibid.*, separate opinion of Judge Martens, para. 16.
[7] *Ibid.*, para. 75.
[8] See, for the above mentioned distinction, O. DE SCHUTTER, 'La coopération entre la Cour européenne des droits de l'homme et le juge national' (1997) 1 *Revue belge du droit international* 21.
[9] Since one of its first judgments (*De Beker v. Belgium*, judgment of 9 June 1958), the ECtHR made it abundantly clear that its privileged perspective was that of individual justice, by affirming that 'the Court is not called upon under articles 19 and 25 of the Convention, to give a decision on an abstract problem relating to the compatibility of that Act with the provisions of the Convention, but on the specific case of the application of such an Act to the applicant and to the extent to which the latter would, as a result, be prevented from exercising one of the rights guaranteed by the Convention'.

accompanying notions of sovereignty are obviously weak in central and eastern Europe it is in the field of protection of individual rights.'[10]

It should also be added that, in support of its new post-enlargement attitude of judicial activism, the ECtHR could count on the remarkable openness of the constitutions of CEE Member States to international law, especially international law on human rights.[11] This openness – a reaction to the very weak, almost non-existent, role played by international law in the legal orders of CEE countries, even at constitutional level, under the Soviet dominance[12] – finds its concrete expression in the monistic vocation of the new constitutions and in the rank granted to international law, which almost everywhere occupies an intermediate position between the constitution and the ordinary domestic law.[13]

On the contrary, the ECJ could not count on the same advantages brought by the EU enlargement to the east. At least five factors, direct or indirect consequences of the said enlargement, dictate against the 'peaceful' impact of EU law on the domestic legal orders of the CEE Member States, and therefore, represent new, problematic challenges for the ECJ.

First of all, there is the risk that the taste of freedom – recently rediscovered after years of humiliation and substantial or formal subjection to the Soviet Union – made the candidate countries from Central and Eastern Europe strongly averse to a (new) transfer of sovereignty to the European Union, albeit in a completely different political and historical context.[14] Against this background, it should be remarked that the protection of national identity acquires a crucial importance in the post-1989 constitutionalism. As Sadurski has pointed out:

---

[10] The main reason, according to Sadurski, is that 'the legacy of Communism under which individual rights were systematically trampled on is still fresh in many people's minds'. See W. SADURSKI, 'The Role of the EU Charter of Fundamental Rights in the Process of the Enlargement', in G.A. BERMANN and K. PISTOR (eds.), *Law and Governance in an Enlarged European Union*, Hart, Oxford 2004, p. 80.

[11] E. STEIN, 'International Law in Internal Law. Toward Internationalization of Central-Eastern European Constitutions?' (1994) 88 *Am. J. Int'l L.* 427.

[12] A. DRZEMCZEWSKI and M.A. NOWICKI, 'Poland', in R. BLACKBURN and J. POLKIEWICZ (eds), *Fundamental Rights in Europe: The European Convention of Human Rights and Its Member States 1950–2000*, Oxford University Press, Oxford 2001, p. 657.

[13] See A. KELLERMAN, J. DE ZWAN and J. CZUCZAI (eds), *EU Enlargement, The Constitutional Impact at EU and National Level*, Asser Press, The Hague 2001; M. CREMONA (ed.), *The Enlargement of the European Union* (Collected Courses of the Academy of European Law 2003); A. KELLERMAN, J. CUZCAI, S. BLOCKMANS, A. ALBI and W.T. DOUMA (eds), *The Impact of EU Accession on the Legal Order of the New EU Member States and (Pre-)Candidate Countries. Hope and Fears*, Asser Press, The Hague 2006.

[14] W. SADURSKI, 'Constitutionalization of the EU and the Sovereignty Concerns of the New Accession States: The Role of the Charter of Rights', *EUI Working Paper Law*, 2003/11, www.iue.it/PUB/Law03–10.pdf, accessed 20.09.2012.

'after the fall of communism, national identity (often perceived in an ethnic rather than civic fashion) has been either the only or the most powerful social factor, other than those identified with social foundations of the *ancien regime*, capable of injecting a necessary degree of coherence into society and of countervailing the anomie of a disintegrated, decentralised and demoralised society'.[15]

Secondly, there is a related argument concerning the 'sovereignist' nature of the CEE legal orders compared with western constitutional models.[16] Thirdly, the emphasis in the constitutions of the CEE countries on the supremacy of the constitution over all other sources of law (including international treaties)[17] is difficult to reconcile with a radical version of the primacy of EU law. Fourthly, we should recall the role of the constitutional courts within these legal orders, as protagonists of the transition period and guardians of regained sovereignty. These courts may be tempted (indeed, it has happened)[18] to raise their voices against Brussels and Luxembourg in order to defend their crucial role, in a domestic dimension, with respect to the national political powers.[19]

Finally, it is not difficult to see that, while, as we noted above, the Council of Europe's enlargement process to the east has been characterized by a generous and benign attitude towards the CEE candidate countries, the same could not be said with regard to the European Union's enlargement to the east. For many reasons this situation was the exact opposite of that which characterized the application of the so-called ex-post conditionality mechanism in the Council of Europe's enlargement to the east. In both cases a double standard was applied to determine the level of human rights protection between the internal and external dimensions respectively of the Council of Europe and the European Union.

In the first case, through ex-post conditionality, the standard of protection required of CEE candidate states by the Council of Europe was less stringent than the standard applied internally to states that were already members of the Council. However, a diametrically opposite situation characterized accession to the European Union of those countries. They had to supply guarantees of

---

[15]   *Ibid.*, p. 12.

[16]   In this regard it is often underlined how the CEE constitutions place much more emphasis than Western European constitutions on the values of independence and sovereignty, which recur almost obsessively in all the CEE constitutions. See A. ALBI, 'Postmodern versus Retrospective Sovereignty: Two Different Discourses in the EU and the Candidate Countries', in N. WALKER (ed.), *Sovereignty in Transition*, Hart, Oxford 2003.

[17]   See Article 8 of the Polish Constitution; Article 153 of the Slovenian Constitution; Article 7 of the Lithuanian Constitution; Article 2(2) of the Slovak Constitution; Article 77 (1) of the Hungarian Constitution; Articles 123(1), 15 and 152 of the Estonian Constitution.

[18]   See A. LAZOWSKY, *The Application of EU Law in the New Member States – Brave New World*, TMC, Asser Press, The Hague 2010.

[19]   W. SADURSKI, 'Partnering with Strasbourg: Constitutionalization of the European Court of Human Rights, the Accession of Central and East European States to the Council of Europe, and the Idea of Pilot Judgments' (2009) 9 *Human Rights L. Rev.* 397.

protection over and above to those required of the 'old' member States by the EU and EC Treaties.

In order to join the EU, the CEE candidate Member States were required not only to adhere to a degree of scrutiny which, at that time, was not applicable to others within the EU (in the absence of a binding Charter of Fundamental Rights), but also to a system of enforcement which simply did not exist internally in the EU. In other words, the candidate countries were required to meet standards that several of the Member States did not even meet at that time, regarding, for instance, the field of minority protection,[20] a key element of the Copenhagen criteria but not at all an integral part of the European *acquis*.[21]

It should be also emphasized that the demand for consistency and reciprocity between internal and external human rights policies, raised almost ten years ago by Philip Alston and Joseph Weiler,[22] was never so neglected at the EU level as it was with regard to the monitoring policy applied to the CEE candidate countries, especially in light of the criteria laid down in Copenhagen in 1993.[23] This policy was based, in the light of the reasons mentioned above, on a core discrimination.[24] In this regard, another element should be taken into account: the conditions to be fulfilled have been entirely set by the EU, without room for any negotiation or differentiation as to each candidate's peculiar position. In the end, the whole European pre-accession strategy was nothing more than a de facto 'take it or leave it' package.[25]

Against this background, the relevant question is whether (and if so, in which direction) the European Court of Justice has somehow developed a new judicial

---

[20]   See C. HILLION, 'On Enlargement of the European Union: The Discrepancy between Membership Obligations and the Accession Conditions as regards the Protection of Minorities' (2004) 27 *Fordham Int'l L. J.* 715.

[21]   See A. WIENER and G. SCHWELLNUS, 'Contested Norms in the Process of EU Enlargement: Non-discrimination and Minority Rights', *Constitutionalism Web-Papers*, ConWEB No. 2/2004; W. SADURSKI, *supra* n. 14, p. 6; G DE BURCA, 'On Enlargement of the European Union: Beyond the Charter: How the Enlargement Has Enlarged the Human Rights Policy of the European Union' (2004) 27 *Fordham Int'l L. J.* 679, 683.

[22]   Philip Alston and Joseph Weiler have in 'not suspicious times' argued that 'a credible human rights must assiduously avoid unilateralism and double standard, and that can only be done by ensuring reciprocity and consistency'. See P. ALSTON and J.H.H. WEILER, 'A European Union Human Rights Policy', in P. ALSTON (ed.), *The European Union and Human Rights*, Oxford University Press, Oxford 1999, pp. 8–9.

[23]   Which, *inter alia*, required the candidate countries to demonstrate the stability of the institutions guaranteeing democracy, rule of law, human rights, and the protection of minorities.

[24]   A. WILLIAMS, 'Enlargement of the Union and Human Rights Conditionality: A Policy of Distinction?' (2001) 25 *EL Rev.* 601, 616.

[25]   András Sajó has observed, making clear that the enlargement was mainly a unilateral process, that 'the accession process was, objectively and subjectively, a process of submission – one that may well have been in the best interest of the new Member States, but a submission nonetheless'. See A. SAJÓ, 'Constitution without the Constitutional Moment: A View from the New Member States' (2005) 3 *Int'l J. Constitutional L.* 243, 252.

sensitivity after the 2004 and 2007 enlargements in order to respond to the change in the dynamic nature of constitutional tolerance. In this respect it has been argued[26] that, in order to prevent potential 'sovereignist' reactions by Member States, and especially in order to enhance this miraculous 'voluntary obedience', in the last few decades the ECJ has resorted to applying the 'majoritarian activist approach'.[27] According to this approach, among the various solutions to a case, the European judges may opt for the final ruling that is most likely to meet the highest degree of consensus in the majority of Member States.[28] The European judges seem to have understood that if such an approach had been partially[29] able to convince Germans and Italians when they were 'invited' to obey the European discipline in the name of the peoples of Europe, the same 'invitation' would have proven much less successful when applied to Estonians or Hungarians.

The post-2004 era has called, then, for a new *ad hoc* judicial strategy to combine with the pre-2004 majoritarian activist approach. After all, what new Member States need to be reassured about seems to be that even if, with regard to those national values relating to a peculiar identity that their constitution protects, they were to find themselves in a minority or isolated position, the European judges would not sacrifice them on the altar of the majoritarian activist approach. It does not seem a coincidence, indeed, that some months after the 2004 enlargement, the Court stated, against an exclusively majoritarian logic, for the very first time, that 'it is not indispensable in that respect for the restrictive measure issued by the authorities of a Member State to correspond to

---

26   G. MARTINICO and O. POLLICINO, 'Between Constitutional Tolerance and Judicial Activism: The 'Specificity' of the European Judicial Law' (2008) *Eur. J. Law Reform* 99.

27   Miguel Maduro identifies the same judicial approach in the different field of European economic constitution. See M. P. MADURO, *We, the Court. The European Court of Justice and Economic Constitution*, Hart, Oxford 1998, pp. 72–78.

28   In particular, in a previous work the author has tried to prove how the reference to the majoritarian approach has been able to explain how it is not unusual in European case law that a couple of cases, which are very similar in their factual and/or legal background, are decided in an opposite, thus almost schizophrenic, way by the ECJ. The key to the apparent enigma has been found by reflecting upon the impact that a decision can have on the national legal systems by the application of the majoritarian activism approach, as is proved by the analysis of two decisions in the field of protection of sexual minorities. See O. POLLICINO, *Discriminazione sulla base del sesso e trattamento preferenziale nel diritto comunitario. Alla ricerca del nucleo duro del 'new legal order'*, Giuffrè, Milano 2005, p. 283.

29   Doubts about the real persuasive attitude of the aforementioned judicial strategy have been advanced by Matej Avbelj, arguing that 'The damaging effect of the "supranational" counter-majoritarian difficulty on legitimacy appears to be doubled: the whole "national demos" is turned into minority and the prevailing value-based view – the identity of the majority of the "national demos", is compromised in favour of a distinct European demos.' See M. AVBELJ, *European Court of Justice and the Question of Value Choices: Fundamental Human Rights as an Exception to the Freedom of Movement of Goods*, Jean Monnet Working Papers No. 6/2004, Jean Monnet Chair.

a conception shared by all Member States as regards the precise way in which the fundamental right or legitimate interest in question is to be protected'.[30]

Upon closer inspection, the attention to national values, far from being a post-2004 accession novelty, has always been a main feature of the ECJ case law related to the achievement of a European single market. This is true in particular as regards consumer protection and the preservation of public order as legitimate justification for the hindrance to fundamental freedoms in national laws, especially the freedom of establishment and the freedom to provide services.

It is sufficient to consider the case law related to gambling where the ECJ has admitted that moral, religious and cultural factors, and the morally and financially harmful consequences for individuals and societies associated with gambling, could serve to justify the existence, in the hands of the national authorities, of a margin of appreciation sufficient to enable them to determine what kind of consumer protection and public order preservation they should apply.[31]

The innovative element of the post-enlargement phase of the ECJ case law, mainly connected with the need to provide reassurance for the strong, identity-based demands for recognition coming from the new CEE Member States, is instead the willingness of the ECJ to take a step back if the protection of a national constitutional right is at stake. If it is true, as it has been objected,[32] that: 'the phase of justification before the ECJ is a phase in which the Court strikes a balance between the competing values of the Member States and the economic values of the Union and makes the final determination', the added value of the relevant post-enlargement case law[33] is that fundamental rights become a legitimate, justified obstacle to the further enhancement of the European economic constitution even if that ground of justification is not at all enshrined in the founding Treaties.

---

[30]   Case C-36/02, *Omega* [2004] ECR I-9609, para. 37. The same vision, even more clearly expressed, was confirmed in *Dynamic Medien*, in a judgment of 14 February 2008 (C-244/06) which has gone strangely unnoticed.

[31]   Case C-124/97, *Läärä and Others* [1999] ECR I-6067. Along the same lines, more recently, see Case C-243/01, *Gambelli* [2003] ECR I-13031, and Joined Cases C-338/04, C-359/04 and C-360/04, *Placanica* [2007] ECR I-1891, where the Court expressly states that 'context, moral, religious or cultural factors, as well as the morally and financially harmful consequences for the individual and for society associated with betting and gaming, may serve to justify a margin of discretion for the national authorities, sufficient to enable them to determine what is required in order to ensure consumer protection and the preservation of public order' (para. 47).

[32]   See M. AVBELJ, *supra* n. 29.

[33]   *Omega*, anticipated by Case C-112/00, *Eugen Schmidberger Internationale Transporte Planzüge v Republik Österreich* [2003] ECR I-565. See, for an analysis of the two decisions, A. ALEMANNO, 'A la recherche d'un juste èquilibre entre libertés fondamentales et droits fondamentaux dans le cadre du marché intérieur. Quelques reflexions à propos des arrêts "Schmidberger" et "Omega"', (2004) 4 *Revue du droit de l'Union europeenne* 1.

In light of the scenario that we have just tried to delineate, it is perhaps possible to advance further in the attempt to systematize the reactions to the enlargement that have characterized the judicial approach of the ECJ. The ECJ, in fact, seems increasingly committed to working on a self-restriction of the principle of EU primacy when it comes to the protection of identity-based constitutional dimensions of one or more Member States. A precise strategy of the ECJ, whose aim seems, in line with the *Solange* approach, to prevent further positions of the European constitutional courts by somehow 'internalizing', the '*controlimiti*' (counterlimits) doctrine in its case law.

In other words, the 'evolutionary nature of the doctrine of primacy'[34] seems to have undergone another transfiguration phase after the 2004 enlargement, from an uncompromising version[35] to a compromising one. It is not a coincidence that the Treaty establishing the European Constitution[36] of 2004 provided, immediately prior to the codification of the principle of EU primacy, at I-6, the following complementary principle: 'The Union shall respect the equality of the Member States before the constitution as well their national identity, inherent in their fundamental structures, political and constitutional, inclusive of regional and local self-government. It shall respect the entire state functions, including the territorial integrity of the state, maintaining law and order and safeguarding national security'.

Moreover, it does not appear to be a coincidence that whereas the Lisbon Treaty entered into force on 1 December 2009, notwithstanding the lack of an express codification of the principle of the primacy of EU law, the principle enshrined in Article 1–5 of the Treaty establishing the European Constitution has been textually provided by Article 4.2[37] of the Treaty on European Union as amended by the Treaty of Lisbon.[38]

---

[34] See J.H.H. WEILER, 'The Community System, the Dual Character of Supranationalism' (1981) 1 *Ybk Eur. L.* 268, 275.

[35] J.H.H. WEILER, 'The Transformation of Europe' (1991) 100 *Yale L. J.* 2403, 2414.

[36] For an in-depth analysis of the element of identity in the Constitutional Treaty, see A. VON BOGDANDY, 'The European Constitution and the European Identity: Text and Subtext of the Treaty establishing a Constitution for Europe' (2005) 3 *Int'l J. Constitutional L.* 295, 299.

[37] See I. ARONSTEIN, '"The Union shall respect cultural diversity and national identities". Lisbon's Concessions to Euroscepticism – True Promises or a Booby-trap?' (2010) 6 *Utrecht L. Rev.* 89.

[38] It is true that the Treaty of Maastricht included in the former Article 6.4 of the former (pre-Lisbon) TEU the reference to the respect for national identity by providing that 'The Union shall respect the national identities of its Member States'. It is also true that, comparing this succinct formulation with the very wordy formulation in the Lisbon version ('shall respect their national identities, inherent in their fundamental structures, political and constitutional, inclusive of regional and local self-government'), it is quite clear that the political and constitutional aspect is much enhanced in the Lisbon version. To the extent that the Lisbon Treaty here focuses on state structures, there is a shift in emphasis from national identity as such to '*constitutional* identity'. See L. BESSELINK, 'National and Constitutional Identity before and after Lisbon' (2010) 6 *Utrecht L. Rev.* 36, 45.

Despite the undeniably great potential of the identity clause in terms of its enhancement of the ECJ's new interest in the margin of appreciation of the single Member State, there has been some scepticism in the scholarship[39] about the effective use of the clause in the case law of the Luxembourg Court. Against these pessimistic predictions, 'only' one year after the entry in force of the Lisbon Treaty, the ECJ, for the first time, in the seminal judgment *Sayn-Wittgenstein*,[40] expressly referred to the new 'identity clause' provided by Article 4(2) of the TEU.

In this case, the ECJ, recalled, in the light of the *Omega* doctrine, that:

'[I]t is not indispensable for the restrictive measure issued by the authorities of a Member State to correspond to a conception shared by all Member States as regards the precise way in which the fundamental right or legitimate interest in question is to be protected and that, on the contrary, the need for, and proportionality of, the provisions adopted are not excluded merely because one Member State has chosen a system of protection different from that adopted by another State.' (para. 92)

It also felt the need to add: 'It must also be noted that, in accordance with Article 4(2) TEU, the European Union is to respect the national identities of its Member States, which include the status of the State as a Republic' (para. 93). In this regard, it has been correctly pointed out that '[c]onstitutional identity still seems to be an element to be taken into account in operations of balancing. The weight of arguments based on it is perhaps different from what normally happened before the last wave of modifications of the Treaties.'[41]

If this impression is to be confirmed, as *Sayn-Wittgenstein* seems to suggest, in the future, the ECJ would have found, thanks to the new parameter provided

---

[39] See, for instance, the reactions after the *Zambrano* and *Elchinov* cases: E. GUILD, 'The Court of Justice of the European Union and Citizens of the Union: A Revolution Underway? The Zambrano judgment of 8 March 2011' EUDO, http://eudo-citizenship.eu/citizenship-news/453-the-court-of-justice-of-the-european-union-and-citizens-of-the-union-a-revolution-underway-the-zambrano-judgment-of-8-march-2011, accessed 20.09.2012; C. BACKES and M. ELIANTONIO, 'Taking Constitutionalization One Step Too Far? The Need for Revision of the *Rheinmühlen* Case Law in the Light of the AG Opinion and the ECJ's Ruling in Elchinov', Maastricht Faculty of Law Working Paper No. 2010/9, http://papers.ssrn.com/sol3/papers.cfm?abstract_id=1722631, accessed 20.09.2012.

[40] Case C-208/09, *Sayn-Wittgenstein* (not reported yet), ECJ 22.12.2010.

[41] See G. DELLEDONNE, 'Dealing with National Identities: Article 4 TEU', paper presented at Joint Workshop (STALS, EUDO, Max Weber Programme, CSF) 'Treaty Reform beyond Lisbon?', San Domenico di Fiesole, 18.03.2011. As an example of the new approach taken by the ECJ, Delledonne quotes the passage in *Sayn-Wittgenstein* in which the Court stated: 'It must be accepted that, in the context of Austrian constitutional history, the Law on the abolition of the nobility, as an element of national identity, may be taken into consideration when a balance is struck between legitimate interests and the right of free movement of persons recognised under European Union law' (para. 83). See more recently now A. VON BOGDANDY and S. SCHILL, 'Overcoming Absolute Primacy: Respect for National Identity under the Lisbon Treaty', (2011) 48 *CML Rev.* 1417.

by Article 4(2) of the TEU as amended by the Treaty of Lisbon, the appropriate judicial mechanism to prevent the occurrence of the most frequent constitutional conflict between the EC and the national levels – the dualistic tension between the irresistible, overriding vocation of the ECJ's *Simmenthal* mandate and the equally monolithic national constitutional mandate to preserve the core of fundamental domestic values from EC 'invasion'.

3. THE NATIONAL JUDICIAL TREATMENT OF THE SUPRANATIONAL LAWS. CONFIRMATION OR DENIAL OF THE CONVERGENCE PROCESS IDENTIFIED AT THE EUROPEAN LEVEL?

In the light of the results of the research presented above, it is possible to conclude, as regards the supranational scenario, that there is a growing trend in the more recent case law of the ECJ and the ECtHR. Indeed, the two European Courts seem to have involuntarily started to converge in terms of their 'idea' of the domestic effects of EU law and the ECHR in the legal orders of the Member States of the two supranational organizations.

The appraisal by the European Courts at supranational level of the approximation between the domestic effects of EU law and ECHR law needs now, to be combined with a comparative analysis rooted in the national dimension, in order to verify, on the basis of the points outlined in the introduction, the way ordinary and constitutional judges treat EU law and ECHR law.

In the next few pages, some of the most important distinguishing features of national judicial treatment of ECHR and EU law in Europe will be underlined through a select number of references to national experiences. The importance of focusing on internal judicial interpretation and application of supranational laws is very well captured by stressing that 'despite the different quality of the EU and the ECHR supranationalism, one common denominator is the role of the judge'.[42]

The first relevant element that should be underlined is the constantly growing bifurcation between a static reading of the relevant 'European' and 'international' clauses present in the constitutions, which was pointed out in the introduction, and their dynamic judicial interpretation by constitutional courts. In other words, this new climate of European constitutionalism seems to be marked by the need to search for new argumentative techniques and original judicial interaction between national and European courts, by following new 'off-piste' routes with respect to those indicated in the national constitutions.

---

[42] V.P. Tzevelekos and S.E. Vetsika, 'Report on Greece', in G. Martinico and O. Pollicino, *The National Judicial Treatment The National Judicial Treatment of the ECHR and EU Laws. A Comparative Constitutional Perspective*, Europa Law, Groningen 2010, p. 227.

In this regard, the Scandinavian case is particularly significant for EU law, and the Czech and Italian experiences are relevant to ECHR law. With regard to EU Law, one simply has to quote Carl Lebeck who underlined that 'all Scandinavian countries regard EU law from a formal perspective as only a matter of international law, which is clearly not the case insofar as one looks to the case law involving these legal orders'.

In relation instead to the ECHR, it has been pointed out that 'the Czech "Euro" amendment adopted in 2001 clarified that the ECHR does not have a constitutional rank, because all international treaties, including international human rights treaties, "only" enjoy the application priority'.[43] What was clear reading the new constitutional parameter was evidently not so clear to the Czech constitutional judges given that, in a much disputed decision of 2002, they concluded that international human rights treaties have *retained* their constitutional status. Indeed the Court constitutionalized, for the first time, international human rights treaties, including the ECHR.

The same aim, underlying the aforementioned Czech decision, i.e. that of not losing the competence to decide on conflicts between the ECHR and domestic statute law, has been pursued by the Italian Constitutional court. Indeed, although Article 117 of the Italian Constitution seems to put European Union law and ECHR law on an equal footing by stating that 'legislative powers shall be vested in the State and the Regions in compliance with the Constitution and with the constraints deriving from the EU legal order and international obligations'. The Constitutional Court, in 2007, opted, as we have seen, for a diverging approach by upholding the para-constitutional nature of EU law and underlining the sub-constitutional character of the ECHR.

As the Czech and Italian cases thus demonstrate, the 'off-piste' routes followed by constitutional judges with regard to the applicable constitutional parameters are often due to their fear of having to abdicate from their privileged position of final arbiter of the protection of fundamental rights in a critical sphere where the constitutional dimension encounters the supranational dimension.

Returning then to the supranational dimension, it is common knowledge that, with regard to the domestic effects of the decisions of these two European Courts, the ECJ judgments are widely recognized as having *erga omnes* effects of *res intepretata*, while Article 46 of ECHR limits the effects of ECtHR judgments to the Contracting State condemned in Strasbourg. In the previous chapters attempts have been made to show how, more recently, the Strasbourg Court has tried to amplify the indirect effect of its case law, with the aim of extending the obligation to abide by its judgments to states that were not directly involved in the decision.

---

[43]   M. Bobek and D. Kosař, 'Report on the Czech Republic and Slovakia', in G. Martinico and O. Pollicino, *supra* n. 42, p. 133.

This idea is supported by Nikolas Kyriakou when he notes that 'the Strasbourg Court's case law has attained a de facto *'erga omnes'* effect, as *Opuz v Turkey*[44] illustrates'.[45] In particular, in that case, the ECtHR specified that it will consider 'whether the national authorities have sufficiently taken into account the principles flowing from its judgments on similar issues, even when they concern other States'.

By looking to the national dimension, the generally applicable rule seems to be that according to which the majority of the general reforms adopted by the national political and administrative powers has only followed decisions against their own Member State, confirming the self-perception that the Strasbourg decisions only have *inter partes* effects. Among the relevant exceptions to this, it is worth underlining the very open attitude[46] towards accepting the indirect effect of Strasbourg case law in the Netherlands, where, as it has been remarked, 'changes of national law have also been induced by ECtHR judgements concerning other states'[47] and in Slovenia, as has been pointed out.[48]

The Netherlands is also one of the few Member States that has granted the *erga omnes* effects of *res iudicata* to the decisions of the ECtHR. By contrast, it is well known that such an effect is only widely recognized in Europe with regard to the decisions of the ECJ as, *inter alia*, the Italian experience demonstrates.

As regards the attitude of national ordinary judges in the case of conflict between EU law and the ECHR, on the one hand, and national law, on the other, the first premise is that, at supranational level, the two European Courts are not asking the national judges to do the same thing. Indeed, whereas the ECJ has established that EU law has to be applied in the domestic legal orders instead of national law so as to guarantee the *effet utile* and the very existence of EU law, the ECtHR has never, at least not with the same emphasis, requested the national judges to set aside the national statutes in contrast with the ECHR.

Having said this, it should be also highlighted that, in many cases, it is the constitutional mandate of the ordinary judges that obliges them to treat the two sources of supranational law differently. In fact, in the majority of European

---

44   ECtHR, *Opuz v. Turkey*, app. no. 33401/02, 09.06.2009, para. 163.
45   N. Kyriakou, 'Report on Cyprus', in G. Martinico and O. Pollicino, *supra* n. 42, p. 157.
46   This attitude is not surprising considering the extreme openness of the Constitution with regard to international law.
47   See E. Mak, 'Report on the Netherlands and Luxembourg', in G. Martinico and O. Pollicino, *supra* n. 42, p. 310.
48   In particular it has been noted that it is '[…] entirely undisputed that regarding the interpretation of the European Convention on Human Rights, the opinion of the European Court of Human Rights is decisive. Such interpretation is not formally binding on the Constitutional Court, however in reality it must nevertheless be respected considering similar subsequent cases if the Court does not wish to risk Slovenia being found in violation before the European Court of Human Rights. […] The Constitutional Court is naturally not restricted to cases in which the European Court of Human Rights decided on the basis of applications from Slovenia, although the Court pays particular attention to them'. C. Ribičič, 'Položaj slovenske ustave po vključitvi v EU' (2006) 25 *Pravna praksa* 29–30.

states characterized by a system of centralized constitutional justice in which international law is granted a *supra*-legislative status, the power to evaluate the conformity of a national law to ratified international treaties is reserved to constitutional judges.[49] This means that an ordinary judge who ascertains a conflict between the ECHR and a national statute is constitutionally obliged to raise the issue of constitutionality before his or her own constitutional court. On the contrary, it is common knowledge that, under the pressure of the ECJ, constitutional courts have granted ordinary judges the power to derogate from their constitutional mandate with regard to the application of EU law. Indeed, they can put aside national laws that are in conflict with EU law. Furthermore, as underlined in the previous chapters regarding Italy, the Italian Constitutional court has reacted to those 'subversive ordinary judges' that have started to treat the ECHR like EU law.

In this regard, and as seen above, one should underline the judicial creativity of the Czech Constitutional Court, which insists on retaining the power to have the last word in cases of conflict between the ECHR and national statutes, despite a constitutional parameter which says exactly the opposite. Worth noting, in this respect, is Poland, which deviates from the general judicial trend outlined above. Indeed, as Krystyna Kowalik clearly underlined, even though the Polish Constitutional Tribunal has repeatedly stated that the ECHR can be directly applied by domestic courts, the Convention is not used in this manner by the majority of Polish courts which prefer to apply the method of consistent interpretation.[50]

Romania is another interesting case. In fact, as Ioana Raducu has pointed out:

> 'if from a strictly constitutional point of view, national court's mandate is primarily bound to obey national provisions as long as they are not declared incompatible with the Constitution, the doctrine unanimously uphold that the article 11 and 20 of the Constitution implies that the national judge's mandate is to give precedence to the ECHR provisions as interpreted by the ECtHR over domestic law'.[51]

Among the few systems of centralized constitutional justice which allow ordinary judges to set aside a national law that is in contrast with international law, is that of France. As outlined by Maria Fartunova, according to this principle the conventionality control is granted to the ordinary judges who consequently apply the same rules for settling conflicts between ordinary statutes and ECHR law and EU law respectively. There is a similar situation in

---

[49]   France, and to some extent, Portugal, Spain and Belgium, as will be underlined below, represent a notable exception in this regard.

[50]   K. KOWALIK-BAŃCZYK, 'Report on Poland', in G. MARTINICO and O. POLLICINO, *supra* n. 42, p. 326.

[51]   I. RADUCU, 'Report on Romania', in G. MARTINICO and O. POLLICINO, *supra* n. 42, p. 372.

Luxembourg where, in case of conflict between domestic legislation and the ECHR, the courts usually give precedence to the Treaty.

In Belgium, the ordinary courts directly apply the ECHR and EU law in case of conflict with national statutes, because, as it has pointed out, 'the Constitutional Court has no competence to review Acts of Parliament directly to international or supranational law, but it does so indirectly via the Articles 10 and 11 of the Constitution'.[52]

With particular regard to the ECHR, the Court has been very keen not to centralize the control of 'conventionalité' by stating that,

> 'ni l'article 26 par.1 de la loi spéciale du 6 janvier 1989 sur la Cour d'Arbitrage, ni aucune autre disposition, constitutionnelle ou législative, ne confère à la Cour de pouvoir de statuer à une disposition d'une convention internationale. En tant que la question invite à un control direct au regard de la Convention européenne des droit de l'homme, la Cour n'est pas compétente pour y répondre.'[53]

The same does not apply to Portugal and Spain. Indeed, even if in Portugal the Constitution itself, and in Spain much less equivocally the case law of the Constitutional Tribunal, would entitle the common judges to put aside the national law in the event of conflict with the ECHR, the judges do not use this possibility, preferring instead to apply the method of consistent interpretation or to raise the issue of constitutionality before their own constitutional court.

In brief, as shown by the judicial practices in the Baltic States, Bulgaria, Poland, the Czech Republic, Slovakia, Romania, Portugal and Spain,[54] in centralized systems of constitutional review consistent interpretation is acquiring a growing importance among the tools at the disposal of the ordinary judges so as to avoid conflict between the ECHR and EU law, on one hand, and the national law, on the other. In decentralized systems of constitutional justice the interpretative tool of consistent interpretation is instead already by far the one most privileged by the ordinary judges. The Scandinavian experience is very significant in this respect because, as it has been pointed out with specific reference to the ECHR:

---

[52]   P. POPELIER, 'Report on Belgium', in G. MARTINICO and O. POLLICINO, *supra* n. 42, p. 89.

[53]   *Cour d'Arbitrage*, Decision 25/200. Interestingly enough, in the Belgian experience an expression of the convergence trend between the domestic impact of the EU and ECHR legal orders is given by a recent intervention of the legislative power in reaction to a clear position of the Belgian Constitutional Court. When, in fact the Constitutional Court clarified that it would have considered itself competent to decide on the preliminary reference related to the constitutionality of EU Treaties or the ECHR, 'the law maker deprived the Court of its jurisdiction to answer to preliminary references concerning an Act of assent to a EU Treaty or to the European Convention of Human Rights or a Protocol'.

[54]   It should also be emphasized that the Spanish, Portuguese and Romanian Constitutions expressly provide that they must be interpreted in the light of the International Declaration of Human Rights.

'the role of consistent interpretation has over time evolved from being a matter of presumption that national law is consistent with the requirements of the ECHR, to that national law as far as possible should be made to conform with the ECHR.'[55]

With regard to the two European countries where there is no constitutional review (the United Kingdom and the Netherlands), the fact that Dutch judges, who cannot ascertain the contrast between national law and the Constitution, are entitled to put aside the national statutes conflicting with ratified international treaties has obviously had the effect not only of reinforcing the ECHR as a 'shadow Constitution' but has also brought about a convergence in the judicial treatment of the ECHR and EU law in the Netherlands.

As far as the United Kingdom's experience is concerned, when it is not possible for judges to interpret primary and subordinate legislation in a way which is compatible, respectively, with Convention rights and EU law, the solution that is adopted is quite different. As Cian Murphy has pointed out:

'unlike national law found to be contrary to EU law, law incompatible with the Convention is not disapplied or declared invalid. A declaration of incompatibility does not affect the 'validity, continuing operation or enforcement' of the law, nor does it bind the parties before the Court. Instead, a procedure is provided to allow Parliament to fast-track an amending bill.'[56]

Still with regard to the UK, even if a cooperative judicial attitude emerges in the attempt to interpret primary and secondary legislation, as requested by the Human Rights Act, 'so far as it is possible to do so, in a way which is compatible with the Convention rights interpret the national law', recently, nevertheless, objections have been raised with respect to the very activist period of the ECtHR. It is worth recalling the fierce criticism, mentioned in the introduction, formulated by Lord Hoffmann when he underlined that:

'the fact that the 10 original Member States of the Council of Europe subscribed to a statement of human rights in the same terms did not mean that they had agreed to uniformity of the application of those abstract rights in each of their countries, still less in the 47 states which now belong. [...] The Strasbourg court has no mandate to unify the laws of Europe on the many subjects which may arguably touch upon human rights.'[57]

---

[55] C. LEBECK, 'Report on Scandinavian Countries', in G. MARTINICO and O. POLLICINO, *supra* n. 42, p. 418.
[56] C. MURPHY, 'Report on the UK and Ireland', in G. MARTINICO and O. POLLICINO, *supra* n. 42, p. 488.
[57] L. HOFFMAN, 'The Universality of Human Rights' (2009) *LQR* 416.

It would be difficult to find a better expression of the feeling of betrayal,[58] which is quite widespread among the founding Member States of the Council of Europe, with respect to their original expectations of the role and the limits of the European Court of Human Rights and the recent period of judicial activism.

These expectations were clearly underlined by Lord Hoffmann himself some years ago when he pointed out that:

> 'when we joined, indeed, took the lead in the negotiation of the European Convention, it was not because we thought it would affect our own law; but because we thought it right to set an example for others and to help to ensure that all the Member States respected those basic human rights which were not culturally determined but reflected our common humanity.'[59]

It should not then be surprising if, as the more recent case law of the Italian Constitutional Court shows, resistance has emerged in the old Member States with respect to the European Court of Human Rights' new self-perception as a pan-European Constitutional Court.

This resistance, as emerges from the analysis carried out in the book, has been weaker in the Central and Eastern European (CEE) Member States, not only because as late comers they did not have any illusions that the ECHR would only be a 'normal' international treaty and that the ECtHR would have acted as a normal international court, but also because, as Sadurski has underlined, 'if there is a domain in which concerns over national identity and accompanying notions of sovereignty are obviously weak in Central and Eastern Europe it is in the field of protection of individual rights'.[60]

If those are among the main reasons which can explain the cooperative attitude of the CEE Constitutional Courts to Strasbourg, the same cannot be said with regard to the attitude of the CEE ordinary judges towards supranational law in general. In comparison to the constitutional judges of this area, who are in general quite open 'to the partisans of the transition and to the innovative spirits',[61] the ordinary judges are, although much less than before, 'still enslaved by textual positivism.'[62]

While the CEE Constitutional Courts, as third-generation constitutional courts, were born into a flourishing international human rights jurisdiction, the ordinary judges, especially in comparison with their colleagues in the West, are

---

[58]   The point was first raised by W. Sadurski, *supra* n. 19.
[59]   L. Hoffman, 'Human rights and the House of Lords' (1999) 62 *MLR* 159.
[60]   W. Sadurski, 'Constitutionalization of the EU and the Sovereignty Concerns of the New Accession States: The Role of the Charter of Rights', in *EUI Working Paper Law*, no. 11/03, www.iue.it/PUB/Law03–10.pdf, accessed 20.09.2012.
[61]   L. Solyom, 'The Role of Constitutional Courts in the Transition to Democracy: With Special Reference to Hungary' (2003) *International Sociology* 136.
[62]   Z. Kühn, 'Words Apart, Western and Central European Judicial Culture at the Onset of the European Enlargement' (2004) 52 *Am J. Comparative Law* 549.

still very deferential to the literal interpretation of the law and are thus not exactly in a mood for dialogue[63] with the European Courts. In other words, they are more keen on keeping a good relationship with their hierarchically superior colleagues, if not with the political powers.

As emerges, for example, from the Polish and Czech-Slovak experience, the constitutional courts have tried to indicate to the ordinary judges a path towards emancipation, especially with regard to their role as European judges and the immediate application of EU law and the dialogue, through the preliminary reference procedure, with the ECJ.[64]

However, equivocal indications to the ordinary judges may come from the extremely 'ECHR-friendly' attitudes of some CEE Constitutional Courts that, on one hand, invite the ordinary judges to go beyond the black letter of the law and make use of their hermeneutical powers, while on the other hand, urging them to deprive themselves of the margin of appreciation by declaring, as the Slovak Constitutional Court recently did, that the case law of the ECHR and ECtHR represents 'binding interpretative guidelines for interpretation and application of statutory rules on the relevant aspects of the right to a fair trial'.[65]

As far as the issue related to the convergence between the domestic impact of EU law and the ECHR is concerned, the Baltic States could be declared the champions in this regard (besides the symmetry underlined with respect to ordinary judges' national mandate in France, Luxembourg, Poland, Belgium and the Netherlands). Indeed in a recent analysis it has been pointed out that 'the jurisprudence of the Constitutional Courts (and the Supreme Court of Estonia) clearly demonstrates the convergence of views towards the ECHR and EU law as special sources of supranational legal orders'.[66]

It seems much more difficult to identify the same trend in Slovenia, Slovakia, the Czech Republic, Portugal, Greece, Germany and Austria where the ECHR and EU law mechanisms are still understood to play different roles and have a different scope and objective.

Pal Sonnevend has raised an interesting point when, after stating that neither the judiciary nor legal scholarship seem to support any trend towards convergence between the domestic impact of ECHR law and EU law, he goes on to underline

---

[63]   G. Martinico, 'Preliminary Reference and Constitutional Courts. Are You in the Mood for Dialogue?' in F. Fontanelli, G. Martinico and P. Carrozza, *Shaping Rule of Law through Dialogue. International and Supranational Experiences*, Europa Law, Groningen 2009, p. 219.

[64]   As has been stated, 'The Czech Constitutional Court and the Slovak Constitutional Court have also declared themselves ready to function as *de facto* enforcers of the last instance ordinary courts' duty to submit a request for a preliminary ruling, similar to the approach elaborated in the case law of the German Federal Constitutional Court and the Austrian Federal Constitutional Court'. See M. Bobek and D. Kosař, *supra* n. 43, p. 127.

[65]   Judgment of the SCC of 19 December 2001, I. ÚS 49/01, available at www.concourt.sk.

[66]   I. Jarukaitis, 'Report on Baltic States', in G. Martinico and O. Pollicino, *supra* n. 42, p. 202.

that 'it is to be expected, however, that such convergence will rather follow from EU law itself and this may lead to a different approach at national level'.[67]

With regard to the Irish and British experiences, the fact that EU law and the ECHR are incorporated in different ways in both jurisdictions means that there is little scope for convergence without much greater judicial activism. In the Scandinavian states, as Lebeck noted, there is convergence in the sense that both ECHR and EU law tend to take precedence over national law and that both work as a substitute for constitutional judicial review. Formally there is no convergence, but in practice there is a certain convergence, and in both cases it seems possible only because of the long tradition of 'pragmatism' in relation to constitutional issues that is characteristic of the Scandinavian countries.[68]

In Romania, as it has been pointed out, there is, according to legal scholarship, a consensus 'on the idea that the ECHR and EU law should converge in the national judicial treatment. However, the practice still presents inconsistencies in applying the ECHR and EU standards.'[69] The same asymmetry between legal scholarship and the judiciary can be found in Spain, where Aida Torres Perez has underlined that:

> 'on the whole, from a scholarly standpoint, it is increasingly the case that the impact of both systems upon constitutional structures is the object of combined research projects. Indeed, the judiciary tends to be at the core of legal analysis which addresses the interaction between legal systems. Judicial practice, however, is more divergent towards ECHR and EU law.'[70]

In Italy, as we have seen, the convergence suggested by the Constitution, following the amendment of 2001, is denied by more recent case law of the Italian Constitutional Court, which is concerned about the risk of losing its role as final arbiter for the protection of national fundamental rights. The trend that is emerging in many European countries for the constitutional court to have the last say on the adequate standards of protection of fundamental rights when there is a conflict between the national legal order, on the one hand, and the ECHR and EU law, on the other hand, does not imply a devaluation of the role played by national ordinary judges. On the contrary, while constitutional courts have the last say, the ordinary judges have the first. Indeed in many cases the first say may also be the last say, if the ordinary judge is successful in his/her attempt to solve the contrast between national and supranational law by using the tool of consistent interpretation.

---

67   P. SONNEVAND, 'Report on Hungary', in G. MARTINICO and O. POLLICINO, *supra* n. 42, p. 265.
68   C. LEBECK, 'Report on Scandinavian Countries', in G. MARTINICO and O. POLLICINO, *supra* n. 42, p. 435.
69   I. RADUCU, 'Report on Romania', in G. MARTINICO and O. POLLICINO, *supra* n. 42, p. 387.
70   A. TORRES PEREZ, 'Report on Spain', in G. MARTINICO and O. POLLICINO, *supra* n. 42, p. 473.

In this respect, consistent interpretation, being the privileged interpretive technique of nearly all the jurisdictions examined, is the real *trait d'union* between the domestic impact of the two European legal orders.

Perhaps one could consider this as the first (judicial) stone in the construction of a unitary theory of supranational law.

NATIONAL CONSTITUTIONS AND THE ECHR

Comparative Remarks in Light of Germany's Experience

Alessandra Di Martino

1. INTRODUCTION

Like other European constitutional courts, in recent years the German Federal Constitutional Tribunal (GFCT) has dealt with the effects of the judgments of the European Court of Human Rights (ECtHR) on the national legal order. As is well known, the relationship between the European Convention on Human Rights (ECHR) and domestic law varies quite considerably from country to country.[1] The German Basic Law (BL) follows a dualist model, according to which international treaties need a national statute to be executed in the domestic legal order (Article 59 FL). Here they rank as ordinary law. The dualist model is also adopted by the Italian Constitution (IC) and – albeit in a particular constitutional setting – by the UK Human Rights Act.

Such a perspective on the relationship between the constitution and the ECHR, centred on their hierarchical rank as sources of law, has not proved fully successful over time. Hence, it has been partially replaced by an interpretive approach. In the following paragraphs, I will outline this process and suggest a comparison of the German experience with Italian developments in the same issue.

---

[1] A. Stone Sweet and H. Keller (eds.), *A Europe of Rights. The Impact of the ECHR on National Legal Systems*, Oxford University Press, Oxford 2008; R. Blackburn and J. Polakiewicz (eds.), *Fundamental Rights in Europe*, Oxford University Press, Oxford 2001; O. Pollicino, *Allargamento dell'Europa ad Est e rapporto tra Corti costituzionali e corti europee*, Giuffrè, Milano 2010, pp. 184 ff., 334 ff.; L. Montanari, *I diritti dell'uomo nell'area europea tra fonti internazionali e fonti interne*, Giappichelli, Torino 2002.

2. THE GERMAN FEDERAL CONSTITUTIONAL TRIBUNAL AND THE EUROPEAN COURT OF HUMAN RIGHTS

At the very beginning, not only was the ECHR mainly considered just like an ordinary statute, but its substantial relevance in protecting human rights was extremely narrow. This was due to the fact that the ECtHR was only set up in 1959 and very few cases were decided until the mid-1960s. Moreover, after the establishment of the GFCT, the *Grundrechte* (fundamental rights of the BL) assumed a central function of legitimacy and integration in the new German Federal Republic.[2] At the same time, German scholars developed a deep and coherent dogmatic construction to systematize the case law of the GFCT.

In a second period, while the ECtHR had been assessing violations of the Convention rights (especially Articles 6, 8 and 10 ECHR) committed by Germany, the GFCT began to stress the Convention's hermeneutic value. This passage was marked by a 1987 decision on the presumption of innocence: referring to Article 6 ECHR, the GFCT emphasized the constitutional relevancy of the ECHR as an *Auslegungshilfe* (interpretative aid) of the BL. Drawing on the constitutional principle of *Völkerrechtsfreundlichkeit* (openness to international law), the ECHR specified the content and extent of *Grundrechte*.[3] From that moment on, this idea was to be central in the GFCT's case law.

In the same period, the GFCT issued the first decision on the effects of the ECtHR's judgments on the German legal order according to Article 46 ECHR (*Pakelli-Beschluß*).[4] The case dealt with the reopening of criminal proceedings after the ECtHR found a violation of the right to a fair trial (Article 6 ECHR). The GFCT stressed the subjective, objective and temporal limits of the *res iudicata* (material legal force) of the Strasbourg decision.

Public law scholarship also developed several arguments to provide the ECHR with a constitutional basis. Amongst them, particularly worth mentioning are the theses built on Article 3 BL (applicable against arbitrary acts), on Article 2 section 1 BL (the subsidiary norm on personal liberties), and on Articles 24 and 25 BL (relating respectively to the participation to international organizations and to international custom).[5]

---

[2]   Cf. R. WAHL, 'Das Verhältnis der EMRK zum nationalen Recht', in S. BREITENMOSER ET AL. (eds.), *Human Rights, Democracy and the Rule of Law*, Dike, Zürich 2007, pp. 873 ff.; J.M. SCHILLING, *Deutscher Grundrechtsschutz zwischen staatlicher Souveränität und menschenrechtlicher Europäisierung*, Mohr, Tübingen, 2010, pp. 43 ff.

[3]   BVerfGE 74, 358, 26.03.1987.

[4]   2 BvR 336/85, 11.10.1985, (1986) 46 ZaöRV (*Zeitschrift für ausländisches öffentliches Recht und Völkerrecht*), 289. In 1998, a remedy for the re-opening of criminal proceedings was introduced by §356 n. 6 StPO.

[5]   T. GIEGERICH, 'Wirkung und Rang der EMRK in den Rechtsordnungen der Mitgliedstaaten', in R. GROTE and T. MARAUHN (eds.), *EMRK/GG Konkordanzkommentar*, Mohr, Tübingen 2006, pp. 84 ff.

Since the individual application to the Strasbourg Court was made automatic in 1998 by Protocol no. 11, a shift in the relationship between the German BL and the ECHR has occurred. Such an important change in access to the European Court led to increasing discrepancies between the ECtHR's and the national courts' decisions. Thus, the need to resolve urgent practical problems moved the GFCT to assess the theoretical constitutional framework of the ECHR anew.

Before examining in detail the GFCT's most important decisions of the last decade, I would like to anticipate that the GFCT has been much more aware than the Italian Constitutional Court (ICC) of the conceptual and legal implications of an integrating 'system of European protection of rights'.[6]

2.1. THE *GÖRGÜLU-BESCHLUß*

The pivotal decision on the effects of the ECtHR's judgments on the German legal order is the *Görgülu-Beschluß* of 2004.[7] The case concerned a family law dispute: in several internal proceedings including a *Verfassungsbeschwerde* (individual complaint to the GFCT), the father Görgülu had been refused the right to visit and the parental custody of his natural child. Having exhausted the internal remedies, Görgülu lodged a complaint with the ECtHR, which found a violation of the protection of family life (Article 8 ECHR), with specific regard to the 'best interest of the child' clause.

Since some appeal tribunals of the *Länder* persisted in interpreting German family law neglecting the Strasbourg case law, Görgülu filed a second complaint with the GFCT. The latter credited it and, for the first time, explicitly confirmed that the ECHR could be integrated into the parameters of the BL. In particular, if a *Verfassungsbeschwerde* had to be declared admissible, it should refer to the principle of *Rechtsstaat* ('German' rule of law) in conjunction with relevant fundamental rights of the BL and the parallel rights of the Convention.

Reformulating the principle according to which the ECHR is an 'interpretive aid' of the BL, the GFCT stated that all German authorities, first of all the judges, have an 'obligation to take into account' both the ECHR and related case law (para. 30). Such an obligation is complied with by making use of a 'methodologically tolerable interpretation,' placed halfway between the 'lack of confrontation' and the 'schematic implementation' of the ECHR (paras. 47–48, 62). The appropriate stage – as the Tribunal argued – for the interpretive consideration of the ECHR and related case law is the review of proportionality.

---

6   P. RIDOLA, *Diritto comparato e diritto costituzionale europeo*, Giappichelli, Torino 2010, pp. 200 ff., 256 ff.

7   BVerfGE 111, 307, 14.10.2004. I have discussed the case considering relevant issues of international law in 'L'efficacia delle decisioni della Corte europea dei diritti dell'uomo nel diritto tedesco' (2006) *Dir. pubbl. comp. eur.* (*Diritto pubblico comparato ed europeo*) 911.

If a judge reaches a different outcome from that of the ECtHR, he or she shall provide thorough reasons for it.

Almost all commentators pointed out that the *Görgülü-Beschluß* was a reaction to the ECtHR's *Caroline* judgment (see *infra*, Section 2.2). Hence, the Tribunal developed in *Görgülü* the concept of 'multipolar relations of fundamental rights,' corresponding to a 'partial system of domestic law, balanced in its legal consequences [... and] dogmatically defined.' Within the scope of such a sub-system, national courts may diverge from the ECtHR's jurisprudence in the event of 'contrast with superior, especially constitutional law' (paras. 50, 57–58).

Debate on this point has been quite heated: immediately after the decision was delivered, some scholars feared too narrow an interpretation of such a sub-system, with a close and impenetrable set of national values being opposed to the values of the ECHR.[8] Indeed, such a fear was supported by statements in the *Görgülü-Beschluß* re-affirming the rigid Triepelian dualistic model and the 'saving sovereignty clause,' according to which 'the last word' had been granted to the BL (paras. 34–36). Such concerns, however, have been put into perspective by later GFCT's decisions and no use has so far been made of the hypothetical power of non compliance.

At a later stage, other scholars have outlined the difference between bipolar relations (between the individual and the state), and multipolar relations (between individuals or between individuals and collective subjects).[9] Whereas in the former the conflict between the ECHR and the BL can be solved by the most favourable clause (Article 53 ECHR), this is not possible in the latter: the minimum standard for one right also represents the maximum standard for the other. Therefore, it quite clearly appears that what the GFCT has called the 'partial system' of fundamental rights corresponds, from the Convention's perspective, to the margin of appreciation. Focusing on national legal and cultural specificities, a widespread consent has been achieved by the idea of the 'corridor solution.' This is a metaphor that indicates, along with a core of protection drawn directly from the ECHR, a sphere of 'conventional indifference' open to various national solutions equally consistent with the ECHR.[10] This

---

8   I. PERNICE, 'BVerfG, EGMR und die Rechtsgemeinschaft' (2004) 15 *EuZWR* (*Europäische Zeitschrift für Wirtschaftsrecht*) 705; H. CREMER, 'Zur Bindungswirkung von EGMR-Urteilen' (2004) 31 *EuGRZ* (*Europäische Grundrechtezeitschrift*) 683, 687–9.

9   W. HOFFMANN-RIEM, 'Kontrolldichte und Kontrollfolgen beim nationalen und europäischen Schutz von Freiheitsrechten in mehrpoligen Rechtsverhältnissen', (2006) 33 *EuGRZ*, 492; C. GRABENWARTER, 'Das mehrpolige Grundrechtsverhältnis im Spannungsfeld zwischen europäischem Menschenrechtsschutz und Verfassungsgerichtsbarkeit', in P.M. DUPUY et al. (eds.), *Völkerrecht als Wertordnung*, Engel, Kehl 2006, pp. 193 ff.

10   W. HOFFMANN-RIEM, *supra* n. 9, pp. 497–499; G. LÜBBE-WOLFF, 'Der Grundrechtsschutz nach der Europäischen Menschenrechtskonvention bei konfligierenden Individualrechten', in M. HOCHHUT (ed.), *Nachdenken über Staat und Recht*, Duncker & Humblot, Berlin 2009, pp. 200–202.

approach is complemented by the insistence upon a careful graduation of the intensity of the ECtHR's scrutiny.

In another significant passage of the *Görgülü-Beschluß*, the constitutional judges have seen themselves as the guardians of respect for international obligations, so that the GFCT is entitled to apply a stricter scrutiny even when the horizontal effects of fundamental rights are at stake. This depends on the need to avoid Germany's international responsibility, but also on the recognition of a 'common European development of fundamental rights' integrating both the ECHR and the BL. The GFCT has also placed upon the national judiciary an obligation to construe domestic law in harmony with the Convention. This obligation has been based on Article 1 section 2 BL (para. 62), according to which 'The German people acknowledge inviolable and inalienable human rights as the basis of every community, of peace and of justice in the world': significantly, this norm has been adequately appreciated only in recent times.[11]

2.2. THE *CAROLINE-URTEIL II*

The second key judgment of the GFCT on the effects of the ECHR in the German legal order is the *Caroline-Urteil II* of 2008,[12] which followed both the GFCT's *Caroline I* decision (1999) and the ECtHR's decision on the same issue.[13] As is well known, the case concerned a conflict between freedom of the press and the right to privacy. The conflict had arisen because the boulevard press had published some pictures of Princess Caroline and members of her family without her consent. Whereas in *Caroline I* the GFCT did not hold that the balancing struck by the *Bundesgerichtshof* (BGH) – with the freedom of the press prevailing over privacy – was unconstitutional, the opposite outcome was reached by the ECtHR. In this regard, some commentators have critically stressed the unilateral approach of the Strasbourg Court, which manifestly ignored the arguments – drawn on well-established German information law – deployed by the GFCT.[14] The ECtHR failed to consider the specific context of the controversy, nor did it apply the consensus standard test. Instead, it built its reasoning mainly upon a quite marginal resolution of the Council of Europe's Assembly on the protection of private life.

---

11 Cf. M. HERDEGEN, 'Art. 1 Abs. 2', in T. MAUNZ and G. DÜRIG (eds.) *Kommentar zum GG*, Beck, München 2006, paras. 1 ff., 39 ff., 47 ff.; T. RENSMANN, *Wertordnung und Verfassung*, Mohr, Tübingen 2007, pp. 208–214.

12 BVerfGE 120, 180, 26.02.2008, see W. HOFFMANN-RIEM, 'Die Caroline II-Entscheidung des BVerfG', (2009) 62 *NJW*, 20; C. STARCK, 'Anmerkung', (2008) 63 *JZ* (*Juristenzeitung*), 627, 634–635.

13 BVerfGE 101, 361, 15.12.1999, and ECtHR, *Von Hannover vs. Germany*, 24.06.2004.

14 M. SCHEYLI, 'Konstitutioneller Anspruch des EGMR und Umgang mit nationalen Argumenten' (2004) 31 *EuGRZ* 628.

Given this background, the *Caroline II* decision was anticipated with fear of an imminent open clash between the GFCT and the ECtHR. However, like similar cases in the field of European law, not only did the conflict between the two Courts not come to a fully-fledged battle, but it was also absorbed through an interpretive integration of the ECHR into the constitutional parameter.

Applying the rule of construction developed by the *Görgülü-Beschluß*, the GFCT has 'taken into account' the Strasbourg case law at the stage of the proportionality test. In particular, the GFCT's reasoning was centred on the reciprocity of rights' limits. On the one hand, the 'general laws' limitation clause to free speech (Article 5 BL) was read in conjunction with the right to respect for private life (Article 8 ECHR). On the other hand, the 'constitutional order' limitation clause to the general right to personality (Article 2 section 1 BL) was interpreted in the light of Article 10 ECHR on freedom of expression. The GFCT also made abundant use of ECtHR's judgments relating both to Article 8 and 10 ECHR, thus expanding the field of balancing to the convention rights. The reference to Strasbourg's decisions not only on Article 8 but also on Article 10 ECHR helped the GFCT to confirm its previous jurisprudence without neglecting the ECtHR's evaluations.

A second interesting aspect of the *Caroline-Urteil II* relates to the extent of the obligation, incumbent on national courts, to 'adapt' domestic law to Strasbourg case law (see *Görgülü-Beschluß*, para. 58).

In *Caroline I*, the BGH's interpretation of relevant norms was found not unconstitutional – but not constitutionally imperative. The BGH had applied arguments and dogmatic categories well-established in information law, including that of the *Person der Zeitgeschichte* (person of contemporary history). This person can be 'relative' or 'absolute', depending on whether the interest he or she raises in public opinion is linked to a particular event.[15] The BGH had considered the princess Caroline to be an 'absolute' *Person der Zeitgeschichte*. The ECtHR, however, contested the application of such a general qualification to Caroline, since it would imply a disproportionate restriction of the private sphere. In *Caroline-Urteil II*, the GFCT took into consideration the critique made by the Strasbourg Court, abandoned the reference to the 'absolute' person of contemporary history and emphasized the concrete elements to be weighed against each other in single judicial cases.

Other interpretive trends and dogmatic categories have instead been confirmed. Amongst them is the principle according to which the entertainment press also falls within the scope of Article 5 BL, since it can stimulate public debate on value issues and lifestyle choices. In contrast, the ECtHR had not granted the entertainment press full protection, because of its asserted triviality.

---

[15] W. Hoffmann-Riem, 'Nachvollziehende Grundrechtskontrolle' (2003) 128 *AöR* (*Archiv des öffentlichen Rechts*) 173, 201 ff.

In the end, the 'adaptation' of the ECHR into domestic law was achieved more by the BGH than by the GFCT. Making use of its own margin of interpretation, the BGH left aside the first *Schutzkonzept* (concept of protection) and substituted it with a second one, equally compatible with the BL. The successful outcome of such a judicial cooperation appeared in the last *Caroline* decision in Strasbourg, where the ECtHR 't[ook] note of the changes made by the [BGH] to its earlier case law' as well as of the GFCT having 'undertaken a detailed analysis' of the ECtHR's jurisprudence, thus respecting the fair balance struck by German courts.[16]

2.3. THE JUDGMENT ON PREVENTIVE DETENTION

The third important judgment on the effects of ECtHR's decisions in domestic law is from 2011 and concerns the *Sicherungsverwahrung* (preventive detention),[17] a preventive and corrective measure ordered on the basis of dangerousness. A series of reforms passed in recent years have retrospectively provided for the elimination of the 10-year maximum cap to preventive detention, and have retrospectively authorized its imposition.

In a 2004 decision, the GFCT had held that such provisions were not unconstitutional. The opposite view was taken by the ECtHR: in several judgments issued since 2009, the Strasbourg Court had found that the German regulation violated the right to liberty and security (Article 5 ECHR) and the prohibition of retrospective application of criminal law (Article 7 ECHR). According to the ECtHR, the breach of Article 5 was due to the lack of a causal link between the deprivation of personal liberty and a judicial assessment of any guilt whatsoever. As for the breach of Article 7, the ECtHR moved from the idea of 'autonomous concepts' under the ECHR and inferred the practical equivalence between prison sentence and preventive detention. In domestic law, instead, these two measures are dogmatically incomparable.

The 2011 judgment reversed the precedent of 2004: the Strasbourg jurisprudence has been considered like a relevant legal change able to overcome the binding legal force of the 2004 decision. The obligation 'to take into account' the Convention, formulated by the *Görgülü-Beschluß*, has been better defined. The GFCT has stated that in so-called 'parallel cases' (concerning the same state but not the same private party) the ECtHR's decisions gain 'at least a factual efficacy of precedent'. According to the GFCT, reference to the ECHR shall be

---

[16] ECtHR (Grand Chamber), *Von Hannover vs. Germany (no. 2)*, judgment of 7 February 2012, paras. 114, 125.

[17] 2 BvR 2365/09; 2 BvR 740/10; 2 BvR 2333/08; 2 BvR 1152/10; 2 BvR 571/10, 04.05.2011, see A. Windoffer, 'Die Maßregel der Sicherungsverwahrung im Spannungsfeld von Europäischer Menschenrechtskonvention und Grundgesetz' (2011) 64 *DöV* (*Die öffentliche Verwaltung*) 590; U. Volkmann, 'Fremdbestimmung – Selbstbehauptung – Befreiung' (2011) 66 *JZ* 835.

ergebnisorientiert (aim-oriented), since its purpose is to avoid the incurrence of German international liability through the 'harmonization of domestic law with the Convention' (paras. 89–91). The 'sovereignty reservation' – which in the *Görgülü-Beschluß* had a rather decisionist flavour – has become 'a concept of sovereignty that not only doesn't oppose inter- and *supra*-national obligations, but that assumes and promotes them.' In addition, 'the 'last word' of the German BL is not incompatible with an international and European dialogue, but constitutes its legal basis' (para. 89). New emphasis has been put on Article 1 section 2 BL, since the '*Grundrechte* have to be understood also as an expression of the human rights', including them 'as a minimum standard' (paras. 90–91).

Further considerations have been dedicated to the notion of the Convention's 'adaptation' into the national legal system. The GFCT has insisted on the specificity of national contexts. Significantly, the implementation of the principle of 'openness to international law' has been associated with the use of the comparative argument by the courts. Like principles developed in foreign law, human rights granted by international treaties need to be re-thought 'in an active [reception] process' when they enter the domestic legal order. Therefore, the 'adaptation' of the Strasbourg case law into the 'national and dogmatically differentiated system' needs to be as undetrimental as possible (paras. 92 and 94).

These theoretical observations paved the way for a legal reconstruction of preventive detention which differed from that of the ECtHR. Indeed, the GFCT confirmed the dogmatic distinction, well-established under German criminal law, between prison sentence and preventive detention because they serve two separate purposes (retaliation and prevention). Thus, the choice of the alleged violated norm was not coincident: the GFCT did not refer to the prohibition of retrospective application of criminal law (Article 103 BL) but to the principle of the protection of legitimate expectations (Articles 2 section 2, 104, and 20 section 3 BL).

Notwithstanding the different dogmatic approach, the ECtHR's judgments have been fully employed by the GFCT to strengthen the effectiveness of the so called *Abstandsgebot* (imperative of distance), which prescribes an obligation to differentiate the execution of preventive detention and the detainee's treatment from the execution of a prison sentence.

Like previous GFCT judgments, the Convention was given consideration when dealing with the review of proportionality. Here, another difference between the ECtHR and the GFCT can be found: while the former has considered the case under a classical bipolar relation, the latter has tended to construct a multipolar scheme (e.g. including potential victims of serious crimes), even if the Tribunal has not formulated a clear positive obligation of the state to protect the whole of society from dangerous subjects. This has led to another feature typical of GFCT's decisions: after having reversed the 2004 statement on the margin of 'prognosis and evaluation' of the legislator in criminal law, the Tribunal fixed a detailed catalogue of measures to be adopted by Parliament in order to comply with the 'imperative of distance'. Such an intervention has been widely criticized as expressing the Tribunal's paternalistic attitude.[18]

3. COMPARATIVE REMARKS

Among other European countries, Italy provides a good case for comparison with the German experience. Indeed, both countries follow the dualist model of incorporation of the ECHR. As already mentioned, such a model is also used by the UK Human Rights Act, albeit in the specific constitutional framework marked by the interaction between the principle of parliamentary sovereignty and the principle of the rule of law.[19]

3.1. THE ECHR IN THE ITALIAN LEGAL ORDER

In Italy, the relationship between domestic law and the ECHR has shown features similar to those in Germany. While initially the Convention was considered mainly as treaty law implemented by an ordinary statute, its interpretative role was later to gain more consensus. An original and so far isolated approach was adopted by judgment no. 10 of 1993 of the ICC, according to which the Convention is an atypical source of law. In parallel, scholarship anchored the ECHR to the constitutional provisions regarding general international law (Article 10 section 1 IC), the limitations of national sovereignty implied by participation in international organizations (Article 11 IC) and the general clause on inviolable rights (Article 2 IC).[20]

Such a linear path has suffered a slight deviation in recent years, starting from the ICC's well-known decisions no. 348 and no. 349 of 2007. They have provided the first and comprehensive systematization of the new Article 117 section 1 IC (introduced by constitutional act no. 3 of 2001) concerning respect for international obligations. According to judgment no. 348, the ECHR is an 'interposed norm',[21] i.e. the ECHR is a sub-constitutional source of law that is

---

18   C. Hillgruber, 'Ohne Rechtes Maß?' (2011) 66 JZ 861, 863; U. Volkmann, *supra*, n. 17, pp. 840–841. On the BVerfG see now critically M. Jestaedt, O. Lepsius, C. Möllers and C. Schönberger, *Das entgrenzte Gericht*, Suhrkamp, Berlin 2011.

19   H. Fenwick, R. Masterman and G. Phillipson (eds.), *Judicial Reasoning under the UK Human Rights Act*, Cambridge University Press, Cambridge 2007.

20   D. Tega, 'La Cedu e l'ordinamento italiano', in M. Cartabia (ed.), *I diritti in azione*, Il Mulino, Bologna 2007, pp. 71 ff.

21   On this notion, see M. Siclari, *Le 'norme interposte' nel giudizio di costituzionalità*, CEDAM, Padova 1992.

subject to a scrutiny of compatibility with the Constitution in order to be integrated into the constitutional parameter.

Such an outcome has reflected the self-perception of the ICC that it is the sole authority for constitutional adjudication in Italy, which is assumed by Kelsen's well-known theory[22] and which was also backed by remains of the old liberal *Stato di diritto* ('Italian' rule of law). A self-perception of this kind implies a strong separation between supremacy of the constitution and force of law, and is very much opposed to the idea of judicial review being carried out by ordinary judges.[23]

Over a longer period of time, however, the rigid separation between constitutional supremacy and force of law has been partially reduced by the widespread construction of statutes in a way compatible with the constitution (and with the Convention)[24] as well as by the use of balancing and reasonability tests.[25]

Similarly, the rigid approach of judgment no. 348 has been relatively tempered by judgment no. 349 and later case law. As stated by the ICC, 'since the ECHR integrates Article 117 section 1 IC, it reproduces the latter's rank in the system of the sources of law, with all that follows in terms of interpretation and balancing' (case no. 317 of 2009). Such a proposition, which implicitly gives the Convention the rank of a constitutional norm, is incompatible with the thesis of the ECHR as an 'interposed parameter.' Thus, the constitutional parameter has been read in the light of the ECHR (see also judgment no. 113 of 2011).[26] In addition, the duty of constructing ordinary law in harmony with the Convention has increasingly been stressed by the ICC as a precondition of the admissibility of a question of constitutional legitimacy (QCL).[27]

3.2. NON-APPLICATION AND CONSTRUCTION OF ORDINARY LAW IN HARMONY WITH THE CONVENTION

A second distinction between the Italian and the German approach on the issue of the ECHR relates to the problem of common judges not applying domestic statutes incompatible with the Convention. Before the ICC delivered decisions no. 348 and no. 349 of 2007, it was not unusual for Italian judges to apply the ECHR, while leaving conflicting ordinary norms non-applied. The ICC reacted to such a trend with the theory of the 'interposed norm' in order to 'reappropriate

---

[22] See, on this point, P. RIDOLA, *supra* n. 6, 197.
[23] C. MEZZANOTTE, *Il giudizio sulle leggi, I*, Giuffrè, Milano 1979, pp. 71 ff.
[24] From ICC, case no. 356 of 1996.
[25] G. SCACCIA, *Gli strumenti della ragionevolezza nel giudizio costituzionale*, Giuffrè, Milano 2000; A. MORRONE, *Il custode della ragionevolezza*, Giuffrè, Milano 2001; A.A. CERVATI, *Per uno studio comparativo del diritto costituzionale*, Giappichelli, Torino 2009, pp. 178ff.
[26] G. REPETTO, 'Corte costituzionale e CEDU al tempo dei conflitti sistemici' (2011) 56 *Giur. Cost. (Giurisprudenza costituzionale)* 1548.
[27] Especially since ICC's judgments no. 239 of 2009 and no. 311 of 2009.

the constitutional parameter'.[28] On the one hand, the ICC's response was due to the aforementioned 'Kelsenian' self-perception. On the other, however, the Italian solution reflected specific procedural aspects and a questionable emphasis placed on the rigid distinction between non-application of ordinary statutes and their construction in harmony with the Convention (and the constitution).

A comparison will make the point clearer. In Germany, the separation between the GFCT and national courts has been reduced by the *Verfassungsbeschwerde*. Since the GFCT's jurisdiction is given after exhaustion of ordinary remedies, the GFCT gains a 'relative' superiority over common courts. Thus, the latter will almost follow the GFCT's rule of construction of ordinary law consistent with the constitution (or with the Convention).[29] This has also happened with the *Görgülü-Beschluß*, whose starting point was quite the opposite to the Italian one: the common judges were not making an abundant use of the ECHR, but were rather avoiding its application. Indeed, after *Görgülü* the reluctant Naumburg *Oberlandgericht* finally complied in 'taking into account' the ECHR. In turn, the GFCT has respected the interpretative competence of German federal jurisdictions, as is shown by the two *Caroline* judgments, thus reinforcing a relationship of cooperation with them. Finally, the GFCT has shown a self-perception which is rather more substantial-axiological than 'Kelsenian'; indeed, the idea of the protection of *Grundrechte* has been so central in Germany after World War II that the GFCT has been seeing itself as the guarantor of fundamental rights and values. Such a self-perception has furthered an approach to the ECHR that aimed to achieve the fundamental rights' effectiveness.

As has been stated (*supra*, section 3.1), after judgment no. 348 the ICC has also furthered the construction of ordinary law in harmony with the ECHR, so that the margins for national courts to implement the Convention have been fixed by the thin line between (illegitimate) non-application of ordinary law and (legitimate) construction of it in a way that is compatible with the Convention.

3.3. BALANCING AND REASONABILITY TESTS

A third difference between the Italian and the German legal order regards the use of *Abwägung* (careful weighing) and the balancing test in the decision's reasoning.

---

[28] C. PINELLI, 'Sul trattamento giurisdizionale della CEDU e delle leggi con essa confliggenti' (2007) 52 *Giur. Cost.* 3518, 3522.

[29] M. JESTAEDT, *Phänomen Bundesverfassungsgericht*, in ID., O. LEPSIUS, C. MÖLLERS, and C. SCHÖNBERGER, *supra* n. 18, pp. 92–95, 112 ff.; A. VOSSKUHLE, '*Theorie und Praxis der verfassungskonformen Auslegung von Gesetzen durch Fachgerichte*' (2000) 125 *AöR* 177, 178–179.

In Germany, the technique of *Abwägung* is deeply entrenched in the *Wertordung* (order of values) of the BL. While this perspective can be traced back to the Weimar period, it has gained new prominence since the 50s, when the GFCT emphasized the value-dimension of *Grundrechte* and their mutual relationship through operations of *Abwägung*. In this regard, the principle of proportionality – the proper site for the 'obligation to take into account the Convention' to be carried out – graduates the weighing of competing rights and values and proves the adequacy of the means deployed to the aim pursued. The object and the intensity of the intervention are duly considered, in order to make the final decision as unarbitrary as possible. Key formulas such as *schonender Ausgleich* (caring balancing) and *praktische Konkordanz* (practical consistency) mean that neither of the positions at stake is fully neglected. Quite the opposite: according to the *Optimierungsgebot* (optimization imperative), each of them aspire to the greatest effectiveness.[30]

At first glance, the Italian framework appears less clear. The ICC has indeed spoken in judgment no. 348 of a 'reasonable balance'. However, the goods to be balanced are not homogeneous: while a general and abstract 'constraint deriving from international obligations' is mentioned, its counterpart should be a more substantial 'protection of other constitutional interests' (para. 4.7). Instead of operating entirely on the level of content-harmonization, which includes the ECHR's evaluations, such a balancing is asymmetrical and mainly inspired by a formal perspective.

Upon deeper examination, however, the Italian case law appears more complex. The ICC also makes use of a 'homogeneous' balancing – and it couldn't be other way, since balancing and reasonability tests are typical of neo-constitutionalism in contemporary pluralistic democracies – but in a less apparent way. There are many examples of covert decisions 'on balance' concerning the ECHR.[31] Unfortunately, they also reflect – from a formal and procedural point of view – the main fault in the Italian reasonability test. While both the US Supreme Court and the GFCT have made an effort to improve their scrutiny 'on balance', developing logical protocols for better controlling the legal reasoning,[32] the ICC has shown a deficiency in this regard.[33] The judgments on

---

[30]   See respectively P. Lerche, *Übermaß und Verfassungsrecht* (1961), 2nd ed., Keip, Goldbach 1999, pp. 125 ff.; K. Hesse, *Grundzüge des Verfassungsrechts der Bundesrepublik Deutschland*, 20th ed., Müller, Heidelberg 1999, pp. 28, 142–144; R. Alexy, *Theorie der Grundrechte* (1985), Suhrkamp, Frankfurt a.M. 1994, pp. 75 ff.

[31]   See, ICC cases nos. 348 and 349 of 2007 on the right to property; nos. 93 of 2010 and 80 of 2011 on the principle of public hearing; nos. 311 of 2009, 257 of 2011, 303 of 2011, 15 of 2012, and 78 of 2012 on the retroactivity of interpretative statutes; and no. 236 of 2001 on the retroactivity of *lex mitior*.

[32]   For related differences, see M. Cohen-Eliya and I. Porat, 'The Hidden Foreign Law Debate in Heller: The Proportionality-Approach in American Constitutional Law' (2009) 46 *San Diego L. Rev.* 367, 384 ff.; 'American Balancing and German Proportionality: The Historical Origins' (2010) 8 *ICON (International Journal of Constitutional Law)* 263.

[33]   For all, G. Scaccia, *supra* n. 25, pp. 182–186.

the ECHR have confirmed such observations: while the GFCT has clearly affirmed that the ECHR is to be taken into account at the stage of the proportionality-scrutiny, no such statement has been made by the ICC.

From a substantive point of view, a difference relates to the goods between which the balancing test occurs. The GFCT's *Abwägung* refers to constitutional values, weighed against each other in the light of a 'scientific-spiritual interpretation' which makes use of 'systematic and value-laden arguments.' In contrast, in recent years the ICC has operated mainly on the level of interests, coming closer to American 'on balance' decisions mainly inspired by a scientific-empirical reasoning.[34] The degree to which the ECHR is taken into account seems to fit into this divide: in Germany, the ECHR has been immediately coupled with the value-content of the *Grundrechte*; in Italy, the ECHR has favoured the emergence of new spheres of interests which have gained constitutional relevancy.[35] This development can be partially explained with the reasoning of the ICC having switched from constitutional values and their function of orientation to constitutional interests and their mediation.

However, it cannot be said that the ICC's decisions 'on balance' consist of a simple transaction of interests and that the value-dimension has completely disappeared. Indeed, it seems that the ECHR has stimulated a new consideration of the values anchored in the IC – on which the national identity has been built over time – in the context of a European system of integration and rights protection. Thus, the reference to the ECHR has not only made the reasonability test stricter but has also enhanced the axiological significance of some constitutional rights and principles, especially with regard to the guarantees of the criminal process. A look at recent ICC case law shows that reference to the ECHR has become decisive in judgments concerning rights and liberties, enhancing the 'constitutional tone' of such decisions.[36]

Like other constitutional courts, the ICC has not schematically implemented Strasbourg case law, but on some occasions has referred to the 'margin of appreciation' doctrine to preserve the relative autonomy of the national 'evaluation of constitutional, political, economical, administrative and social profiles' (judgment no. 311 of 2009, para. 9).[37]

It has been rightly said that a perspective based on values and their balancing results in 'the breaking up of [...] the approach [...] based on the exclusivity of normative qualifications stemming from single legal orders', as well as the

---

[34]   A. CERRI, *Ragionevolezza*, in *Enciclopedia Giuridica*, Ist. dell'Enciclopedia italiana, Roma 1994, pp. 6 ff.; F. MODUGNO, *Ragione e ragionevolezza*, ESI, Napoli 2009, pp. 96–98.

[35]   See also ICC cases no. 236 of 2011 and no. 393 of 2006 (para. 11).

[36]   The expression has been applied to the ECHR by S. PANUNZIO, 'I diritti fondamentali e le Corti in Europa' in S. PANUNZIO (ed.), *I diritti fondamentali e le Corti in Europa*, Jovene, Napoli 2005, p. 33.

[37]   See also ICC cases no. 257 of 2001 and 303 of 2011.

breaking up of the hierarchical model.[38] In this light, the weakness of the thesis of the ECHR as a sub-constitutional interposed parameter is confirmed. The ICC has corrected it in various ways: not only explicitly in judgment no. 317 of 2009, but also implicitly, employing – albeit improperly – the *distinguishing* technique.[39] Stressing the link between the facts of the case and relevant Strasbourg decisions, the ICC has reached the same practical outcome (maintaining a distance from Strasbourg case law) of the invalidation of the Italian statute executing the ECHR (the solution initially formulated by judgment no. 348 of 2007). The consequences, of course, have been much less disruptive for the relations between the two legal orders.

3.4. THE IMPACT OF THE ECHR AND RELATED CASE LAW ON NATIONAL COURTS AND LEGISLATORS

A fourth relevant aspect concerns the impact of the ECHR and related case law on the national balance of powers, i.e. constitutional courts, national legislators and common judges.

In order to adequately evaluate the implications of the ECtHR's jurisprudence on institutional relations at a national level, some specific features of the Strasbourg system need to be considered. First, ECtHR judgments are merely of a declaratory nature and may not invalidate national legislation. Second, the Strasbourg system lacks a democratically elected legislator that 'cooperates' with the ECtHR in reinforcing the Convention rights' effectiveness and that where necessary 'corrects' the Court's excessively unilateral approaches. Third, the Convention organs lack the productive Weberian tension between *Wertrationalität* (value-rationality) and *Zweckrationalität* (purpose-rationality), which distinguishes the roles of constitutional courts and legislators in mature systems of judicial review.[40]

Nonetheless, the ECHR value-dimension cannot be denied, given that the Convention guarantees a *minimum standard* of rights protection inspired by a

---

[38] F. Rimoli, 'Costituzione rigida, potere di revisione e interpretazione per valori' (1992) 37 *Giur. Cost.* 3712, 3772–3773, arguing for a re-consideration of the textual limit in constitutional interpretation.

[39] E. Lamarque, 'Gli effetti delle sentenze della Corte di Strasburgo secondo la Corte costituzionale italiana' (2010) *Corr. Giur.* (*Corriere Giuridico*) 955, 960–961 and, more critically, A. Guazzarotti, *Uso e valore del precedente CEDU nella giurisprudenza costituzionale e comune posteriore alla svolta del 2007*, available at www.diritti-cedu.unipg.it, accessed 24.04.2012. It must be said, however, that later UK developments have differentiated the 'duty to take into account' the Convention from the traditional binding precedent (see n. 19).

[40] C. Mezzanotte, *Corte costituzionale e legittimazione politica*, Tipografia Veneziana, Roma 1984, pp. 115 ff.; A. Bickel, *The Least Dangerous Branch*, Bobbs-Merrill, Indianapolis 1962, pp. 24 ff.

differentiated principle of 'rights priority'[41] and operates as part of a 'European public order'. On the other hand, the ECtHR's increasing resort to an 'evolutive construction' of the Convention, adapting it to changing and shared social needs, can be read as a compensation for the lack of a legislator in Strasbourg.

As for the 'margin of appreciation' doctrine – which graduates the balancing of Convention rights with cultural diversity and with the democratic principle at national level – it has been noted that the ECtHR tends to be more deferent when faced with coherent and comprehensive legislative reforms, backed by the consensus of national political forces and by uniform judicial application. Instead, the ECtHR tends to strike down such measures when social and institutional support at the national level is lower.[42]

In such a context, constitutional courts occupy a key position: they transmit to national legislatures and judges the task of making effective the proper balance between the ECHR and constitutional values and principles. Thus, national constitutional courts represent an 'element of integration' between the Strasbourg and the domestic system of rights protection.[43]

A common trend has emerged so far in Germany and Italy: the integration of the ECHR into the constitutional parameter has rendered the constitutional scrutiny stricter, especially after the ECtHR has found systematic infringements of the Convention and has indicated specific instruments to put an end to the violations. This may have strengthened the constitutional courts' position before national parliaments. But such a conclusion is only a half-truth, because both the GFCT and the ICC have called on national courts and legislators for the full reparation of the violations ascertained by the ECtHR.

There is, however, also a relevant difference between the two countries, which concerns the relationship between constitutional courts and legislators. In Germany, the *Bundestag* (Federal Assembly) is particularly 'reactive' to the GFCT's judgments, responding very quickly to its demands. The negative side of this is that the *Bundestag* also accepts quite easily the paternalistic stance of the GFCT. In Italy, on the contrary, the legislator has long been famous for its inertia in implementing the ICC's warnings and annulment decisions. This attitude has been confirmed by some key pronouncements relating to the ECHR.

---

[41]   S. GREER, *The European Convention on Human Rights*, Cambridge University Press, Cambridge, 2006, pp. 203 ff.

[42]   A. GUAZZAROTTI, 'Interpretazione conforme alla CEDU e proporzionalità e adeguatezza: il diritto di proprietà', in M. D'AMICO and B. RANDAZZO (eds.), *Interpretazione conforme e tecniche argomentative*, Giappichelli, Torino 2009, pp. 187–188.

[43]   Outlining the Smendian perspective, see P. SALADIN, *Wozu noch Staaten?*, Stämpfli, Bern 1995, pp. 189 ff. Critically C. MÖLLERS, 'Legalität, Legitimität und Legitimation des Bundesverfassungsgerichts', in ID., M. JESTAEDT, O. LEPSIUS, and C. SCHÖNBERGER, *supra* n. 18, pp. 299–302.

4. CONCLUSION

To conclude, it may be stated that since 2004 the GFCT has focused on the idea of national judges taking the Convention 'into account', constructing German fundamental rights in harmony with the ECHR. In contrast, the ICC's leading judgments of 2007 showed a more formal approach, based upon the dogmatic figure of the 'interposed parameter.' Later developments of the ICC have pointed to a closer link between the two legal orders, because of a certain affinity between the German principle of proportionality and the Italian reasonability test, in context of which the Convention's norms are generally applied. In addition, the ICC and the GFCT have used similar arguments in applying the margin of appreciation doctrine and distinguishing the ECtHR's from national case law.

However, relevant divergences still remain, which are due to the different understanding of the principle of constitutionality and to the different operation of the balancing test in the two countries. Even if the reasonability test represents a form of reasoning typical of all contemporary pluralistic democracies, its operation in Italy is particularly weak. The relative shift from values to interests as objects of the reasonability test may also be seen in this perspective.

ICC case law concerning the ECHR presents ambivalent features: if the formal perspective remains in the background, the consideration of the ECHR has enriched the sphere of relevant constitutional interests and 'elements of value.' While the ECHR has made the scrutiny stricter, reasoning and logical protocols concerning the reasonability test are still unsatisfactory.

In contrast, the GFCT has been much more aware of the axiological dimension of the ECHR in a European system of rights protection. The principle of constitutional supremacy has been anchored, from the first steps of constitutional adjudication, to the rights and values of the BL, so that it has been easier to conceive the ECHR as an element integrating the constitutional parameter. Far from being dogmatically too vague a category, the 'duty to take into account' tries to cope with the specific problems posed by European legal pluralism.[44] Only flexible concepts like this can provide satisfactory responses to the challenges faced by the contemporary 'open constitutional state',[45] reconciling unity and difference in the structure of a *pluralisme ordonné*.[46]

---

[44]   M. HERDEGEN, 'Menschen- und Grundrechte: Wechselwirkungen im modernen Verfassungsstaat', in S. BREITENMOSER ET AL. (eds.), *supra* n. 2, p. 331.

[45]   P. HÄBERLE, 'Der Kooperativer Verfassungsstaat' (1978), in ID., *Verfassung als öffentlicher Prozeß*, Duncker & Humblot, Berlin 1996, pp. 407 ff.; more recently T. GIEGERICH (ed.), *Der "offene Verfassungsstaat" des Grundgesetzes nach 60 Jahren*, Duncker & Humblot, Berlin 2010; A. DI MARTINO, *Il territorio: dallo stato-nazione alla globalizzazione. Sfide e prospettive dello stato costituzionale aperto*, Giuffrè, Milano 2010, pp. 295 ff., 411 ff., 477 ff.

[46]   M. DELMAS-MARTY, *Le pluralisme ordonné*, Seuil, Paris 2006, pp. 26 ff., 78 ff., 268 ff.

PART II

INNER AND OUTER BOUNDARIES: THE RELATIONSHIP OF THE EUROPEAN COURT OF HUMAN RIGHTS WITH CONTRACTING STATES AND WITH THE EU

PART II.A

JUST DEFERENCE?
THE MULTIPLE FACETS OF
THE DOCTRINE OF MARGIN
OF APPRECIATION

TEACHING OF RELIGION AND MARGIN OF APPRECIATION
The Reluctant Liberalism of the Strasbourg Court

Alberto Vespaziani

1. THE DOCTRINE OF THE MARGIN OF APPRECIATION

The recent Brighton declaration of the High Level Conference on the Future of the European Court of Human Rights[1] expressed hope that the margin of appreciation might one day be codified. Despite its absence from the text of the European Convention on Human Rights, and status as the mere creation of Strasbourg Court jurisprudence, the 'doctrine' of the margin of appreciation has been acclaimed in the legal literature, testified by the numerous academic analyses dedicated to it.[2]

The doctrine of the margin of appreciation has often been celebrated as a flexible tool for harmonizing international Convention rights with contested national norms, and often praised for its virtue in promoting the acceptance of

---

[1]   High Level Conference on the Future of the European Court of Human Rights – Brighton Declaration: 'The High Level Conference meeting at Brighton on 19 and 20 April 2012 at the initiative of the United Kingdom Chairmanship of the Committee of Ministers of the Council of Europe ("the Conference") declares as follows: [...] 12. The Conference therefore:
   a)   Welcomes the development by the Court in its case law of principles such as subsidiarity and the margin of appreciation, and encourages the Court to give great prominence to and apply consistently these principles in its judgments;
   b)   Concludes that, for reasons of transparency and accessibility, a reference to the principle of subsidiarity and the doctrine of the margin of appreciation as developed in the Court's case law should be included in the Preamble to the Convention and invites the Committee of Ministers to adopt the necessary amending instrument by the end of 2013, while recalling the States Parties' commitment to give full effect to their obligation to secure the rights and freedoms defined in the Convention': www.coe.int/en/20120419-brighton-declaration/.

[2]   For a general overview of the doctrine see I. DE LA RASILLA DEL MORAL, 'The Increasingly Marginal Appreciation of the Margin-of-Appreciation Doctrine' (2006) 7 *German Law Journal* 611–624 (www.germanlawjournal.com/index.php?pageID=11&artID=736).

ECtHR rulings by national political and judicial authorities.[3] At the same time, the doctrine has also met with harsh criticism, even by the same Strasbourg judges that appeal to it, for its excessive vagueness and unpredictability.[4]

This contribution analyzes two important decisions of the Strasbourg Court, concerned with religious instruction in public schools, and discusses the Court's use of the margin of appreciation doctrine. An initial discussion of the individual decision will pave the way for a critical evaluation of the use of the margin of appreciation in the area of freedom of expression and religion more generally.

The concept of the margin of appreciation refers to the discretionary zone granted by the ECtHR to national authorities in fulfilling their obligations under the ECHR. It therefore relates to the relationships between the Strasbourg Court and national jurisdictions.

Academic commentators tend to regard the margin of appreciation doctrine as an expression of judicial restraint, by which the Court wisely shifts the burden of evaluating the 'marginal' content of contested national norms to national authorities, who are assumed to be in a better position to appreciate the law in question. In addition to its association with judicial restraint, the margin of appreciation is also frequently linked to the principle of subsidiarity. According to this principle, rooted in the requirement that parties exhaust domestic remedies, national courts remain the most appropriate fora to assess the contents of a fundamental right, because they are 'closer' to the individual rights-bearers in question.

Looking at the origins of this dominant formula in the prehistory of the ECHR, we can evaluate its path-dependency more critically: in 1958, the year before the establishment of the Strasbourg Court, the European Commission on Human Rights stated that, in the context of Article 15 of the Convention, the

---

[3]   See, for example, D. SPIELMANN, 'Allowing the Right Margin the European Court of Human Rights and the National Margin of Appreciation Doctrine: Waiver or Subsidiarity of European Review?', CELS Working Paper, February 2012 (www.cels.law.cam.ac.uk/cels_lunchtime_seminars/Spielmann%20-%20margin%20of%20appreciation%20cover.pdf) and T.A. O'DONNELL, 'The Margin of Appreciation Doctrine: Standards in the Jurisprudence of the European Court of Human Rights' (1982) 4 *Human Rights Quarterly* 474.

[4]   See, for example, Judge Malinverni's dissenting opinion in ECtHR, Grand Chamber, *Lautsi and others v. Italy*, judgment of 18 March 2011: 'Whilst the doctrine of the margin of appreciation may be useful, or indeed convenient, it is a tool that needs to be handled with care because the scope of that margin will depend on a great many factors: the right in issue, the seriousness of the infringement, the existence of a European consensus, etc. The Court has thus affirmed that 'the scope of this margin of appreciation is not identical in each case but will vary according to the context. [...] Relevant factors include the nature of the Convention right in issue, its importance for the individual and the nature of the activities concerned. The proper application of this theory will thus depend on the importance to be attached to each of these various factors. Where the Court decrees that the margin of appreciation is a narrow one, it will generally find a violation of the Convention; where it considers that the margin of appreciation is wide, the respondent State will usually be "acquitted"' (para. 1).

government should be able to exercise *'une certaine marge d'appréciation'*.[5] Already in the Court's first decision in *Lawless v. Ireland* (1961),[6] we see that the Commission made reference to the margin of appreciation left to States in determining the existence of a public danger that can threaten national security. The first use of the term 'margin of appreciation' by the Court itself dates back to the inter-state case of *Ireland v. the United Kingdom*.[7]

The origins of the doctrine thus reside in the area of interpretation of Article 15, specifically in the vital interests of the nation, an area in which the Convention institutions were reluctant to intervene. Faced with the extreme situation of the suspension of Convention rights in cases of emergency or war, the Court appealed to the margin of appreciation to justify its deference to the national evaluation of sensitive political issues.

This paper aims to challenge the presumed link between the margin of appreciation and judicial self-restraint, by showing how the Strasbourg Court appeals to the margin of appreciation both when it censors the decisions of national courts, as well as when it affirms them. In its rich and inevitably inconsistent jurisprudence, the Strasbourg Court has not actually developed a meaningful legal doctrine of margin of appreciation. It remains instead a kind of magic formula by which the Court seeks to justify both activism *and* deference. The Court has not developed legal criteria by which citizens may evaluate the arguments justifying the Court's activism or deference to national authorities. A critical examination of the values considered by the Court in its judgments reveals the margin of appreciation as neither a legal doctrine nor a filter argument, but rather an argumentative black hole in which the constitutional antimatter collapses, an Hegelian night in which all the appreciations are grey.

2. THE *FOLGERØ V. NORWAY* CASE

In the *Folgerø* case,[8] the non-Christian parents of students in Norwegian public schools claimed that mandatory Christian instruction violated their rights under under Article 9 of the Convention[9] and even more importantly, under Article 2

---

5   Application no. 176/56, *Yearbook of the European Convention on Human Rights*, vol. 2, pp. 174, 176.
6   ECommHR, *Lawless v. Ireland (no. 3)*, judgment of 1 July 1961, series A no. 3.
7   ECtHR, *Ireland v. the United Kingdom*, judgment of 18 January 1978, §207, series A no. 25.
8   ECtHR, *Folgerø and others v. Norway*, judgment of 29 June 2007.
9   Article 9 ECHR states: '1. Everyone has the right to freedom of thought, conscience and religion; this right includes freedom to change his religion or belief and freedom, either alone or in community with others and in public or private, to manifest his religion or belief, in worship, teaching, practice and observance. 2. Freedom to manifest one's religion or beliefs shall be subject only to such limitations as are prescribed by law and are necessary in a democratic society in the interests of public safety, for the protection of public order, health or morals, or for the protection of the rights and freedoms of others.'

of Protocol No. 1.[10] The Norwegian Constitution, while recognizing the Lutheran Evangelical Religion as the national church, does grant religious liberty to all citizens. While religious instruction has been a part of the public school curriculum since 1739, national norms have granted members of other religious communities the right to an exemption from Christian instruction since 1889. In Folgerø's case, national authorities refused to grant such an exemption, providing the Strasbourg court an opportunity to expound upon the meaning of Article 2 of Protocol No. 1.

This article requires the State to respect parents' religious convictions. The Court recognized that, in a democracy, individual interests must sometimes bend to the will of the majority (para. 84(f)), and that the determination of school curricula falls 'in principle within the competence of the Contracting States. This mainly involves questions of expediency on which it is not for the Court to rule and whose solution may legitimately vary according to the country and the era' (para. 84(g)). Still, the State must take care to insure that any religious instruction is provided in 'an objective, critical and pluralistic manner' (para. 84(h)). This would preclude deliberate indoctrination or proselytism, and other abuses of the State's discretion (para. 85). The Court was impressed by Norway's expressed intention to promote pluralism and an open school environment (para. 88), and was also unperturbed by the heavy weight given to Christianity in the overall curriculum ('In view of the place occupied by Christianity in the national history and tradition of the respondent State, this must be regarded as falling within the respondent State's margin of appreciation in planning and setting the curriculum'(para. 89)). Still, the Court was ultimately unconvinced that Norway took sufficient care to convey religious information in an objective, critical and pluralistic manner, thus violating the parents' Article 2 of Protocol No. 1 rights. The dissenting judges held by contrast that the value of pluralism 'should not prevent a democratically elected political majority from giving official recognition to a particular religious denomination and subjecting it to public funding, regulation and control. Conferring a particular public status on one denomination does not in itself prejudge the State's respect for parents' religious and philosophical convictions in the education of their children, nor does it affect their exercise of freedom of thought, conscience and religion.'

---

[10] Article 2 of Protocol No. 1 ECHR states: 'No person shall be denied the right to education. In the exercise of any functions which it assumes in relation to education and to teaching, the State shall respect the right of parents to ensure such education and teaching in conformity with their own religious and philosophical convictions.'

3. THE *HASAN AND EYLEM ZENGIN V. TURKEY* CASE[11]

Two adherents of the Alevi strand of Islam challenged Turkey before the ECtHR for refusing them an exemption from mandatory Islamic religious instruction in public schools. Under Turkish law, only Christians and Jews may enjoy an exemption from Islamic religious education, but members of minority sects within Islam may not. The Court performed a comparative law analysis of similar policies in other Council of Europe Member States, which revealed great diversity in states' approaches to religious education. 43 out of 46 Member States provide religious education; in 26 states, religious education is compulsory, in some absolutely, in others only partially. 10 states allow for exemptions, under different kinds of conditions, or alternative instruction. In 21 states, religious instruction is available, but optional. Overall, the vast majority of Member States provides families 'at least one route by which pupils can opt out of religious education classes' (para. 71).

Hasan and Eylem Zengin argued that religious instruction in Turkey was not objective, critical and pluralistic, clearly favoring the Sunni interpretation of the Islamic faith and tradition (para. 36). Pertinent to the margin of appreciation, they also argued that a State like Turkey, 'governed by the principle of secularism could not have a wide margin of appreciation in the field of religious education. The State could not teach a religion to children who were educated in state schools' and asserted that 'the State's duty of neutrality and impartiality was incompatible with any power on the State's part to assess the legitimacy of religious beliefs or their means of expression' (para. 36).

Though impressed by the stated objectives of the 'religious culture and ethics' classes to promote peace and tolerance in a secular and free society, and unperturbed by the greater priority given to Islam, the Court was receptive to Zengin's argument that the short shrift given to the Alevi faith compromised the classes' objectivity and pluralism. The Court moreover viewed Turkey's exemption for Christian and Jewish students as evidence of the concrete partiality of the religious instruction: 'if this is indeed a course on the different religious cultures, there is no reason to make it compulsory for Muslim children alone. Conversely, if the course is essentially designed to teach the Muslim religion, it is a course on a specific religion and should not be compulsory, in order to preserve children's and their parents' religious freedoms' (para. 74). While members of other religious communities may seek an exemption, the procedure:

'does not provide sufficient protection to those parents who could legitimately consider that the subject taught is likely to give rise in their children to a conflict of allegiance between the school and their own values. This is especially so where no

---

[11]   ECtHR, *Hasan and Eylem Zengin v. Turkey*, judgment of 9 October 2007.

possibility for an appropriate choice has been envisaged for the children of parents who have a religious or philosophical conviction other than that of Sunni Islam, where the procedure for exemption is likely to subject the latter to a heavy burden and to the necessity of disclosing their religious or philosophical convictions in order to have their children exempted from the lessons in religion' (para. 76).

The Court unanimously agreed that Zengin's Article 2 of Protocol No. 1 rights had been violated by Turkey's imposition of Sunni Islam on members of the Alevi minority in the context of public religious instruction.

4. THE SELECTIVE LIBERALISM OF THE STRASBOURG COURT

The Member States of the Council of Europe do not share a common model of the relationship between political powers and religious powers. The classical doctrine holds that there are three basic models of state-religion relations in Europe: state-church, separation and cooperation, the latter one predominating.[12] Regarding religious instruction in public schools more specifically, there are no signs of a common European model. According to Roe, European States may conform to one of five different approaches:

'(1) compulsory Christian knowledge which the State designs, teaches and funds, but from which parents or pupils may opt out; (2) compulsory denominational education which religious organizations design (perhaps in collaboration with the State) and teach but which the State funds and from which pupils may opt out; (3) opt-in denominational education which religious organizations design (perhaps in collaboration with the State) and deliver but the State funds; (4) opt-in non-denominational education which the State designs, delivers, and may fund; and (5) the prohibition of religious education on the premises of State schools but the State makes provision for pupils to receive religious education externally.'[13]

In the absence of a European consensus on how to regulate the teaching of religion in public schools, the Strasbourg Court would not be justified in

---

[12] N. Doe, *Law and Religion in Europe. A Comparative Introduction*, Oxford University Press, Oxford 2011, p. 5: 'The so-called state-church system operates in the largely Protestant countries of Scandinavia and the United Kingdom, with their national, folk, or established churches and in Greece, with its prevailing religion of Orthodox Christianity. In the separation systems of France and Ireland, religion has a non-formal place in the constitutional life of the State. The cooperation systems of Spain, Portugal, and Italy, and most central and eastern countries have a basic separation of State and religion but there are also formal agreements between the State and certain religious organizations (such as the Catholic Church). The legal evolution of these religion-state models, and how they accommodate religious freedom, has been shaped directly by the religious and political history of Europe.'

[13] N. Doe, *supra* n. 12, p. 191.

imposing one model on any state. Faced with diversity, the Court feels that it must limit itself to scrutinizing the violation of the minimum standard of religious liberty, but not the model itself. Faced with a model which it cannot review, the Court invokes the margin of appreciation that each state has in such matters.

Though the Strasbourg Court regards itself as unempowered to judge the compatibility of national religious instruction models with the Convention, it has censored Norway and Turkey's approaches to exemptions from compulsory religious instruction. Analysing the Court's legal reasoning, we see that the Court in *Folgerø* resorted to an originalist methodology and stressed the intentions of the legislature as they resulted from the drafting reports. While finding a breach of the minimum standard of rights guaranteed in Article 2 of the First Protocol to the Convention, the Court still acknowledged that the determination of school curricula falls within the margin of appreciation of the State 'in view of the place occupied by Christianity in the national history and tradition of the respondent State'. The Court's activism ultimately relied upon a questionable argument, in which the appeal to the intentions of the national legislature was joined by an apodictic invocation of history and national traditions, which in no way the Court proceeded to construct or analyze.

In its *Zengin* judgment, the Court reached a similar conclusion, though by taking a very different argumentative path. The Court avoided invoking the margin of appreciation altogether, and made no reference to the intentions of the national legislator, national history or tradition, but merely stated that 'notwithstanding the State's secular nature, Islam is the majority religion practiced in Turkey' (para. 63). Dealing with the Turkish scenario, in which a formally secular constitutional framework rubs up against a society almost completely dominated by one religion, the Court turned to a comparative study. Though demonstrating a diversity of models for public religious instruction, this information did not trigger the use of the metaphor of the margin of appreciation. Rather such diversity led the Court to the discovery of a common European constitutional principle, namely that 'almost all of the States offer at least one route by which pupils can opt out of religious education classes' (para. 34).

Reading these two decisions together one might get the impression of an activist court, ready to protect the rights of religious minorities against the tyranny of the majoritarian belief. However, placing these decisions in the broader context of the Court's case law on religious freedom, one gets the impression that the Court's activism is somewhat selective. If we read the *Folgerø* and *Hasan* decisions against the background of much more famous hard cases, such as *Sahin v. Turkey*[14] or *Kervanci v. France*,[15] the Court's deference to Turkey and France's rigid secularism in the latter cases is all the more striking.

Faced with a doctrine of strict separation between the religious and the political dimensions, typical of the constitutional frameworks of France and Turkey, the Court invoked the margin of appreciation to defer to national authorities the judgment on Muslim women and girls' religious liberty right to wear the veil in state schools and universities. In other words, the Court used the margin of appreciation to validate the strict liberalism[16] of prohibitive Turkish and French laws.

Conversely, in the broader context of the jurisprudence of the Strasbourg Court on freedom of expression, just think of leading cases such as *Handyside*,[17] *Otto-Preminger Institut*[18] and *Wingrove*.[19] In these cases, the Court used the margin of appreciation to validate national laws that favor the majority religion at the expense of individual freedom of expression.[20] In *Lautsi II*, the Grand Chamber invoked Italy's margin of appreciation to keep the crucifix in public schools, notwithstanding Lautsi's religious liberty claims to the contrary.[21]

Through the doctrine of the margin of appreciation, the Court has been able to validate illiberal, if not confessional, national decisions and national authorities' privileging of a particular religion at the expense of the rights of religious minorities and of freedom of individual expression, be it atheistic or blasphemous.

The approach of the Strasbourg Court in the area of religious freedom is thus very selective: it is secular when faced with Islamic claims but confessional when dealing with anti-Catholic feelings. It is liberal-activist in easy cases

---

[14]   ECtHR, *Leyla Sahin v. Turkey*, judgment of 10 November 2005.

[15]   ECtHR, *Kervanci v. France*, judgment of 4 December 2008.

[16]   See J. HABERMAS, "'The Political': The Rational Meaning of a Questionable Inheritance of Political Theology', in J. BUTLER et al., *The Power of Religion in the Public Sphere*, Columbia University Press, New York 2011, p. 24: 'In a liberal democracy, state power has lost its religious aura. And, in view of the fact of persisting pluralism, it is hard to see on which normative grounds the historical step toward the secularization of state power could ever be reversed. This in turn requires a justification of constitutional essentials and the outcomes of the democratic process in ways that are neutral toward the cognitive claims of competing worldviews. Democratic legitimacy is the only one available today. The idea of replacing it or complementing it by some presumably 'deeper' grounding of the constitution in a generally binding way amounts to obscurantism'.

[17]   ECtHR, *Handyside v. United Kingdom*, judgment of 7 December 1976.

[18]   ECtHR, *Otto-Preminger-Institut v. Austria*, judgment of 20 September 1994.

[19]   ECtHR, *Wingrove v. United Kingdom*, judgment of 25 November 1996.

[20]   For a critique of the excessive vagueness of the margin of appreciation in the context of freedom of expression, see G. REPETTO, *Argomenti comparativi e diritti fondamentali in Europa. Teorie dell'interpretazione e giurisprudenza sovranazionale*, Jovene, Napoli 2011, p. 177.

[21]   ECtHR, Grand Chamber, *Lautsi and others v. Italy*, judgment of 18 March 2011.

involving marginal provisions and minor violations of religious freedom, but deferential-confessional in hard cases involving individual challenges to majoritarian religious powers which might destabilize the national legislative and constitutional framework. The Court favors the majoritarian belief in the hard cases that define the socio-cultural identity of a constitutional community, but has been willing to intervene in favor of minorities in cases where it was just to reformulate specific provisions deemed to be offensive to religious freedom.

THE CRUCIFIX AND THE
MARGIN OF APPRECIATION

Ilenia Ruggiu

1. A CONSTITUTIONAL CONVERSATION OVER A RELIGIOUS SYMBOL

The impact of the ECHR in the Italian legal system can be appreciated in issues concerning particular conflicts as the case around the religious symbol of the Christian cross in schools.[1] The richness and diversity of arguments and legal reasoning that have been used have made the crucifix issue an example of a constitutional conversation in a multilevel judicial setting.

It is a conversation because it is composed of several layers of judicial reasoning, very different from one another, that try to be persuasive, and to integrate different aspects of the case into the public sphere.

It is constitutional not only because it touches directly upon constitutional norms or values but, especially, because this issue concerns the values of coexistence and the changes taking place in society – Italy's above all, but Europe's as well. This reflection on the value of coexistence is made over and over again, through the work of the courts as well.

The 'porous forms of interaction'[2] between the national and ECHR legal systems are also observed in the interplay of values of coexistence. In the case concerning the presence of the Christian cross in Italian schools the ECtHR intervened, including at the same time results of the Italian Courts but with new arguments that enrich the perceptions of, and the points of view on, the issue.

---

[1] European Group of Public Law, Colloquium on *Religions and Public Law–Religions et Droit public*, Esperia, London 2005; A. Morelli, 'Simboli, religioni e valori nelle democrazie costituzionali contemporanee' in *Forum dei Quaderni Costituzionali* (www.forumcostituzionale.it).
[2] G. Repetto in this *Volume*, p. 37.

2. A BRIEF HISTORY OF THE 'CRUCIFIX ISSUE' IN ITALY

'Every school has the national flag; every classroom has an image of the crucifix and the portrait of the king' states article 118 of Royal Decree no. 965/1924 regulating the organization of primary schools in Italy.

'The furnishings, the teaching material in the various classrooms, and all the tools in every school are indicated in schedule C attached'. They are: 'the crucifix, the portrait of the king, the clock…' So states article 119, and the attached table C, of Royal Decree no. 1297/1928 governing the organization of middle schools in Italy.

These two articles represent the normative foundation of the duty to display a crucifix in every primary and middle school in Italy.[3] For decades, the quoted norms were not questioned, giving rise to different practices, with schools in which the cross was not present, and a majority of them in which it was. It was not until about a decade ago that cases regarding the removal of the cross began to be brought in Italian courts.

In 2000, the Italian Supreme Court[4] decided a criminal case of a person accused of 'omission of public service without justified cause' because he had refused to serve at an electoral polling station located in a school until the crucifix was removed. On this occasion, the Supreme Court declared that the presence of the crucifix in public institutions such as schools went against the constitutional principle of secularism and freedom of conscience, and for these reasons the crucifix should be removed. The decision referred to the circumstances of political elections, leaving unresolved the question of the presence of the crucifix during everyday classes.

In 2002, Ms Soile Lautsi asked her children's school board to remove the crucifix from their classroom. After receiving a refusal, she contested the school's decision before the Administrative judge (*tribunale amministrativo regionale*, TAR) in her region. The judge raised a question as to the constitutionality of the royal decrees before the Constitutional Court, asking the Court to invalidate them.

---

[3] Both norms are prior to 1948, the year when Italy became a Democratic Republic – abandoning its previous monarchical and fascist regime – and when the Constitution was enacted. Like every norm prior to 1948, they remain in the legal system unless they conflict with a norm in the Constitution. The so called pre-Republican norms are considered abrogated by the 1948 Constitution if there is a direct conflict with an explicit norm in the Constitution. If there is no direct conflict, it must be the Constitutional Court that declares the unconstitutionality of the previous norms. For example, in the case of the 'portrait of the king', that norm could be considered abrogated because it conflicts directly with Article 1 of the Constitution that establishes a Republic. Conversely, the norm on the presence of the cross in classroom has been considered in force because the Italian Constitution contains no norm explicitly regulating the crucifix.

[4] *Corte di cassazione*, Criminal Section IV, 1 March 2000, no. 439.

In 2004 (ordinance 389/2004), the Constitutional Court declared the question raised by Veneto's TAR to be inadmissible, resorting to a procedural argument: the norms imposing the presence of the crucifix in the schools had no legislative level; they were secondary sources of law (a royal decree is a *regolamento,* not a law), and in Italy, the Constitutional Court can decide only as to the legitimacy of laws.[5] The two decrees could not be strictly connected with other republican laws regarding the organization of schools, as the judge tried to demonstrate in order to obtain a verdict by the Constitutional Court.

With judgment no. 1110 of 2005 the Veneto TAR decided the case, rejecting Ms Lautsi's application. The judicial reasoning aimed to deny the religious nature of the crucifix in the school context. According to the judge: 'the crucifix is a historical/cultural symbol, endowed with a connotation of identity referring to our people'; it is part of Italy's historical heritage; 'the constitutional principles of liberty have many roots, and one of these roots is Christianity'. With this argument, the judge de-religionized the symbol. For this cultural (and not religious) nature of the cross, there was – according to the judge – no violation of the secular principle whatsoever.[6]

The decision was then appealed by Ms Lautsi to the *Consiglio di Stato* (the supreme administrative judge).

With judgment no. 556 of 2006, the *Consiglio di Stato* upheld the TAR's decision. This judge used a similar 'cultural argument', connecting the presence of the crucifix with the Italian constitutional tradition: 'the conditions for using the principle of secularism are determined with reference to cultural tradition, to the living customs of each people [...] inasmuch as these traditions and customs are transferred into their juridical systems. And these change from nation to nation'; 'it is clear that in Italy, the crucifix is appropriate for symbolizing the religious origin of the values of tolerance, solidarity, emphasis on the person, and rejection of all discrimination [...] that are characteristic of Italian civilization. These values, which have imbued the traditions, ways of life, and culture of the Italian people [...] underlie and emerge from the fundamental norms of our constitutional charter'; 'the crucifix aims to affirm the principles safeguarded by the Constitution itself'.[7]

---

5   Italian doctrine saw in this ordinance a way to not decide the question, and implicitly a way not to permit the removal of the crucifix from schools: A. Pugiotto, 'Sul crocifisso la Corte pronuncia un'ordinanza pilatesca' (2005) 3 *Diritto e Giustizia* 102; F. Cortese, 'Brevi osservazioni sul crocifisso come simbolo affermativo e confermativo del principio di laicità dello Stato repubblicano' (2005) *Costituzionalismo.it* 1 (www.costituzionalismo.it). On the contrary, R. Bin, 'Inammissibile, ma inevitabile', in R. Bin, G. Brunelli, A. Pugiotto and P. Veronesi (eds.), *La laicità crocifissa? Il nodo costituzionale dei simboli religiosi nei luoghi pubblici*, Giappichelli, Torino 2004, p. 37, held that the Constitutional Court had no choice.

6   P. Veronesi, 'La Corte costituzionale, il Tar e il crocifisso: il seguito dell'ordinanza n. 389/2004' (2005) *Forum dei Quaderni Costituzionali* (www.forumcostituzionale.it).

7   For a criticism against this equation N. Fiorita, 'Se il crocefisso afferma e conferma la laicità dello Stato: paradossi, incongruenze e sconfinamenti di una sentenza del Tar Veneto' (2005)

Having exhausted the internal remedies offered by the Italian legal system, Ms Lautsi then contested the violation of the European Charter of Human Rights. As is well known, the Court of Strasbourg answered to the claims with two opposing judgments.

Lautsi v. Italy, 3 November 2009 (hereinafter, '*Lautsi I*') stated that the crucifix should be removed, relying two arguments. First, because it violated the freedom of education enshrined in Article 2 of the Protocol 1 of the Convention, which can be assured only if 'there is a school environment open and oriented to inclusion, and not to exclusion'. Second, because it violated Article 9 of the Convention, which also includes the freedom not to believe.

Lautsi v. Italy, 18 March 2011 (hereinafter, '*Lautsi II*') was enacted by the Grand Chamber after the Italian government, joined by more than ten of the Convention's States, contested *Lautsi I*. In this final judgment, the European Court of Human Rights advanced two arguments. The first is that although the crucifix is primarily a religious symbol, it is a 'passive symbol', not capable of offending, indoctrinating, or proselytizing. The second is the margin of appreciation: since there is no standard consensus, but, to the contrary, a great diversity among member states, Italy can decide whether or not to perpetuate this tradition.[8]

In the following paragraphs, I will focus on some arguments raised in the *Lautsi II* decision that are important for seeing how the European Court tries (or does not try) to reshape the values of coexistence. I will use the margin of appreciation as a prism for dealing with this analysis.

3. DOES THE USE OF THE MARGIN OF APPRECIATION LIMIT THE CONVENTION'S RIGHTS?

The first question to be explored is whether the use of the margin of appreciation represents a weakened protection of the Convention's rights, in the sense that the Court uses it to escape affording their protection in cases that are, for example, politically sensitive. In my opinion, the margin of appreciation in the *Lautsi* case does not affect the level of protection of the rights under the Convention.

Osservatorio delle libertà e istituzioni religiose (www.olir.it); S. MANCINI, *Il potere dei simboli, i simboli del potere. Laicità e religione alla prova del pluralismo*, Cedam, Padova 2008; F. LAFFAILLE (ed.), *Laïcité(s)*, Mare & Martin, Paris 2010; A. PACE (ed.), *Problemi pratici della laicità agli inizi del secolo XXI*, Cedam, Padova 2008; M. CROCE, 'C'è un giudice a Valladolid: la rimozione del crocifisso dalle aule scolastiche in Spagna' (2009) *Quaderni costituzionali* 108.

8   The lack of this argument in the *Lautsi I* decision had been criticized by D. TEGA, 'Cercando un significato europeo di laicità: la libertà religiosa nella giurisprudenza della Corte europea dei diritti' (2010) *Quaderni costituzionali* 799.

It should however be pointed out that resorting to it takes place after the Grand Chamber has made a substantial judgment as to the violation of the rights protected by the ECHR: the margin of appreciation is a second argument that is used after assessing that there is no violation of the freedom of education. As mentioned, the argument used to demonstrate this is that: 'a crucifix on a wall is an essentially passive symbol and this point is of importance in the Court's view, particularly having regard to the principle of neutrality [...] It cannot be deemed to have an influence on pupils comparable to that of didactic speech or participation in religious activities' (para. 72).[9]

There is obviously much room for discussion as to whether, in this regard, it is true that the crucifix is a merely passive symbol. In any event, it appears to me that with this argument, *Lautsi II* provides a solution that is 'less difficult', less divisive on the crucifix question than is *Lautsi I* which, by maintaining the violation of the freedom of education, conscience and religion protected under the Convention, closed the constitutional conversation for good, obscuring other possible forms of accommodation for this cultural/religious conflict. In essence, that decision, by construing the presence of the crucifix as a violation of the Convention's freedoms and rights, in some way radicalized the two positions. *Lautsi II*, on the other hand, in using the argument by which 'the crucifix is a passive symbol', does not cause the religious freedom of the majority to prevail over that of the minority, but is in some way deconstitutionalizing – or better, deconventionalizing – the conflict, transforming it from a conflict between rights to one between practices, customs, and traditions not liable to touch upon the sphere of rights. We are not – the Court tells us – dealing with a question of balancing rights.

At times, juridical experience is so complex that the final end of law and juridical argumentation is not always that of seeking the equitable, reasonable, and fair solution to a conflict of interests, but becomes that of seeking the *least difficult* solution. In this way, future constitutional conversation on how to settle it will not be brought to a halt – or at least, this conversation can take place in a cooler climate. It appears to me that this is *Lautsi II*'s strong point, which attempts to provide a suggestion for coexistence: minorities can tolerate the presence of the crucifix because it is not so influential. The solution of keeping the crucifix in the schools is obtained with a milder motivation for the ruling. In fact, the Court does not tell us that Catholics' religious freedom prevails over the free education of atheists. Even if the result is the same, this kind of argument is far more suited to not aggravating the tones of the conflict.

---

9   Italian doctrine has found a contradiction between this reasoning and that in the *Dahlab* case (judgment of 15 February 2001), in which the ECtHR recognized that the veil worn by a Muslim teacher supplemented a proselytization activity, and thus violated the freedom of education: A. SCHILLACI, 'L'ultima sentenza Lautsi: margine di apprezzamento, principio maggioritario e libertà di coscienza' (2011) *Diritti comparati* (www.diritticomparati.it). However, upon closer examination, the Court upheld in the crucifix an element that, in my opinion, differentiates the two concrete cases.

4. WHAT ARE THE CONDITIONS FOR USING THE MARGIN OF APPRECIATION?

Reliance on the margin of appreciation points to a certain continuity with prior jurisprudence.[10] Although often recourse to the margin of appreciation is not subjected to a precise test ensuring the criteria established for its application, it bears noting that *Lautsi II* is part of that vein which, starting from the *Handyside v. UK* judgment of 1976, sees the consensus standard as the chief argument sustaining recourse to the margin of appreciation.

Dealing with the crucifix issue, the Court observed: 'The Court takes the view that the decision whether or not to perpetuate a tradition falls in principle within the margin of appreciation of the respondent State. The Court must moreover take into account the fact that Europe is marked by a great diversity between the States of which it is composed, particularly in the sphere of cultural and historical development' (para. 68). It is thus the lack of a common juridical tradition, of a consensus between the states, that justifies the Court's withdrawal. It also bears observing that in the decision, the Court dictates the limits, albeit abstract, to state sovereignty. Indeed, it specifies: 'the reference to a tradition cannot relieve a Contracting State of its obligation to respect the rights and freedoms enshrined in the Convention and its Protocols'. It is a matter of abstract limits because, in the case of the crucifix, the Court itself has already ascertained that the Convention's rights are in fact not violated. In light of these considerations, it may be stated that in *Lautsi II*, recourse to margin of appreciation is justified and subjected to limits, characteristics that make it a tool that does not serve to surrender to state sovereignty, but simply to circumscribe the space for the ECtHR's intervention in a dispute that – while not, in the Court's opinion, violating any right under the Convention – belongs to another public sphere, limited to the national one. Therefore, it is a public sphere with which the Court is not familiar, and that, from afar, it sees as divided: 'As regards the Government's opinion on the meaning of the crucifix, the Court notes that the *Consiglio di Stato* and the Court of Cassation have diverging views in that regard and that the Constitutional Court has not given a ruling (see paragraphs 16 and 23 above). It is not for the Court to take a position regarding a domestic debate among domestic courts'. By referring the constitutional conversation to the Italian public sphere, the Court does not close the issue.[11]

---

[10]   G. REPETTO, *Argomenti comparativi e diritti fondamentali in Europa. Teorie dell'interpretazione e giurisprudenza sovranazionale*, Napoli, Jovene 2011.

[11]   Nor does the Court explicitly deny the idea that crucifix is culture and not religion. On the difficulties in defining religion L.G. BEAMAN, 'Defining religion: the promise and the peril of legal interpretation' in R. MOON (ed.), *Law and religious pluralism in Canada*, UBC Press, Toronto-Vancouver 2008, pp. 192 ff.

The Grand Chamber's decision is not the final word, but a reference to a public sphere – the national one – which appears the most suited to resolving the conflict.

5. WAS THERE AN ALTERNATIVE TO THE MARGIN OF APPRECIATION?

The Court's choice to rely on the margin of appreciation clearly appears to be the indicator of the lack of a common juridical tradition for resolving religious and cultural conflicts. But is this tradition truly lacking? Could the Court have tried to outline a path of some kind?

In my opinion, the ECtHR could have made a greater effort, by investigating – both comparatively and within its own jurisprudence – whether there is an *idem sentire* as to how to resolve religious or cultural conflicts.

From the comparative standpoint, it bears mentioning that the issue of religious and cultural conflicts is present in all legal systems, and standards – recurrent models for resolving conflicts of this kind – begin to emerge.[12] Both national courts (particularly in the United States and Canada) and supranational bodies (the United Nations Human Rights Committee) have worked out sophisticated technical/juridical instruments: religious tests and cultural tests. Tests are motivational techniques organized by logical, argumentative and consequential steps that guide the judges in their argumentation, expressing the formation of a consensus on when culture or religion demand recognition. Embryonic forms of tests are also found in British, German, and, to a certain extent, Italian jurisprudence.[13]

Even in the juridical literature in recent decades, a number of authors have suggested some 'cultural tests' in order to submit cultural claims to some standards.

The first author to suggest a cultural test was Alison Dundes Renteln,[14] according to whom a judge, before accepting a cultural claim, should ask: Is there a cultural practice? Do the people belong to the group? Does the group have that cultural practice?

In the Canadian literature, Avigail Eisenberg[15] suggested that a cultural claim should demonstrate three conditions: a jeopardy condition (the group should demonstrate a risk to its cultural survival); a harm condition (the cultural

---

[12] On the use of foreign law B. Markesinis and J. Fedtke, *Judicial recourse to foreign law. A new source of inspiration?*, Routledge-Cavendish, London 2006.

[13] I. Ruggiu, 'Test e argomenti culturali nella giurisprudenza italiana e comparata' (2010) *Quaderni costituzionali* 531.

[14] A. Dundes Renteln, *The cultural defense*, Oxford University Press, Oxford 2004, p. 207.

[15] A. Eisenberg, *Reasons of identity. A normative guide to the political and legal assessment of identity claims*, Oxford University Press, Oxford 2009, p. 12.

practice must not cause harm to others); a validation condition (the practice should have been validated, through procedures inside that community).

In Italy, Cristina De Maglie[16] recently suggested a set of questions that judges should ask before giving recognition: Is there a cultural practice? Would the average person in that cultural group behave the same way? De Maglie calls this requirement 'coincidence in reaction', in the sense that a person should behave as an average person in that culture would behave. Is there any violation of other rights?

Moving from scholarship to judicial reasoning, we can see that cultural and religious tests[17] vary only slightly from one legal system to another, and are marked by the presence of some recurring requirements, concerning themselves, for example, with the following questions: To what extent is a practice obligatory? To what extent is it essential to the cultural group's survival? To what extent is it shared within a cultural system? Does the disputed cultural practice cause harm? How reasonable is its preservation in a democratic society?

In the first place, according to each cultural test, the judge should analyze whether or not the practice is obligatory. From this standpoint, the ECtHR could have inquired whether displaying the crucifix in schools is an obligatory practice for Catholics. The demand by a minority (whether they are atheists, as in this case, or belong to other religions) to remove the crucifix does not appear to conflict with any dogma of the Catholic Church. It would have been different if a minority had demanded moving the Sabbath to Saturday or Friday, or if it had requested suppressing the practice of the Communion because the idea of eating the body of Christ is viewed as a cannibalistic ritual. In these cases, given that going to Mass and taking Communion are obligatory practices, the majority could not have been asked to make a sacrifice of this kind.

Secondly, the cultural tests existing on a comparative level require the practice to be essential to the group's survival: this is certainly not the case with the crucifix. The group of Catholics would not be placed at risk by the elimination of this tradition – not only because there are so many other places (churches, religious images on public streets) that consolidate Christian identity, but above all because the crucifix's display in schools is not required by dogma.

Thirdly, the tests evaluate to what extent the practice is shared – or disputed – within the culture. It appears to me that on this point, the ECtHR is too hasty in upholding the Italian petition sustaining that Italy wishes to perpetuate an 'age-old tradition'. The tradition may in fact be old (the obligatory crucifix in

---

[16] C. De Maglie, *I reati culturalmente motivati. Ideologie e modelli penali*, ETS, Pisa 2010, pp. 31, 253–260.

[17] For tests in Canada, M. Asch, 'The judicial conceptualization of culture after Delgammukv and Van der Peet' (2000) 2 *Review of Constitutional Studies* 119; in the USA, A. Dundes Renteln, 'In defense of culture in the Courtroom' in R.A. Shweder, M. Minow and H.R. Markus (eds.), *Engaging cultural differences. The multicultural challenge in liberal democracies*, Russell Sage Foundation, New York 2002, p. 194.

schools dates back to the Casati law of 1857), but what the ECtHR should have ascertained is whether the tradition is alive and deeply felt today. As is known, the presence of the crucifix in schools expresses first of all an endocultural conflict within Italian society, which appears divided between atheists and practising Catholics, but also among progressive Catholics claiming the public sphere's greater autonomy from the Church's influence. As a case in point, the *Lautsi* case was raised not by a Muslim or Jew, but by an atheist Italian citizen. This is clear proof of how we are dealing not so much with a minority opposing a majority as with a society divided within itself, and that has begun to question its own cultural practice.

Another element that cultural tests assay is whether tradition causes harm. Certainly, in the case of the crucifix, the harm is not physical, but in some way its presence may appear as a form of cultural imperialism, a symbolic submission.

In the tests, a judgment also often appears as to how reasonable it is to conserve the practice in a free and democratic society. From this standpoint as well, the deep transformations experienced by Italian society might lead one to conclude there is no longer any reason to preserve a single symbol in an increasingly heterogeneous society.

One may then reply that these tests do not belong to us, that they come from another juridical tradition, that the comparative argument cannot be excessively forced to the point of taking on a prescriptive function. Why should we import argumentation techniques present in Canada or the United States? However, this observation is belied by the fact that on other occasions, the Court, in its reasoning, has applied similar if not identical standards, when investigating the conditions under which to leave – or not to leave – room for a cultural tradition.

For example, in *Chapman v. United Kingdom* of 2001, in which a Rom woman claimed violation of Article 8 of the Convention over the fact that she was denied permission to park a caravan on a piece of land she herself had bought, the ECtHR ended up according her, in the abstract, a full-blown 'right to a nomadic way of life', developing its argumentation upon these considerations which virtually mirror the steps in the examined cultural tests. The Court says that to protect the minority's cultural practice, the following assessments must be made: the practice must be integral and essential to, and characteristic of the group; the practice must be traditional; if the practice is of a vulnerable group, as with the Roms in this case, it deserves greater consideration; cultural practice ought to be defended 'not only for the purpose of safeguarding the interests of these minorities, but to preserve a cultural diversity that has value for the entire community'; a quantitative distinction may be made between 'alteration' and total 'destruction' of a cultural practice or of a culture; and lastly, once these elements are ascertained, the practice ought to be balanced.

If the ECtHR has come to apply these standards to a minority, it should apply them all the more when it is a tradition of the majority that comes into relief.

For these reasons, it seems to me that the Court could have avoided resorting to the margin of appreciation by constructing a different decision: that is to say, it could have said that precisely because the crucifix is a passive symbol, whose presence in classrooms is a historic fact but is not essential and obligatory for the majority, the majority could have given it up.

In this sense, in choosing to connect the use of the margin of appreciation to the choice of whether or not to perpetuate a tradition, the Court missed the opportunity to establish rules on when and under what conditions a tradition should be admitted or not. The *Lautsi* decision had greater constitutional potential than this.

It is my hope that this potential will be grasped at the national level, when the crucifix issue comes back into discussion.

THE UNBEARABLE LIGHTNESS OF THE MARGIN OF APPRECIATION: ECHR AND 'BIO-LAW'

Antonello Ciervo

1. THE MARGIN OF APPRECIATION DOCTRINE IN ECHR CASE LAW ON 'BIO-LAW': GENERAL PROFILES OF RECONSTRUCTION

The subject of this work is the analysis of the use by the Strasbourg Court of the criterion of state margin of appreciation in the case law concerning issues of 'bio-law'. Before going into the analysis, a preliminary survey of these two expressions, namely of the concept of 'state margin of appreciation' and of 'bio-law' is needed.

State margin of appreciation is the discretional space that the Strasbourg Court recognizes the States as having to regulate certain matters, even if such regulation could lead to a concrete violation of the ECHR. Therefore, state margin of appreciation could be regarded as a sort of 'border' between the authorized measures (because they are within the margin of appreciation itself) and the excluded measures (because they go beyond the margin and therefore constitute violations of the Convention). It is a 'border' that is necessarily 'mobile,' and that, indeed, is nothing but a point of equilibrium, found by the Strasbourg Court, to enable the Member States to reconcile their indefeasible sovereignty with the conventional duties.[1]

Among the various definitions of the margin of appreciation that have been provided, we recall the one by Arai-Takahashi, which relies on the implementation of ECHR rights by the Member States. According to this definition, the margin of appreciation can be considered as 'the measure of

---

[1] See, on the contrary, D.U. Galetta, 'Il principio di proporzionalità nella Convenzione europea dei diritti dell'uomo, fra principio di necessarietà e dottrina del margine di apprezzamento statale: riflessioni generali su contenuti e rilevanza effettiva del principio' (1999) *Rivista Italiana di Diritto Pubblico Comunitario* 750, who considers the margin of appreciation an attitude of self-restraint by the Court, dictated by reasons of institutional fairness.

discretion allowed to the Member States in the manner in which they implement the Convention standards, taking into account their own particular national circumstances and conditions'.[2] Another important definition is the one by Macdonald, who states 'the doctrine of margin of appreciation illustrates the general approach of the European Court of Human Rights to the delicate task of balancing the sovereignty of Contracting Parties with their obligations under the Convention'.[3]

State margin of appreciation is often considered in the light of the so-called 'doctrine of consensus': this expression indicates the verification carried out by the Strasbourg Court on the existence or not of a common understanding among the legal systems of the Member States of the Council of Europe. As shown by Benvenisti,[4] the application of the doctrine of consensus is inversely proportional to the margin of appreciation: thus, when the Court finds a rather broad consensus on the protection of a certain right, it leaves a smaller margin of appreciation to the States.

Nevertheless, an enhancement of the margin of appreciation risks leading to a relativistic drift on the content of fundamental rights, and to an abdication by the Court of its role as guardian of the common European standard of human rights protection.[5] Indeed, from this point of view, the judgments of the ECHR concerning issues related to 'bio-law' seem to confirm these risks.

Since the late eighties of the last century, the term 'bio-law' has indicated a new branch of legal studies attempting to broaden the debate on bioethical issues and, in particular, on those concerning the redefinition of the beginning and the ending of human life. Therefore, 'bio-law' can be defined as the area of law that deals with the phenomena related to human life, once they are invested by the action of bio-medical sciences.[6] The contribution that medical and scientific thought can give, in order to suggest solutions for the issues affected by 'bio-law',

---

[2]   Y. ARAI-TAKAHASHI, 'The Defensibility of the Margin of Appreciation Doctrine in the ECHR: Value-Pluralism in the European Integration' (2001) *Revue Européenne de Droit Public* 1162.

[3]   R. ST. J. MACDONALD, 'The Margin of Appreciation in the Jurisprudence of the European Court of Human Rights' (1992) *Collected Courses of the Academy of European Law* 95.

[4]   E. BENVENISTI, 'Margin of Appreciation, Consensus, and Universal Standards' (1999) 31 *New York University Journal of International Law and Politics* 843–845. This is particularly evident, for instance, in the decisions concerning the protection of transsexuals' rights, at least in its first phase: see G. LETSAS, 'Two Concepts of the Margin of Appreciation' (2006) 26 *Oxford Journal of Legal Studies* 705, 732.

[5]   In this sense, A. CARDONE, 'Diritti fondamentali (tutela multilivello)' in *Enciclopedia del diritto. Annali. IV*, Giuffrè, Milano 2011, p. 405. See also P. MAHONEY, 'Marvellous Richness of Diversity or Invidious Cultural Relativism?' (1998) 19 *Human Rights Law Journal* 1–10, and R. SAPIENZA, 'Sul margine di apprezzamento statale nel sistema della Convenzione europea dei diritti dell'uomo' (1991) *Rivista di Diritto internazionale* 571–573.

[6]   In this sense, P. DE STEFANI, 'Dimensioni del biodiritto nella giurisprudenza della Corte europea dei diritti umani. Aspetti penalistici', in S. RODOTÀ and M. TALLACCHINI (eds.), *Ambito e fonti del biodiritto*, Giuffrè, Milano 2011, p. 657.

is thus clearly essential and can play a significant role in the current international legal framework.

With regard to the application of the margin of appreciation to the solution of 'bio-law' questions, the ECHR has defined a procedure designed as a sort of pyramid, whose base is the factor most closely linked to ECHR purposes. If this factor exists, the possibility of room for the margin of appreciation tends to be excluded. Placed towards the top of this pyramid are the other elements that, in descending order, influence the Court in its decision whether or not to grant some discretion to the States.[7] The doctrine has thus tried to schematize these factors according to a decreasing degree of influence: of the most important, the following have been identified: (a) the nature of the right guaranteed, (b) the purpose of the restriction, and finally (c) the common consensus inferable from national laws.[8]

Therefore, once the content of the concepts of 'state margin of appreciation' and 'bio-law' have been clarified, in the forthcoming pages I will analyse the contradictions emerging from ECHR case law when the margin of appreciation is used by the Court itself to solve legal issues concerning the beginning and the ending of human life.

2. STATE MARGIN OF APPRECIATION AND BEGINNING OF LIFE ISSUES

The Grand Chamber of the Strasbourg Court ruled, in *Vo v. France*, that Article 2 of the ECHR is 'silent as to the temporal limitations of the right to life and, in particular, does not define "everyone" ("*toute personne*") whose "life" is protected by the Convention. The Court has yet to determine the issue of the "beginning" of "everyone's right to life" within the meaning of this provision and whether the unborn child has such a right'.[9] Therefore, the Court has always refused to assess in the abstract the consistency of national laws regulating access to abortion with Article 2 of the ECHR, not only because of the necessity of guaranteeing the life and health of pregnant women – and of the foetus during pregnancy[10] –

---

[7] In this sense, P. TANZARELLA, 'Il margine di apprezzamento', in M. CARTABIA (ed.), *I diritti in azione. Universalità e pluralismo dei diritti fondamentali nelle Corti europee*, Il Mulino, Bologna 2007, p. 159.

[8] *Ibid.* For a comparative analysis of this issue, see G. REPETTO, *Argomenti comparativi e diritti fondamentali in Europa. Teorie dell'interpretazione e giurisprudenza sovranazionale*, Jovene, Napoli 2011.

[9] Judgment of 8 July 2004, para. 75. For greater depth, see D. CANALE, 'La qualificazione giuridica della vita umana prenatale' in S. CANESTRARI, G. FERRANDO, M.C. MAZZONI, S. RODOTÀ and P. ZATTI (eds.), *Il governo del corpo*, Giuffrè, Milano 2011, pp. 1253–1265.

[10] In this sense, ECommHR, *X v. Great Britain*, decision of 12 July 1978, paras. 7 and 12.

but also because such a protection necessarily implies granting a degree of discretion to the States.[11]

Therefore, the Court has never taken a stand on the issue of the beginning of human life, nor has it considered it appropriate to assess the choices made by national lawmakers with regard to the balance between the life of the foetus and the one of the pregnant woman, because: 'The "life" of the foetus is intimately connected with, and it cannot be regarded in isolation from, the life of the pregnant woman'.[12] In *Evans v. UK*, the Grand Chamber defined its position on this point, stating that '… in the absence of any European consensus on the scientific and legal definition of the beginning of life, the issue of when the right to life begins comes within the margin of appreciation which the Court generally considers that States should enjoy in this sphere'.[13]

Despite this neutral approach to the problem of the beginning of human life, the concrete use of the margin of appreciation by the Court of Strasbourg in the issues involving 'bio-law' appears inconsistent.

Paradigmatic is the case of the Austrian law on access to the techniques of medically assisted procreation: with a judgment by the first Section, dated 1 April 2010, the European Court of Human Rights decided on the appeal of two Austrian couples who asked that the law of their country (FmedG – 'Fortpflanzungsmedizingesets') be declared to conflict with Articles 8 and 14 of the ECHR. With regard to the clinical situation of the first couple, they complained that in their case only the use of a heterologous *in vitro* fertilization would have allowed the start of a pregnancy, while Austrian law allows donation of sperm and its use only through *in vivo* fertilization. With regard to the clinical situation of the second couple, the woman needed both the donation of an ovum and an *in vitro* fertilization, both prohibited by FmedG.

The Strasbourg Court, in pointing to violation of Articles 8 and 14 of the ECHR, nevertheless considered it appropriate to distinguish its arguments with regard to the applicants' two different situations. Starting from the second couple, the Court noted that the absolute prohibition of ovum donation is not the only solution that the national legislature can take in order to avoid a 'eugenic' selection of embryos. Indeed, the codes of conduct of Austrian doctors already prohibit performing a selective intervention.

With regard to the situation of the first applicant couple, it is necessary, according the Court, to consider whether the different discipline of the situation of a couple who, to satisfy the desire to have a child, can resort to sperm donation

---

[11]   See ECommHR, *H v. Norway*, decision of 19 May 1992.
[12]   In this sense, *X v. Great Britain*, *supra* n. 10, para. 19.
[13]   See ECtHR, *Evans v. UK*, judgment of 10 April 2007, para. 54. For greater depth, see D. TEGA, 'La procreazione assistita per la prima volta al vaglio della Corte di Strasburgo' (2006) *Quaderni costituzionali* 587–592. See also C. CAMPIGLIO, 'La procreazione medicalmente assistita nel quadro internazionale e transnazionale' in *Il governo del corpo, supra* n. 9, pp. 1497–1513.

for an *in vitro* fertilization, and another couple who, instead, can legitimately use sperm donation for *in vivo* fertilization, is supported by a justifiable and reasonable difference.

On this point, the Court affirmed that: 'Even if one were to accept this argument submitted by the Government as a question of mere efficiency it must be balanced against the interests of private individuals involved. In this respect the Court reiterates that where a particularly important facet of an individual's existence or identity is at stake, the margin allowed to the State will be restricted [...]. In the Court's view the wish for a child is one such particularly important facet and, in the circumstances of the case, outweighs arguments of efficiency. Thus, the prohibition at issue lacked a reasonable relationship of proportionality between the means employed and the aim sought to be realized' (para. 93). For this reason, in the opinion of the judges, in both cases can be found a violation of Article 14 of the ECHR, read in conjunction with Article 8.

Subsequently, however, the Grand Chamber gave a different assessment of the facts (judgment *S, H and others v. Austria* of 3 November 2011). It is worth noting how the judges of the Grand Chamber outline in very clear and sharp terms, in paragraph 85, the focus of the case in point. In the opinion of the judges, in fact, 'The next step in analyzing whether the impugned legislation was in accordance with Article 8 of the Convention is to identify whether it gave rise to an interference with the applicants' right to respect for their private and family lives (the State's negative obligations) or a failure by the State to fulfil a positive obligation in that respect'.

Therefore, according to the Grand Chamber, Article 8 of the ECHR protects individuals from arbitrary interferences by public authorities and there is no obligation for the States to abstain from such interferences only in a negative way.

Thus, in the opinion of the judges, the ECHR obliges States to respect the private and family life of individuals, engaging in positive actions aimed at this specific goal. However, the question, in the case at issue, was precisely to see if Austria had a positive obligation to allow access to techniques of heterologous medically assisted procreation or, instead, if a prohibition by the national legislation could be considered an interference with the private life of Austrian citizens.

While the first section of the Court had expressed itself in the latter sense, by finding a violation of the ECHR, the Grand Chamber instead believed that 'having regard to the above considerations, the Court therefore concludes that, neither in respect of the prohibition of ovum donation for the purposes of artificial procreation nor in respect of the prohibition of sperm donation for in vitro fertilisation under section 3 of the Artificial Procreation Act, the Austrian legislature, at the relevant time, exceeded the margin of appreciation afforded to it' (para. 115).

However, the Strasbourg judges continue in paragraph 117 of the judgment, 'Nevertheless the Court observes that the Austrian parliament has not, until now, undertaken a thorough assessment of the rules governing artificial procreation, taking into account the dynamic developments in science and society noted above. The Court also notes that the Austrian Constitutional Court, when finding that the legislature had complied with the principle of proportionality under Article 8 §2 of the Convention, added that the principle adopted by the legislature to permit homologous methods of artificial procreation as a rule and insemination using donor sperm as an exception reflected the then current state of medical science and the consensus in society'.

In this way – that is, by addressing an admonition to the Austrian Parliament in order to reconsider the scientific (and legal) basis of domestic legislation – the Grand Chamber assessed differently from the first Section the question at issue, considering Austrian legislation not inconsistent with Articles 8 and 14 of the Convention.[14]

Another paradigmatic example of how state margin of appreciation is used by the Court of Human Rights to hide specific policies of the Court itself, is certainly the Grand Chamber's judgment in *A, B and C v. Ireland*, 16 December 2010.[15] Since 1861, the Irish legal system has punished abortion caused by a woman with life imprisonment (as provided for by articles 58 and 59 of the Offences Against the Person Act) and the Irish Constitution has stated an absolute prohibition of abortion since 1983, when the eighth amendment to article 40, para. 3, entered into force.

However, the Irish Supreme Court – in case *X* of 26 February 1992 – has determined that it is always possible for a woman to terminate her pregnancy in the event of a serious and real risk for her life, but not for her health. Then, it was the Court of Strasbourg itself that declared that the Irish Constitution breached Article 10 of the ECHR, by prohibiting certain associations to provide information on the opportunities for women to have abortions abroad, even for

---

[14] For an initial analysis of the judgment by Italian doctrine, see C. Di Costanzo, 'Ancora sul margine di apprezzamento: frontiera costituzionale o crinale giuridicamente indefinibile?' (2011) *Forum dei Quaderni Costituzionali* (www.forumcostituzionale.it), accessed 02.12.2011; B. Liberali, 'Il margine di apprezzamento riservato agli Stati e il cd. Time factor. Osservazioni a margine della decisione della Grande Camera resa contro l'Austria' (2012) *Rivista telematica giuridica dell'Associazione italiana dei Costituzionalisti* 1 (www.rivistaaic.it), accessed 17.01.2012, 1–10; C. Grabenwarter and B. Krauskopf, 'S.H. and Others vs. Austria: a Larger Margin of Appreciation in Complex Fields of Law' (2012) *Quaderni costituzionali* 155–158; A. Osti, 'La sentenza *S.H. e altri c. Austria*: un passo "indietro" per riaffermare la legittimazione della Corte europea' (2012) *Quaderni costituzionali* 159–164.

[15] On the subject, see D. Tega, 'Corte europea dei diritti: l'aborto tra margine di apprezzamento statale e consenso esterno nel caso *A, B e C contro Irlanda*' (2011) *Forum dei Quaderni Costituzionali* (www.forumcostituzionale.it), accessed 02.03.2011; G. Repetto, 'Obblighi positivi dello Stato e salute della donna in una recente decisione in tema di aborto' (2011) (https://diritti-cedu.unipg.it), accessed 21.02.2011.

health reasons.[16] This judgment had a substantial influence on Irish law: one month after its publication, in fact, a referendum was voted on that transposed the effects of the judgment and led to a revision of article 40, para. 3, of the Constitution.

The case *A, B and C* refers once again to the substance of the regulation of abortion in Ireland, by means of the appeal by three women (namely A, B and C). The first two complained of having suffered serious psychological and physical trauma as a result of their abortion abroad, without being properly treated by Irish health facilities upon their return. The third applicant complained that she was unable to get a clear diagnosis of her pregnancy's compatibility with a serious form of cancer she was suffering. In fact, if the tumour had been correctly diagnosed, she could have terminated her pregnancy in her country, without having to go – as she had to do – to England.

In this regard, the Court stated that there was a violation of Article 8 of the ECHR only with reference to Mrs C, because Irish law did not provide for a clear legal-medical procedure that could allow the woman to have an abortion in her country. With regard to the position of the other two applicants, on the contrary, the Court held there was no violation of Article 8, arguing its decision in light of the *X* judgment, which stated, in fact, that it is always possible to voluntarily terminate pregnancy, but only when there is a danger to the woman's life, and not in the event of threat to her health.

Strasbourg judges formulated the matter with the usual neutral approach to beginning of life issues, saying that 'The Court does not therefore consider it necessary to determine whether these are moral views stemming from religious or other beliefs or whether the term "others" in Article 8 §2 extends to the unborn'.[17]

However, although Irish women cannot legally have an abortion when their health is at risk, the Constitution granted them the right to terminate their pregnancy abroad, because of 'profound moral views of the Irish people as to the nature of life and as to the consequent protection to be accorded to the right to life of the unborn'.[18] For these reasons, the Court concluded, the interference of Ireland in the private lives of women A and B does not breach Article 8.

This ruling is paradigmatic of how the Strasbourg Court contradicts itself when using its neutral method in order to resolve the disputes concerning the beginning of human life. While in almost all countries of the Council of Europe – except Andorra, Malta and San Marino – a woman can have an abortion to protect her health, the Court does not believe that it is an element to be considered (although, incidentally, it is precisely the one that defines the width of the state margin of appreciation in the specific facts), giving precedence instead

---

[16] ECtHR, *Open Door and Dublin Well Woman v. Ireland*, judgment of 29 October 1992.
[17] Para. 228 of the judgment.
[18] As may be found in para. 241 of the judgment.

to the 'profound moral views of the Irish people'. Moreover, in para. 88 of the judgment, the Court itself reports the results of a survey promoted by the Irish government in 2003. This survey, which, to a selected sample of 3,000 Irish citizens, men and women between 18 and 45 years of age, posed once again the same questions that were submitted to an identical sample in 1986, yielded very interesting conclusions that the Court should have taken into account. In fact, 90% of respondents thought it right that a woman could have an abortion in case of danger of her life (while in 1986 the percentage was 57%), and 86% believed the pregnancy could be terminated in the event of a psycho-physical health risk for the woman, while in 1986 only 46% of respondents approved of this proposition.

The last judgment we will analyze – and which is again paradigmatic of the use of the margin of appreciation in issues of 'bio-law' – is the judgment of 26 May 2011 in which the fourth section of the Court settled the case *R.R. v. Poland*. Mrs R.R. had given birth to a daughter suffering from Turner syndrome, and, for this reason, complained of an infringement of Articles 3 and 8 of the ECHR. The woman, in fact, was denied access to the prenatal genetic tests she demanded during pregnancy: if she had known the foetus's illness in time, she could have demanded an abortion, as permitted by domestic law.[19]

In para. 188, the Court affirms: 'in the present case the Court is confronted with a particular combination of a general right of access to information about one's health with the right to decide on the continuation of pregnancy. Compliance with the State's positive obligation to secure to their citizens their right to effective respect for their physical and psychological integrity may necessitate, in turn, the adoption of regulations concerning access to information about an individual's health [...]. Hence, and since the nature of the right to decide on the continuation of pregnancy is not absolute, the Court is of the view that the circumstances of the present case are more appropriately examined from the standpoint of the respondent State's positive obligations arising under this provision of the Convention'.

From this perspective, in the Court's opinion, since Poland allows – albeit with specific restrictions – women to have abortions, then it must logically structure its law so as not to restrict the actual possibility of access to abortion techniques. This is inferable, in the judges' opinion, by the fact that the State bears a positive obligation to create a 'procedural framework' aimed at enabling women to exercise the right to access legal abortion. If this right is guaranteed, then the Polish State must also provide access to prenatal genetic testing, which must be considered a pre-requisite to accessing legal abortion procedures, allowed in this case until the sixth month of pregnancy.

---

[19] On the argument, see M.T. ANNECCA, 'Test genetici e diritti della persona' in *Il governo del corpo, supra* n. 9, pp. 389–423. For a first analysis of the judgment, see A. OSTI, 'L'interruzione di gravidanza nella sentenza *R.R. c. Polonia*' (2011) *Quaderni costituzionali* 963–968.

Although it is possible, in the abstract, to agree with the conclusions reached by the fourth section of the Court – which in this case declared a violation of Article 8 – the fact remains that Polish legislation only generically provides for the possibility of resorting to legal abortion, and only when the foetus has severe or mortal abnormalities. Evaluating Turner's syndrome as falling within this general class of cases, the Court made an evaluation of the merits of the case, thus replacing the legislature and the Polish judge, and not merely formally applying – as it claims to have done – the criterion of margin of appreciation to the case.

In my opinion, this judgment should be positively evaluated, because it broadens the spectrum of the rights of Polish women to access legal abortion. Nevertheless, the fact remains that this assessment of the merits of the Polish legislation is carried out by the ECHR through a use of the margin of appreciation to assert its own policy. Then, unlike the previous judgments analyzed, in this case the Court uses the criterion of the margin of appreciation to assert its own point of view, rather than to 'hide' it. Perhaps, it is precisely the judgment *R.R. v. Poland* that shows us, unequivocally, how in the field of 'bio-law' the Court uses the state margin of appreciation in a way that is not neutral at all.

3. STATE MARGIN OF APPRECIATION AND END OF LIFE ISSUES

In contrast with what occurred as regards the beginning of human life, the questions before the Strasbourg Court involving issues of euthanasia are few.[20] The Court never took a clear position in favour of certain practices, and instead, very often, the arguments used seem, rather, aimed to avoid the issues in question.

This has been clear since the first ruling in which the Strasbourg judges solved a problem that concerned passive euthanasia: this was the case *Widmer v. Switzerland* (judgment of 24 August 1998) with which the EHR Commission declared inadmissible a Swiss citizen's application for a ruling against his country because it did not provide for a specific incrimination of passive euthanasia.

Another case in which the Court decided not to decide concerned the affair of Ramon Sampedro, a quadriplegic Spanish citizen, who remained motionless

---

[20] See, on this matter, C.H. BARON, 'The Right to Die: Themes and Variations' in *Il governo del corpo, supra* n. 9, pp. 1841–1865; A. DI STASI, 'Human Dignity: From Cornerstone in International Human Rights Law to Cornerstone in International Bio-Law?' in S. NEGRI (ed.), *Self-Determination, Dignity and End-of-Life Care. Regulating Advance Directives in International and Comparative Perspective*, Martinus Nijhoff, Leiden-Boston 2011, pp. 3–22; P. MERKOURIS, 'Assisted Suicide in the Jurisprudence of the European Court of Human Rights: A Matter of Life and Death', in S. NEGRI, above, 107–126.

in his bed for over twenty years, and who, through his sister-in-law's appeal, asked the Strasbourg Court for recognition of his right to suicide. In this case (judgment of 26 October 2000), the Court declared the application inadmissible because Sampedro's sister-in-law could not replace him as a claimant.

But the most famous and disputed case approached by the Strasbourg Court in this area is the one activated by Mrs Pretty against the United Kingdom (judgment of 29 April 2002). The facts are well-known: Diane Pretty, a British citizen born in 1958, was about to die of a neurodegenerative illness in an advanced stage. The woman was by that time paralyzed from the neck down, but was perfectly capable of understanding and expressing free will. Article 2 §1 of the English Act of 1961 on suicide (the 'Suicide Act'), however, qualified helping a person to commit suicide as a criminal offence: Mrs Pretty wished to obtain her husband's assistance to end her days, but the Director of Public Prosecutions refused to approve her application.

Appearing before the Strasbourg Court, the applicant argued that Article 8 provided for a right of self-determination for every individual: this right would entail not only disposing of one's own body, but also the right to choose when and how to die. Therefore, the British authorities' refusal to help her, and the related general prohibition of assisted suicide provided by the 'Suicide Act', allegedly infringed her rights. The judges' answers were contradictory: on the one hand, they recognized that, in this case, Mrs Pretty was impeded from making a free and conscious choice to avoid a painful and undignified death, and, therefore, that there was a violation of her private life under Article 8, para. 1. Nonetheless, the judges considered that the general prohibition of suicide was not disproportionate and that, given a wide margin of state appreciation, it was appropriate to apply the 'Suicide Act', which forbade her husband to help her commit suicide.

In my opinion, the contradiction from a legal-argumentative point of view is very evident. In fact, English law can be applied – because of a very wide margin of appreciation granted to States – only to protect so called 'vulnerable subjects', that is people incapable of discernment, people who perhaps could be instigated by others to commit suicide (e.g. by doctors, friends, acquaintances or even their own family). As the *ratio legis* of the 'Suicide Act' is to protect this category of persons from possible abuses, it is clear that English law was not to be applied to the case of Mrs Pretty.

The incongruities of the *Pretty* judgment also emerge in light of a recent case decided by the Strasbourg Court: *Haas v. Switzerland* (judgment of 20 January 2011). This is the case of a Swiss citizen, Ernst Haas, suffering from severe bipolar disorder, who, for this reason, twice tried to commit suicide. Mr Haas resorted to the Strasbourg Court, arguing that Swiss authorities denied him the possibility of being prescribed a medicine needed to end his life. According to the claimant, the refusal of the request for a medical prescription and of administration of the drug in question, even after a clinical examination that ascertained the impossibility of alternative treatments to cure his illness, led to a violation of Article 8.

Referring to the arguments used by the Swiss Federal Court to resolve the dispute, the Court held that in this case 'The subject of dispute in this case is whether, under Article 8 of the Convention, the State must ensure that the applicant can obtain a lethal substance, sodium pentobarbital, without a medical prescription, by way of derogation from the legislation, in order to commit suicide painlessly and without risk of failure'. The Court noted that, unlike Mrs Pretty, 'the Court observes that the applicant alleges not only that his life is difficult and painful, but also that, if he does not obtain the substance in question, the act of suicide itself would be stripped of dignity. In addition, and again in contrast to the Pretty case, the applicant cannot in fact be considered infirm, in that he is not at the terminal stage of an incurable degenerative disease which would prevent him from taking his own life' (para. 52).

Still relying on the interpretation given by the Swiss Federal Court of Article 2 of the ECHR, the Court stated, however, that 'the right to life guaranteed by Article 2 of the Convention obliges States to establish a procedure capable of ensuring that a decision to end one's life does indeed correspond to the free wish of the individual concerned. It considers that the requirement for a medical prescription, issued on the basis of a full psychiatric assessment, is a means enabling this obligation to be met. Moreover, this solution corresponds to the spirit of the International Convention on Psychotropic Substances and the conventions adopted by certain member States of the Council of Europe' (para. 58).

In my opinion, this passage of the judgment is of great interest because the Court changed the *Pretty* perspective. In fact, it does not only recognize that the right to choose when and how to end one's life can be inferred from Article 2 of the Convention, but it also establishes that the States have an obligation to allow an assisted suicide motivated by reasons of dignity. Therefore, the State must identify specific medical-legal procedures that, after the verification of the patient's free and independent will, can make his or her right to die feasible.

It may then be inferred from this judgment that a patient's will to die can not force a State to ensure recourse to assisted suicide, while the will to die expressed by persons completely capable of understanding and expressing free will obliges the State, under the combined provisions of Articles 2 and 8 of the ECHR, to ensure that third parties help them end their existence with dignity.

On closer inspection, this legal principle emerging from *Haas* decision was exactly the request by Mrs Pretty that the Strasbourg Court, nine years earlier, had decided to refuse. In the writer's opinion, the Court decided correctly in the *Haas* case, though it absolutely confirmed how contradictory and illogical the *Pretty* judgment was. In conclusion, it may be argued that if Mrs Diane Pretty were still alive today – and still capable of discernment – perhaps the Court could agree with her and allow her husband to help her commit suicide.

4. CONCLUDING REMARKS ON THE ROLE OF THE STRASBOURG COURT ON THE SIDELINES OF THE ECJ JUDGMENT *BRÜSTLE V. GREENPEACE*

The neutral approach of the European Court of Human Rights in matters of 'bio-law' is not consistent with its use of state margin of appreciation, which showed itself to be a formalistic tool through which the Court tried to resolve specific disputes in this topic, while only apparently maintaining this neutrality. In this way, the ECHR tried to hide its policies, to avoid 'disastrous' normative consequences in the various national legal systems that, in turn, were involved in its judgments.

Lastly, the risk of this approach is that the Court might be considered an unreliable interlocutor in the definition of a common standard of fundamental rights protection in Europe. Moreover, this could even affect the role that the ECtHR has found for itself in its relations with the Luxembourg Court: the one as judge of the 'concrete case,' deciding in equitable terms.[21]

Consider, for instance, the Luxembourg Court's recent judgment *Brüstle v. Greenpeace* of 18 October 2011:[22] the case involved Mr. Brüstle, a holder of a patent on embryonic stem cells and their use for the treatment of genetic abnormalities. Starting from an application by Greenpeace, the *Bundespatentgericht* contested the nullity of the patent, because it related to progenitor cells derived from human embryonic stem cells. When the *Bundesgerichtshof* raised an interpretive question, the Luxembourg Court affirmed that human embryos are non-patentable for commercial purposes, establishing that article 6(2)(c) of the Directive 98/44/EC on the legal protection of biotechnological inventions must be interpreted as meaning that '... any human ovum after fertilisation, any non-fertilised human ovum into which the cell nucleus from a mature human cell has been transplanted, and any non-fertilised human ovum whose division and further development have been stimulated by parthenogenesis constitute a "human embryo"'.

Apart from the consideration that such a definition of a human embryo seems too broad and generic, it must nevertheless be noted that the Luxembourg Court has taken a position on the point, giving a definition of the concept of

---

21   For a detailed analysis of the role played by the margin of appreciation in the jurisprudence of the two Courts, reference is made to I. Anrò, 'Il margine di apprezzamento nella giurisprudenza della Corte di giustizia dell'Unione europea e della Corte europea dei diritti dell'uomo' in A. Odennino, E. Ruozzi, A. Viterbo, F. Costamagna, L. Mola and L. Poli (eds.), *La funzione giurisdizionale nell'ordinamento internazionale e nell'ordinamento comunitario: atti dell'Incontro di studio tra i giovani cultori delle materie internazionalistiche, VII edizione, Torino 9–10 ottobre 2009*, Jovene, Napoli 2010, pp. 7–28.

22   In C-34/10, not yet published. For a first analysis of the case, see A. Spadaro, 'La sentenza *Brüstle* sugli embrioni: molti pregi e... altrettanti difetti' (2012) *Forum dei Quaderni Costituzionali* (www.forumcostituzionale.it), accessed 03.05.2012.

embryo in the light of European law. In my opinion, such a stance is aimed at unequivocally excluding the possibility of using human embryos for commercial purposes and must be understood as an exigency of the Court of Luxembourg – used to think rather in 'economic' terms – of defining the area of what is commercially permitted.

However, this heterogeneity of intents induced the EU Court itself to take a clear position, albeit in a perspective of self-restraint. Therefore, it will be interesting to see how, in the coming years, questions of 'bio-law' will be examined by the Luxembourg Court, and how it can enter 'competition' with the Court of Human Rights in the resolution of these issues.

HISTORIES, TRADITIONS AND CONTEXTS IN THE JURISPRUDENCE OF THE EUROPEAN COURT OF HUMAN RIGHTS

Andrea BURATTI

1. THE PROBLEM OF THE USE OF HISTORY IN STRASBOURG'S JURISPRUDENCE

The past, its public representation, and its shared memory are the foundations upon which peoples forge their identities. They are thus a matter of a public 'use' and debate that raises inevitable conflicts.[1] It cannot come as a surprise that this debate has also ended up conditioning the catalogues of human rights, especially in less established democracies.

In dealing with disputes that involve questioning the past and traditions, the European Court of Human Rights is often forced to sit in judgment over the history of peoples and nations.[2] Nevertheless, it is the Convention's own text – through such general clauses as 'common heritage of political traditions [and] ideals,' the 'general principles of law recognised by civilised nations,' the notion of 'necessary in a democratic society,' the 'protection of public order [...] or morals,' 'public emergency threatening the life of the nation,' 'religious and philosophical convictions,' and the 'free expression of the opinion of the people' – that encourages a historical and contextual interpretation.[3]

But dealing with the history of European peoples poses specific difficulties for the Court, determined by its 'distance' from national experiences. First among these is the information gap, which the Court seeks to bridge through the

---

1   On which see the contributions by E. NOLTE and J. HABERMAS on the so-called *Historikerstreit* collected in G.E. RUSCONI (ed.) *Germania: un passato che non passa. I crimini nazisti e l'identità tedesca*, Einaudi, Turin 1987.
2   J.L. FLAUSS, 'L'Histoire dans la jurisprudence de la Cour européenne des droits de l'homme' (2006) 65 *Revue trimestrielle des droits de l'homme* 5.
3   L. BÉGIN, 'L'internationalisation de droits de l'homme et le défi de la "contextualisation"' (2004) 53 *Revue interdisciplinaire d'études juridiques* 64–66.

analyses by such support and study bodies as the Venice Commission, accompanied by the cultural and information resources deriving from the dialectics between the parties and the *amici curiae*.[4] But certainly, the Court's lying outside the national public debate aggravates the perception that its historical judgments are arbitrary.

Thus, the problem of assessing and using history in juridical reasoning – which involves the activity of every judge, Constitutional Court, or international tribunal[5] – acquires a marked specificity in the Strasbourg Court, as demonstrated by the attention that the Court has had to give to reflecting upon the 'historical method' that characterizes its own jurisprudence.

In this work, I shall attempt to reconstruct the approach the Strasbourg Court has taken towards history, memory, and national historic traditions, and the use of historical and contextual analysis in its jurisprudence. I shall first analyze the various strands of jurisprudence in which national history becomes an element for resolving disputes, and I will then go on to examine more specifically the jurisprudence accumulated in cases of historical denial, in which the historical method guiding the Court becomes more explicit.

Therefore, in this study's chosen outlook, reference to historical argument does not coincide with the notion of 'historical interpretation' in the manner of Savigny, or with the problem of originalism, also discussed with regard to appealing to the intentions of the parties to the Rome Convention, which has marked some of the European Court's motivations.[6] Rather, with the notion of 'historical argument,' I am referring to a 'practice of contextual interpretation'[7] that makes use of historical references in reconstructing cases and in providing motivations for judicial decisions.

---

[4]   A. PECORARIO, 'Argomenti comparativi e giurisprudenza Cedu: il ruolo della Commissione di Venezia in materia di diritto elettorale'(2010) *Diritti comparati* (www.diritticomparati.it).

[5]   R. UITZ, *Constitutions, Courts and History. Historical Narratives in Constitutional Adjudication*, Ceu Press, Budapest-New York 2005, pp. 5–14, which among other things reconstructs the debate over and the criticism of 'law-office history' in the United States (*ibid.*, pp. 17 ff.).

[6]   B. RANDAZZO, 'Il giudizio dinanzi alla Corte europea dei diritti: un nuovo processo costituzionale' (2011) 4 *Rivista dell'Associazione italiana dei costituzionalisti* 1, 29–30, which insists on the marginality of reliance on historical interpretation in Strasbourg's jurisprudence. F. OST, 'The Original Canons of Interpretation of the European Court of Human Rights', in M. DELMAS-MARTY (ed.), *The European Convention for the Protection of Human Rights: International Protection versus National Restrictions*, Martinus Nijhoff, Dordrecht 1992, p. 283.

[7]   In the sense proposed by L. BÉGIN, *supra* n. 3, p. 64 (n. 1), pp. 76 ff.

2. HISTORICAL ARGUMENT IN STRASBOURG'S JURISPRUDENCE

2.1. HISTORICAL CONTEXTUALISATION AND CONSTITUTIONAL TOLERANCE

Historical argument can normally be found to take on highly significant prominence in the judgments most contaminated with political struggle. This is the case with the current of jurisprudence on the so-called 'anti-system parties':[8] in the well-known case *Refah Partisi (the Welfare Party) and others v. Turkey* (2003), the Grand Chamber confirmed the Section's judgment finding that the measure dissolving *Refah* had not violated Article 11 of the Convention, given the party's programme and its action aimed at affirming Sharia law. To strengthen the Section's argument and justify a measure that, in many other cases, was found to violate the rights protected by the Convention, the judges reconstructed the historical path of the building of the Turkish national state, which – as is known – was marked by having radically overcome the theocratic conception of public power and of statehood (paras. 124–125).

But the influence of historical context in the Court's decisions is even clearer in the jurisprudence on election law in the Contracting States, which arose in certain Commission decisions[9] in the 1970s: in rejecting arguments that England's majoritarian electoral system violated the Convention, the Commission observed that this system was part of the 'common heritage of political traditions referred to in the Preamble' (*X v. the United Kingdom*, 1976, my translation). Even more evident is the appeal to national historical tradition in the judgment *W, X, Y and Z v. Belgium* (1975): under discussion here was the legitimacy of the constitutional rule under which the claimant to the throne was automatically entitled to a seat in the Senate – a seat acquired at eighteen years of age, as against the threshold of forty years prescribed for general candidates. Here as well, the Commission rejected the petitions, finding 'a tradition of Belgian constitutional monarchy' in the challenged regulation. When in 1982 an English citizen residing on the Island of Jersey petitioned the Strasbourg Court to complain of being barred from taking part in elections for the House of Commons, the Commission answered that the Convention's principles were not such as to undermine 'exceptional constitutional ties based upon historical reasons preceding the Convention' (*X v. the United Kingdom*, 1982). And there is more: in 1984, it was the 'historical tradition of the Commonwealth' that upheld

---

[8]   On which see P. Ridola, 'Commentary on Art. 11' in S. Bartole, B. Conforti and G. Raimondi (eds.), *Commentario alla Convenzione europea per la tutela dei diritti dell'uomo e delle libertà fondamentali*, Cedam, Padova 2001, 359–363.

[9]   F. Bouchon, 'L'influence du cadre historique et politique dans la jurisprudence électorale de la Cour européenne des droits de l'homme' (2001) 85 *Revue trimestrielle de droits de l'homme* 153, 155.

the United Kingdom against the petition by a Northern Irish deputy who had been barred from standing for election in the Parliaments of other Commonwealth countries (*M v. the United Kingdom*, 1984).

In *Mathieu-Mohin and Clerfayt v. Belgium*, (1987), it was the Grand Chamber that reconstructed the historical background of the gradual 'federal pattern of organisation' in the Belgian constitutional system, basing upon the country's specific political conditions the legitimacy of electoral rules that set aside certain elective offices for members of the cultural communities:

> 'Any electoral system must be assessed in the light of the political evolution of the country concerned; features that would be unacceptable in the context of one system may accordingly be justified in the context of another (para. 54)'.

These are merely the initial episodes in a considerable body of jurisprudence, recently reproduced following largely similar patterns. In *Yumak and Sadak v. Turkey* (2008), the clause requiring the threshold of 10% in national political elections was found not to violate the Convention, despite the conclusions to the contrary in all the documents of the Council of Europe and the Venice Commission, in light of the dangers that political instability held for the stability of democracy: to demonstrate this, the Court retraced the events in Turkish political history starting from the elections of the 1950s (para. 44).

Whether called upon to rule on recognizing the rights to vote or stand for office, or assessing the electoral system, how elections are organized, or how electoral challenges are dealt with, the Court legitimizes a wide margin of appreciation for the States in moulding the electoral process to the specific context.[10] If we go on to search for 'recurring themes' in electoral jurisprudence, we may isolate three steps of major importance: a first one, according to which any electoral legislation 'must be assessed in the light of the political evolution of the country concerned';[11] then, establishing that 'there are numerous ways of organising and running electoral systems and a wealth of differences in historical development, cultural diversity and political thought within Europe which it is for each Contracting State to mould into their own democratic vision';[12] lastly, the conclusion by which 'features unacceptable in the context of one system may be justified in the context of another'.[13]

The last of these statements is confirmed in the recent judgment *Grosaru v. Romania* (2010), in which the Court ruled that the system of electoral challenge in Romania, which was entirely entrusted to parliamentary verification of powers, was incompatible with the Convention. The Court – after affirming, in

---

[10] F. BOUCHON, *supra* n. 9, pp. 164–5, especially n. 34–39, with further indications of jurisprudence.
[11] As with, first of all, the already cited judgment *Mathieu-Mohin and Clerfayt v. Belgium* (1987).
[12] Starting with *Hirst v. the United Kingdom* (2004).
[13] See, again, *Mathieu-Mohin and Clerfayt v. Belgium* (1987).

line with the opinions from the Venice Commission, that this parliamentary oversight over the validity of elections lacked impartiality – wondered whether this judgment should also be extended to the other Contracting States that adopted a similar system (Italy, Belgium and Luxembourg): the negative response is based on the following argument: 'These three States benefit from a long democratic tradition which would seem to dispel doubts on the legitimacy of such a practice' (para. 28).

2.2. THE INSUFFICIENCY OF HISTORICAL ARGUMENT (*SEJDIĆ AND FINCI V. BOSNIA-HERZEGOVINA*)

Specific national features and reconstruction of the historical background do not always end up sparing state regulations:[14] in *Matthews v. the United Kingdom* (1999), the Court, distancing itself from the aforementioned precedent of 1982 rendered in the case of the island of Jersey, ruled against the State for barring a resident of Gibraltar from voting for the European Parliament. In 2004, 'blind and passive adherence to a historical tradition' did not exempt the United Kingdom from a ruling against it for its law disenfranchizing convicted prisoners, always and under any circumstance (*Hirst v. the United Kingdom*, 2004).[15] Also, when called upon to rule on the conditions for the right to vote for Cyprus's Turkish population (which had been essentially prevented from voting by the separation regime imposed by the Cypriot constitution and by the Turkish military occupation of the northern part of the island), the Court ruled against Cyprus, while however finding that its own criteria of judgment may vary according to the historical and political factors peculiar to each State (*Aziz v. Cyprus*, 2004, para. 28).

More recently, the Court then ruled against Moldova on a law that allowed only those with Moldovan citizenship to stand for election (*Tânase v. Moldova*, 2010): in *Tânase*, the Court stressed that 'particular historical and political considerations may justify more restrictive measures' (para. 172), and dwelt on 'Moldova's special situation', reconstructing its national history from the Middle Ages (para. 173), but concluded that Article 3 of the Protocol had been violated, 'notwithstanding Moldova's special historical and political context' (para. 180).[16]

---

14 F. BOUCHON, *supra* n. 9, p. 166.
15 '… the Court does not consider that a Contracting State may rely on the margin of appreciation to justify restrictions on the right to vote which have not been the subject of considered debate in the legislature and which derive, essentially, from unquestioning and passive adherence to a historic tradition' (para. 41).
16 F.R. DAU, 'Il diritto a elezioni libere tra attivismo della Corte EDU e argomenti storici: in merito alle pronunce *Tanase c. Moldavia* e *Aliyev c. Azerbaijan*' (2011) *Diritti comparati* (www.diritticomparati.it).

But the most important case – to exemplify how appreciation of the historical context does not always orient the Court's decision towards tolerance of state restrictions of fundamental rights – was *Sejdić and Finci v. Bosnia-Herzegovina* (2009), a case with an extraordinary impact on international public opinion: the applicants were two Bosnian citizens complaining of their ineligibility to stand for election to parliament and the national presidency on the grounds of their respective Roma and Jewish origins. Now, the Bosnian constitution is an attachment to the Peace Treaty dating back to the Dayton Agreements of 1995, which had put an end to the Yugoslavian conflict: it introduced a state organisation founded upon a rigorous partition of functions between the Bosnian, Serbian, and Croatian ethnic groups, attributing veto powers exercisable by the representatives of the constituent peoples and a collective presidency. Because of this rigid partition, only those who declared their membership in one of the three constituent communities could acquire the right to stand for election.

Although the Court was not unaware of this special model of constitutionally guaranteed ethnic integration (paras. 6–7) or of the events in the difficult coexistence between the three peoples (para. 45), it considered the critical moment of the Constitution's genesis to have passed (para. 46), concluding that it was discriminatory to bar from a fundamental right those who, in belonging to a different community, do not intend to declare their membership to any of the three constituent peoples.

But dissenting opinions struck at the heart of the Court's reasoning, contesting the shortcomings in the reconstruction of the historical background and the low importance given to it: according to the judges Mijović and Hajiyev, the Court 'has failed to analyze both the historical background and the circumstances in which the Bosnia and Herzegovina Constitution was imposed'; according to the judge Bonello, the Court shoved 'history out of its front door' and thus 'divorced Bosnia and Herzegovina from the realities of its own recent past':

> 'With all due respect to the Court, the judgment seems to me an exercise in star-struck mirage-building which neglects to factor in the rivers of blood that fertilised the Dayton Constitution. It prefers to embrace its own sanitised state of denial, rather than open its door to the scruffy world outside. Perhaps that explains why, in the recital of the facts, the judgment declined to refer even summarily to the tragedies which preceded Dayton and which ended exclusively on account of Dayton. *The Court, deliberately or otherwise, has excluded from its vision not the peel, but the core of Balkan history.*' (My emphasis.)

And with reference to the question central to the Court's decision – whether the critical post-war moment, which had justified adopting the contested measures, had truly passed – Mijović and Hajiyev opposed the majority's analysis, while Bonello criticized not only the analysis, but the Court's very legitimacy to judge the historic transition:

'I also question the Court's finding that the situation in Bosnia and Herzegovina has now changed and that the previous delicate tri-partite equilibrium need no longer prevail. That may well be so, and I just hope it is. *In my view, however, a judicial institution so remote from the focus of dissention can hardly be the best judge of this. In traumatic revolutionary events, it is not for the Court to establish, by a process of divination, when the transitional period is over, or when a state of national emergency is past and everything is now business as usual. I doubt that the Court is better placed than the national authorities to assess the point in time when previous fractures consolidate, when historical resentments quell and when generational discords harmonise.*' (My emphasis.)

2.3. THE FLIGHT FROM THE COMMUNIST PAST

Despite the importance of these pronouncements, the cases in which the Court overcame historic specifics are still in the minority in comparison with the tendency to safeguard a wide margin of appreciation enjoyed by the state in electoral matters. We see this more clearly in the jurisprudence regarding the political transition processes in the countries belonging to the old Communist Bloc, where reliance on historical argument has become central and disputed to the point that the Court has been forced to set out a full-blown 'doctrine' on the use of history in its own jurisprudence.

Rekvényi v. Hungary (1999) debated whether the Convention was violated by the constitutional law introduced in 1994, prohibiting police officers from engaging in political life, on the ground of the police corps being compromised with the past Communist regime. According to the Court, the 'particular history of some Contracting States' may justify these kinds of restrictions on political freedoms, in order to consolidate and safeguard democracy (para. 46). In the case in point, the state measures were oriented 'against this historical background' and thus answered a pressing social need (para. 48).

In *Ždanoka v. Latvia* (2006), the Grand Chamber held that the Convention was not violated by the Latvian law prohibiting those who had been members of the Communist Party before 1991 from standing for election – a restriction that, as the Court stated, was to be assessed 'with due regard to this very special historico-political context', thus giving rise to a wide margin of appreciation for the state (paras. 121 and 133). In the case in point, however, it is the very interpretation of the historical context that is subject to debate: the applicant in fact called upon the Court to judge the interpretation, provided by the national authorities, of the events of the spring of 1991, characterized by the Soviet attempt to repress Lithuanian independence and the Lithuanian Communist Party's responsibilities in these affairs. Background is no longer – as it was in *Rekvényi* – the reassuring objective element, removed from contestations, that offers jurisprudence a solid rhetorical foothold for solving a dispute. On the contrary, it becomes the ground for the dispute. This gives rise to setting out an initial, swift doctrine on the use of history:

'Furthermore, the Court will abstain, as far as possible, from pronouncing on matters of purely historical fact, which do not come within its jurisdiction; however, it may accept certain well-known historical truths and base its reasoning on them.' (para. 96)

By endorsing the interpretation of the historical facts supplied by the national jurisdictional authorities, and justifying the restrictive state measures, the Grand Chamber deviated from the section's judgment (*Ždanoka v. Latvia*, 2004), in which the restriction on standing for election had been deemed justified in the very first years after Latvian independence, but out of proportion once many years had passed.

Just two years later, the *Âdamsons v. Latvia* (2008) judgment returned to the point, circumscribing the value of *Ždanoka*. In *Âdamsons*, analysis of the historical context is highly thorough and takes on the utmost importance, but does not result in justifying a measure of general restriction on standing for election against those who were KGB agents during the Soviet regime. The restriction of the political rights of KGB agents provided for by the Latvian law was 'defined too generically' (para. 125, my translation), and may be applied solely with reference to persons for whom, on a case-by-case basis, a role of active threat to the democratic system is proved. Here, the historical background is traced to its ambivalence and problematic nature: it does not condemn and it does not absolve, but rather invites appreciation of, the case at hand.

Another step towards reducing the weight of history in the democratic transitions in the former Communist countries may be seen in *Linkov v. Czech Republic* (2006). The judgment was born from the application by a leader of a liberal political party that had been refused registration on the ground of its pursued goals of rejecting Communism and breaking the state's continuity with the Communist period. In particular, the party's statute cast doubt on the content of the Czech legislation adopted in the aftermath of the democratic transition, aimed at safeguarding the state's continuity with the Communist period,[17] and proposed retroactive criminal measures with the purpose of punishing the behaviour by the leaders of the previous regime, that would otherwise be covered by impunity.

Upholding the party's application, the Court ruled out that an arrangement of pacification based upon the irretroactivity of criminal law for Communist

---

[17]   In the same vein was the law on irretroactivity in criminal law during the Hungarian transition (on which: J. ELSTER, *Closing the Books: Transitional Justice in Historical Perspective*, Cambridge University Press, Cambridge 2004). For a general overview of the problem, in addition to J. Elster's already cited volume, cf. also R.G. TEITEL, 'Transitional Justice Genealogy' (2003) 16 *Harvard Human Rights Journal* 69, 78 ff.; A. LOLLINI, *Costituzionalismo e giustizia di transizione*, Il Mulino, Bologna 2005, pp. 161 ff., especially pp. 201–5.

crimes could become an asset to protect and remove from the exercise of the freedoms of communication. While recognizing in two passages that its decision must 'take into account the historical and political context of the question' (paras. 37 and 42), the Court ruled out having to pronounce on 'facts taking place in the territory of Czechoslovakia between 1948 and 1989' (para. 42). But, also with the aid of the Convention's preparatory proceedings, it stressed that the admissible exceptions to the principle of retroactivity of criminal law respond, among other things, to the need to check areas of criminal immunity to crimes against humanity, thus deeming legitimate a project aimed at calling past guilt back into discussion.

In so doing, the *Linkov* judgment stands in continuity with the previous one in the case of *Streletz, Kessler and Krenz v. Germany* (2001), regarding the legitimacy of the convictions handed down by German courts after reunification against the leaders of the Socialist Party of the dissolved German Democratic Republic. Accused of having incited military personnel to assassinate those who attempted to flee the country and cross the minefields at the Berlin Wall, the applicants claimed application of the law in force at the time of the facts, and therefore also of the laws on national security, to justify their conduct. The Court resolved the dramatic affair by recognizing the right 'for a State governed by the rule of law to bring criminal proceedings against persons who have committed crimes under a former regime' (para. 81). According to the Court, these states, 'having taken the place of those which existed previously, cannot be criticized for applying and interpreting the legal provisions in force at the material time in the light of the principles governing a State subject to the rule of law' (para. 81).[18]

Therefore, the *Âdamsons* and *Linkov* judgments show a clear detachment from the reasoning used in *Rekvényi* and *Ždanoka*, where the transition context justified state restrictions of rights: as the years passed, the legislation adopted after the transitions, the result of delicate legitimizing balances, ceased to be afforded absolute protection.[19]

2.4. PRINCIPLE OF SECULARISM AND HISTORICAL TRADITIONS

Another area in which historical argument takes on enormous importance is that of disputes between religious freedom, freedom of conscience, and the principle of secularism. Here, deeper analysis of the historical framework starts from a dual line of argument: on the one hand, the need to contextualize the

---

[18] The problem of the applicable law in cases of justice of transition is discussed in the fundamental work of G. VASSALLI, *Formula di Radbruch e diritto penale*, Giuffrè, Milan 2001, pp. 68 ff., especially pp. 85 ff.

[19] On the importance of 'the passage of time' for the Strasbourg Court's jurisprudence cf., in a different context, the judgment *Éditions Plon v. France* (2004), para. 53.

dispute in a specific culture, depending on the particular features of each national experience in articulating the relationship between religion and the public sphere; on the other hand, and more strategically, the emphasis on the specific historical context opens the way to recognizing a wide margin of appreciation for the state – and therefore for operations justifying measures restricting the fundamental freedoms.[20]

As early as *Dogru v. France* (2008), the premise of the judgment's motivation lay in the French conception of the principle of secularism – 'arising out of a long French tradition' and a founding principle of the Republic, rooted in the *Déclaration* of 1789 (paras. 17–18). And the same argument in support of and confirming the indissoluble link between the principle of secularism and the national historical tradition is found in the pronouncements on the prohibition against displaying religious symbols in Turkey: in the most well-known one, *Leyla Şahin v. Turkey* (2005), the Grand Chamber reconstructed the role of the principle of secularism in the origins of the foundation of the Turkish national state, leading it to state that in the Turkish context, secularism was guarantor of democratic values (para. 30).

But the national tradition is also appreciated and protected when it establishes preferential positions for given religions in the public sphere, at the sacrifice of freedom of conscience and of the principle of nondiscrimination. In *Folgerø and others v. Norway* (2007), the Court, while upholding the application of some parents complaining of the compulsory nature of Lutheran religious instruction in the schools, did not fail to formulate a general principle based upon 'the place occupied by Christianity in the national history and tradition of the respondent State' (para. 89).[21] Then, in the well-known *Lautsi v. Italy* (2011), the Grand Chamber, starting from the assumption that Europe 'is marked by a great diversity between the States of which it is composed, particularly in the sphere of cultural and historical development', stated that 'the decision whether or not to perpetuate a tradition falls in principle within the margin of appreciation of the respondent State.'[22] Also, in the case *F v. Switzerland* (1987), a law under the civil code was disputed, which authorized a three-year prohibition against remarrying for a divorced, adulterous wife. Despite the vast European consensus, the Court refused to resort to homogenizing treatment of adultery, since the matter of marriage is 'closely bound up with the cultural and historical traditions of each society' (para. 33), although concluding that the right had been violated due to the seriousness of the fault.

---

[20]   In this sense, reference must be made to the ruling *Otto Preminger Institute v. Austria* (1994). But see also a decisive rethinking – also referring to the Austrian context – in *Vereinigung Bildender Künstler v. Austria* (2007). The different effects of 'cultural contextualization' in the Strasbourg Court's jurisprudence are discussed by F. HOFFMANN-J. RINGELHEIM, 'Par delà l'universalisme et le relativisme: la Court européenne des droits de l'homme et le dilemme de la diversité culturelle' (2004) 52 *Rev. interdisc. d'etudes jur.* 109, 119 ff.

[21]   For a critique of this passage of the judgment, see the contribution of A. VESPAZIANI in this *Volume* at p. 142.

[22]   *Lautsi v. Italy* (2011) para. 68.

2.5. THE USE OF HISTORICAL ARGUMENT: OPEN QUESTIONS

Therefore, in these currents of jurisprudence, contextual analysis extends to a consideration of national history, placing within historic processes the reasons for given laws or state measures, as well as the reasons for the needs, claims, and behaviours of groups and of individuals. At times, history is presented in the guise of long-standing tradition that deserves to be understood and respected; at times, on the other hand, it takes on the dimension of recent political history, of a transition process yet to be entirely consolidated, which contextualizes and justifies delays and contradictions in current legislation. Historical argument often ends up determining the sense of the decision of the concrete case. In most cases, it justifies and legitimates state measures restricting fundamental rights, by identifying through historical reconstruction 'contextual' reasons prevailing over the objective affirmation of universally held principles.

But when the court summarizes in a few lines of motivation a complex and often disputed historical experience, obtaining from it a purportedly objective reflection on a system's fundamental traits, what type of historical research has it done? And how thoroughly? What sources did it prefer in reconstructing national history? And what space did it grant to other histories, the histories of the defeated, the alternative histories? In particular, with reference to cases involving transitions to 'recent' or 'fragile' democracies, is the risk not run of objectivizing, behind the label of historical tradition, disputed, still-open questions as to the interpretation of the past and of collective memory? And is the risk not run, then, of removing from public debate ideological premises that are not entirely shared in memory? Do the Strasbourg judges not end up then selecting, by way of assessment, a 'single' tradition over the 'other' ones? And in so doing, are they not contributing towards consolidating a historical memory that is not necessarily affirmed and shared, thus conditioning a nation's future even more than its past?[23]

But above all: what idea of Europe descends from the argument's reliance on national histories and traditions? It is certainly clear that historical traditions – which first in the jurisprudence of the Union's Court of Justice, and later in the writing of the Treaties, played a fundamental role in integration and in building a common heritage of values[24] – establish, in the outlook of the Strasbourg Court, culturally defined identities and carve the fracture lines in European civilisation.[25]

---

[23]   On valuing historical traditions, reference must be made to E.J. HOBSBAWM and T. RANGER, *The Invention of Tradition*, Cambridge University Press, Cambridge 1983. But see also E.J. HOBSBAWM, *Nations and Nationalism since 1870. Program, Myth, Reality*, Cambridge University Press, Cambridge 1990, and T. TODOROV, *Les abus de la mémoire*, Arlea, Paris 1995.

[24]   See P. RIDOLA, *Diritto comparato e diritto costituzionale europeo*, Giappichelli, Turin 2010, pp. 52 ff., 171–5, 233–40.

[25]   It is true, however, as a partial correction of this view, that elsewhere the court has stated that 'diversity and the dynamics of cultural traditions, ethnic and cultural identities, religious

3. DENYING HISTORICAL TRUTH: AN ABUSE OF LAW

These are questions that re-emerge if we analyze the Strasbourg Court's jurisprudence on cases of historical denial, which in many ways makes explicit options that have remained in the background in the use of historical argument.

When having to assess the compatibility with the Convention of these state criminal-law measures aimed at suppressing the formulation of opinions expressing Holocaust denial, the Court avoided treating these issues in accordance with the perspective of Article 10 of the Convention, shifting the dispute onto the ground of prohibiting abuse of law.[26] Although this canon is recessive in European jurisprudence,[27] it all the same re-emerges as an exceptional technique in treating these cases, with the purpose of removing the Court from operations of balancing freedom of expression, and ruling out any need to contextualize denialist opinions in a public debate, while measuring them against the objective canon of historical facts that are definitively clear and no longer the object of historical investigation.

While in *X v. Federal Republic of Germany* (1982) the Commission had already held Holocaust denial to be counter to notorious historical facts, established with certainty by damning evidence of all kinds, in *Marais v. France* (1996), the denial of definitively clear historic facts is no longer merely apt to cause harm to others' rights, but 'runs counter to basic ideas of the Convention, as established in its preamble, namely peace and justice [...] and would contribute to the destruction of the rights and freedoms guaranteed by the Convention'. Then, even more explicitly, *Lehideux and Isorni v. France* (1998) states that:

'the justification of a pro-Nazi policy could not be allowed to enjoy the protection afforded by Article 10 [...]. [There is a] category of clearly established historical facts – such as the Holocaust – whose negation or revision would be removed from the protection of Article 10 by Article 17.' (paras. 53 and 47)

In *Garaudy v. France* (2003), the Court rendered a judgment that the *Loi Gayssot-Fabius*, which criminalized Holocaust denial, was fully compatible with the Convention – integrating it through the conduct of disputing the Nuremberg Court's ruling, which was thus raised to objective canon of historical truth:[28]

---

beliefs, artistic, literary and socio-economic ideas and concepts' are the basis of the principle of pluralism (*Gorzelik and others v. Poland* (2004), para. 56). On this point, it is essential to refer to F. HOFFMANN and J. RINGELHEIM, *supra* n. 20, p. 135.

26 The line of argument is well described by E. STRADELLA, *La libertà di espressione politico-simbolica e i suoi limiti: tra teorie e 'prassi'*, Giappichelli, Turin 2008, pp. 126 ff.

27 C. PINELLI, 'Commentary on Art. 17', in BARTOLE, CONFORTI and RAIMONDI (eds.), *supra* n. 8, pp. 455 ff.

28 P. WACHSMANN, 'Libertà di espressione e negazionismo' (1999) 12 *Ragion Pratica* 57, 58. On the *Garaudy* judgment, more broadly, see A. BURATTI, 'L'affaire *Garaudy* di fronte alla Corte

'There could be no doubt that disputing the existence of clearly established historical events, such as the Holocaust, did not constitute historical research akin to a quest for the truth.'

As may be seen, in this thread of jurisprudence, the Court's reasoning starts from an extremely rudimentary conception of historical investigation: by parsing the categories of certainty and falsehood for statements through which it expresses its own results, it appears to ignore the very assumptions of historical research.[29] It is a now long-standing (in historiographical research) methodological given that historical truth is nothing more than a continuous recasting into discussion of truths taken as acquired. In fact, even when one wants to consider the material content of an event that is the object of historical investigation to be definitively ascertained, despite this, the mere change in the viewer's perspective, in his or her personal inclinations, in how he or she interrogates the documentary material, and in the cultural context being worked in, can only result in a different 'historical knowledge.'[30]

When it does not go into cases of denial of the Jewish Holocaust, the Court abandons the canon of abuse of law and re-expands the area of application of Article 10 of the Convention: thus, it has a way to appreciate the irreducible relativity of historical research. In the already cited *Lehideux* judgment – concerning writings aimed at rehabilitating the figure of Marshall Pétain – the Grand Chamber recognizes that:

'the events referred to in the publication in issue had occurred more than forty years before. Even though remarks like those the applicants made are always likely to reopen the controversy and bring back memories of past sufferings, the lapse of time makes it inappropriate to deal with such remarks, forty years on, with the same severity as ten or twenty years previously. That forms part of the efforts that every country must make to debate its own history openly and dispassionately.' (para. 55)

Upon consideration, it is not a matter of rethinking the technique of judgment with respect to denialism: in *Lehidueux*, the Court held it was dealing with an issue that did not involve opinions of this kind, a page in French history open to historical criticism. This line of argument was also reproduced in *Chauvy and others v. France* (2004), which regarded a dispute over the historical revision of facts related to the French Resistance during the Second World War. The Court argued:

---

di Strasburgo: verità storica, principio di neutralità etica e protezione dei "miti fondatori" del regime democratico' (2005) 157 *Giurisprudenza italiana* 2243, 2247.

[29]   H.I. Marrou, *De la connaissance historique*, Seuil, Paris 1954.
[30]   M. Bloch, *Historian's Craft*, Manchester University Press, Manchester 1954; P. Ricoeur, *Histoire et vérité*, Seuil, Paris 1955, pp. 23 ff.; H.I. Marrou, *supra* n. 29, p. 54; R. Aron, *Leçons sur l'histoire*, Fallois, Paris 1989; Id., *Paix et guerre entre les nations*, Calmann-Lévy, Paris 1962.

'It is an integral part of freedom of expression to seek historical truth and it is not the Court's role to arbitrate the underlying historical issues, which are part of a continuing debate between historians that shapes opinion as to the events which took place and their interpretation.' (para. 69)

Furthermore, in Hungary in 2004, some right-wing newspapers promoted building a statue to honour Pál Teleki, the country's Prime Minister in the 1940s. The initiative – aimed at rehabilitating a figure held responsible for anti-Semitic legislation, and more generally for having led Hungary into the Second World War – raised enormous and heated debate, which the historian Karsai joined by opposing the proposal and bringing up Teleki's crimes and offences. Convicted of defamation by the national courts, Karsai petitioned the European Court of Human Rights which, in 2009, ruled in his favour. According to the Court:

'the applicant – a historian who had published extensively on the Holocaust – wrote the impugned article in the course of a debate concerning the intentions of a country, with episodes of totalitarianism in its history, to come to terms with its past. The debate was thus of utmost public interest.' (*Karsai v. Hungary*, 2009, para. 35)

Highly interesting in this same vein is the more recent *Fatullayev v. Azerbaijan* (2010): the petitioner was an Azerbaijani journalist convicted by the national authorities for having, in various articles, cast doubt upon the traditionally accredited historical version of the Khojaly massacre perpetrated in 1992 by Armenian and Russian troops against the Azerbaijani population, one of the foundational events in the national historical memory. The Court was aware that in this matter, historic events are not definitively ascertained truth, but a subject for debate and the object of legitimate dispute: 'This judgment is not to be understood as containing any factual or legal assessment of the Khojaly events or any arbitration of historical claims relating to those events' (para. 76). The Court, therefore, could not resolve the case by espousing one version of the historic events or the other, but had to act within criteria upholding application of Article 10 – first and foremost respect for pluralism:

'Owing to the fact that the Nagorno-Karabakh war was a fairly recent historical event which resulted in significant loss of human life and created considerable tension in the region and that, despite the ceasefire, the conflict is still ongoing, the Court is aware of the very sensitive nature of the issues discussed in the applicant's article. The Court is aware that, especially, the memory of the Khojaly victims is cherished in Azerbaijani society and that the loss of hundreds of innocent civilian lives during the Khojaly events is a source of deep national grief and is generally considered within that society to be one of the most tragic moments in the history of the nation. In such circumstances, it is understandable that the statements made by the applicant may have been considered shocking or disturbing by the public. However, the Court reiterates that, subject to paragraph 2 of Article 10, *the freedom of expression is applicable not only to 'information' or 'ideas' that are favourably received or regarded as inoffensive or as a matter of indifference, but also to those that offend, shock or disturb the State or any sector of the population. Such are the demands of pluralism, tolerance and broadmindedness without which there is no 'democratic society'.* (para. 86, my emphasis)

Democracy, which from the perspective of Article 17 is an asset to be protected against historical denial, from that of Article 10 is the foundation for the freedom of historical research (para. 81).

Having been returned to the field of application of Article 10, historical discourse may be appreciated with respect to the content, the state of public debate on the point, and the journalist's intentions, establishing a scrutiny of proportionality. In this way, the Court reappropriates a capacity for mediation between conflicting rights and values, treating historical revisionism as a discourse that, although perhaps unpleasant – and at times repugnant, like any work that excavates historical memory, like any exhumation of an experience that has yet to experience reconciliation – is intimately connected to the exercise of communicative freedoms.

4. TOWARDS A CONCLUSION: PROTECTION OF HISTORICAL TRADITIONS OR CRITICAL HISTORICAL METHOD?

There is a profound ambiguity in the treatment that the European Court reserves for the history of nations and peoples and for its memory: in all the cases examined, historical events break into jurisdictional disputes as foundations that are not unanimously shared and stipulated, as a disputed memory, and the Court addresses these conflicts with ambivalent attitudes.

In most cases, the Court's argument tends to absolutize a historical narrative in a historical tradition, if not in an objective, definitively stable and clearly established history. Whether it is the history of the horrors of the Second World War, or the history of the liberation from religious fundamentalism, or the history of transition from Communist regimes, the Court protects certain selected historical narratives as traditions and foundations of the democratic order. In the Court's vision, history is often a private place for the exercise of public freedoms – in some cases even sacred ground that cannot be trodden upon, criticism of which becomes abuse. Far from being the result of a thorough investigation open to multiple interpretations, historical narrative is most of the time used strategically by a Court in search of a rhetorical legitimacy resting upon apparently objective and factual arguments.[31]

---

[31]   R. Uitz, *supra* n. 5, pp. 5 ff., especially p. 9.

Therefore, it comes as no surprise that the use of historical argument raises so much perplexity within the Court. As the judge Garlicki, in his opinion concurring with the *Âdamson* judgment, writes:

'We are experts in law and legality, but not in politics and history, and we must not venture into these territories unless in cases of absolute need.' (My translation.)

I personally do not share this concern, which is founded upon a simplistic acceptance of juridical interpretation:[32] the Strasbourg Court, due to the specific features that are the hallmarks of its jurisdiction, is inevitably called upon – even more than constitutional judges – to grapple with national histories and traditions that are complex and often disputed; many of the general clauses present in the Convention's text impose historical and contextual analyses. To evade this confrontation would simply mean clouding the underpinnings of the Court's decisions.

But narrating history is the same as writing it: although one cannot require the Court to work out a scientifically rigorous historical method, it is still necessary to be aware of the extraordinary delicateness of these passages of argument, to submit them to heated and open public criticism, within the Court as well as in public opinion, and to proceed towards argument practices capable of refining the method of historical research and balancing the weight of history with the need to protect fundamental rights.

---

[32] On the importance of historical, contextual, and cultural elements in juridical interpretation, the literature is boundless: for the profile considered here, see above all H.G. GADAMER, *Truth and Method*, Continuum, New York 2004, and thus, at least, P. HÄBERLE, *Per una dottrina della costituzione come scienza della cultura*, (1982), Carocci, Rome 2001, pp. 21 ff., but also pp. 46–47, 52, 75 ff., and A.A. CERVATI, *Per uno studio comparativo del diritto costituzionale*, Giappichelli, Torino 2009, especially pp. 1–6, 237 ff.

PART II.B

COOPERATION IN NEED OF COORDINATION: EUROPEAN COURT OF HUMAN RIGHTS AND THE EU

IMMIGRANTS' FAMILY LIFE IN THE RULINGS OF THE EUROPEAN SUPRANATIONAL COURTS

Gianluca Bascherini

1. INTRODUCTION

The importance of the questions linked to the relationships between immigration and family life in the European mechanisms protecting fundamental rights may be seen in the numerous regulatory interventions in the matter, and in the kind of disputes that these questions raise before national and European courts, throwing into relief frequently overlooked connections between the promotion of individual freedom, family life, and socioeconomic integration. In fact, on the one hand, with regard to migration policies more directly, the actual possibilities of maintaining or reconstituting the family nucleus contribute considerably towards limiting migration irregularities and fostering immigrants' rapid social integration. On the other hand, the growing number of families consisting of EU and non-EU citizens, like the importance that immigrant domestic labour has taken on in Europe, are just some of the factors that underscore the complex relationships by which the lives of EU and non-EU families are bound.

From this standpoint, the jurisprudence of the European Court of Human Rights and of the European Court of Justice regarding immigrants' right to family life therefore offer a variety of suggestions for those who wish to reflect upon the European mechanisms of multilevel protection of rights, upon the current trends in building European citizenship, and also upon the relationships that, in the affairs pertaining to family life, bind together law and economics, people, market, and society.

Immigration, and in particular the relationships between immigration and family life, are in fact issues around which a redefinition has been seen in the relationships between national systems and European courts, and a constitutional conversation – in its turn paradigmatic of the mechanisms for the plural protection of rights being articulated within the European constitutional horizon – is being held.

2. THE ECtHR'S JURISPRUDENCE ON IMMIGRANTS' RIGHT TO PRIVATE AND FAMILY LIFE. THE PROGRESSIVE BUT OSCILLATING ENLARGEMENT OF THE PROTECTION AFFORDED BY ARTICLE 8

Article 8 of the ECHR does not require States to absolutely guarantee to the foreigner the right to enter and reside in their territory. The foreigner's claims in this sense must in fact be balanced with the States' general interest in controlling the migration flows involving their territory. However, starting in the 1990s, the ECtHR's jurisprudence considerably restricted the states' room for manoeuvre in this regard. In 1991, for the first time, the Strasbourg Court declared that an expulsion violated Article 8 (*Moustaquim v. Belgium*, judgment of 18 February 1991); ten years later, for the first time it required a Contracting State to admit entry to the daughter of a foreign couple residing in the State's territory, in order to allow her to join her family (*Sen v. the Netherlands*, judgment of 21 December 2001).

The argumentative structure of the ECtHR's jurisprudence regarding Article 8 in fact reveals a tendency towards elaborating a series of common rules on a comparative basis, aimed above all at avoiding measures that clash with the paths of integration of immigrants with residence of long standing, and at the same time shows a substantial vision of the family and of the relations of which it is composed, also aside from their legal formalization.

The logical and argumentative path characterizing Strasbourg's jurisprudence in this area goes through two principal phases.[1] In the first place, the Court verifies the existence of a private or family life deserving of protection. In this regard, it should be stressed that the jurisdiction in this matter, by hingeing upon the nature of the bond in fact and effect, has upheld a broad notion of the family, which, while according special protection to the classical family – nuclear and bound together by marriage – also protects other types of family bonds, provided that elements qualifying the relationship exist, starting with the presence of children.[2] The second phase of the judgment aims instead at ascertaining whether the contested measure infringes the right to family life, assessing in particular whether this is 'in accordance with the law' and 'necessary in a democratic society'. It is in this context that the Court has set important limits on State prerogatives in the matter, pointing out the necessary respect for the principle of proportionality, and therefore holding that injury of the individual sphere may be deemed justifiable only in relation to proven and not otherwise

---

[1]   On this path, cf. for example D. FELDMAN, 'The Developing Scope of Article 8 of the European Convention on Human Rights' (1997) 3 *European Human Rights Law Review* 265.

[2]   See for example, in addition to *Moustaquim*, *Berrehab v. the Netherlands*, judgment of 21 June 1988, *Boughanemi v. France*, judgment of 24 April 1996. N. BLAKE and R. HUSAIN, *Immigration, Asylum and Human Rights*, Oxford University Press, Oxford 2003, pp. 165 ff.

attainable benefits that may be derived for society as a whole. It also bears mentioning that, in examining the contested state measures, the Strasbourg judges are relying on criteria that differ in part depending on the positive or negative nature of the obligations that would be devolved upon the State in the specific case. The protection of the family unit offered by the ECtHR's jurisprudence thus varies depending on whether it is ruling in disputes regarding family reunification, or on non-renewals of permits to stay, or cases of expulsion.

In the presence of positive obligations of the States (and thus in cases of family reunification, but also in disputes regarding the legitimacy of refusing to grant or renew permits to stay to subjects that have already developed, albeit illegally, a private or family life in the country of residence), the European Court of Human Rights tends to express a more restrictive orientation: noting the State's prerogatives in terms of controlling immigration, stressing that Article 8 does not require the States to respect the families' choice regarding the place of residence, and that any state obligation in the matter depends on the assessment of the particular circumstances of the people involved,[3] and paying special attention when minors are involved – minors at any rate whose best interests, for the Court, are not always achieved by according the minor the entitlement to stay in the country where his or her parents reside. There is in fact no lack of cases in which the Court deemed denial legitimate when nothing was preventing the parents from returning to their country of origin, where their children had always lived.[4] However, when the children's interest cannot be otherwise safeguarded, this provides grounds for the right to join the family in the State of residence.[5]

The ECtHR's approach appears partially different when the issue is one of the State's obligations of a negative nature, such as, above all, expulsion measures. In these cases, in fact, the Court – while stressing its acknowledgement of the margin of appreciation that the States enjoy in this matter (and therefore, for example, justifying deportations connected with the commission of offences raising serious social alarm, such as terrorism, narcotics and organized crime) – makes a closer examination of the conditions of legitimacy of these measures and, in particular, as to respect for the principle of proportionality. Measures of this kind in fact have an impact on family lives already in progress. For this reason, the ECtHR's decisions in these cases show greater attention to a series of elements paradigmatically summarized in *Boultif v. Switzerland*, 2 August 2001 (para. 48), including: the nature and gravity of the offence;[6] the period which

---

3   Paradigmatic here is the reasoning in the leading case in the matter: *Abdulaziz, Cabales and Balkandali v. United Kingdom*, judgment of 28 May 1985, para. 67.

4   See for example *Gül v. Switzerland*, judgment of 19 February 1996; *Ahmut v. the Netherlands*, judgment of 28 November 1996, and, more recently, *Chandra and others v. the Netherlands*, judgment of 13 May 2003, *Ramos Andrade v. the Netherlands*, judgment of 6 July 2004.

5   See, in addition to *Sen* already cited, *Tuquabo-Tekle and others v. the Netherlands*, judgment of 1 March 2006.

6   Among the decisions that have held the deportation measure to be disproportionate, see, for example, in addition to *Moustaquim* already cited, the judgments *Ezzouhdi v. France*,

elapsed between the commission of the offence and the enforcement of the expulsion and the applicant's conduct during that period; the duration of residence and the level of integration;[7] the applicant's family situation, including the presence of children and their ages, as well as the actual possibilities of reconstituting family life in the country of origin.[8]

Moreover, in cases of foreigners without family bonds, the Court has not failed to insist on such factors as the duration of the stay, or the level of education in the country of residence, in order to acknowledge that an expulsion measure at any rate interfered with the applicant's right to private and family life.[9] Therefore, in these cases as well, the Court does not renounce appealing to a link to family life, despite the references present in some separate opinions guaranteeing autonomous protection for the foreigner's personal bonds with the country of stay, regardless of the existence of a family life.[10]

Nor can it be overlooked that in this vein of jurisprudence, the Court has had a way, on the one hand, to stress the need for the national law to include measures of protection against arbitrary interference by the public authorities[11] – a point of particular importance, as Strasbourg has always denied application of Article 6 of the ECHR to expulsion procedures – and on the other hand to affirm, especially in the case of not particularly serious offences, the tendential (but not absolute) non-deportability of second-generation immigrants and of those arriving when young in age, also in consideration of the responsibilities that the Contracting States must take on with regard to educating and integrating these persons.[12]

---

     judgment of 13 February 2001; *Yilmaz v. Germany*, judgment of 17 April 2003, and *Radovanovic v. Austria*, judgment of 22 April 2004. On the other hand, for cases where the seriousness of the offence legitimated deportation, see for example (in addition to *Boughanemi* already cited) *Boujlifa v. France*, judgment of 21 October 1997.

[7]   See for example the case *Rodriguez Da Silva and Hoogkamer v. the Netherlands*, judgment of 31 January 2006.

[8]   Among the expulsions that, according to the Court, violated Article 8 of the ECHR because of the difficulties the deportee's family would have encountered in following him to the country of origin, see for example *Boultif* already cited and, more recently, *Omojudi v. the United Kingdom*, judgment of 24 November 2009, in which, for the ECtHR, although the gravity of the offence justified the deportation measure, this measure all the same appeared disproportionate '[h]aving regard to the circumstances of the present case, in particular the strength of the applicant's family ties to the United Kingdom, his length of residence, and the difficulty that his youngest children would face if they were to relocate to Nigeria' (para. 48).

[9]   See for example the already cited cases *Boujlifa* (para. 36) and *Ezzouhdi* (para 26).

[10]   See for example the concurring and separate opinions of Martens and de Meyer in *Beldjoudi v. France*, judgment of 26 March 1992, and the concurring and partly dissenting opinions of Wildhaber, Morenilla and De Meyer in *Nasri v. France*, judgment of 13 July 1995.

[11]   See for example *Al-Nashif v. Bulgaria*, judgment of 20 June 2002.

[12]   See in this regard the already cited opinions of Martens (para. 2) and De Meyer in *Beldjoudi v. France*, judgment of 26 March 1992, as well as the dissenting opinion of Baka and Van Dijk in the already cited case *Boujlifa*. Recently, important confirmation of this tendency has come from the Grand Chamber in *Maslov v. Austria*, judgment of 23 June 2008, which, while starting from the specification of the *Boultif* criteria made by *Üner*, held the ten-year residence

Starting from the mid 1990s, many European countries adopted immigration regulation reforms that broadened the grounds for expulsion, while limiting the possibilities of family reunification. These reforms have led to a greater sensitivity in the ECtHR's jurisprudence to the states' demands to handle the migration flows and to the seriousness of the offences committed, and thus a greater openness to the margin of appreciation the States enjoy in choosing the means necessary for maintaining public order.

Among the most recent judgments that best demonstrate this changed approach, noteworthy is, for example, *Üner* v. *the Netherlands*, 18 October 2006, appl. no. 46410/99. Although the Court in this decision further articulates two criteria already sketched out in *Boultif* – regarding the minors' interests and the solidity of the social, cultural and family bonds linking the interested parties to the country of residence (para. 58) – it is also true that, in this judgment, the comparative argument[13] is used to justify reductive interpretations of the immigrants' right to family life. The wish concluding the dissenting opinion of Costa, Zupančič and Türmen – 'we would have liked to see this dynamic approach to case law tending towards increased protection for foreign nationals (even criminals) rather than towards increased penalties which target them specifically' (para. 18) – sums up in a nutshell the doubts that this judgment raises.

Although judgments like *Üner*[14] bear witness to favouring the State's claims in the matter of expulsion and give little attention to the family situation of the subjects involved, these decisions cannot be said to have marked a turning point, as they appear rather as one of the not infrequent oscillations in the jurisprudence in this matter. In fact, thereafter there was no shortage of judgments, as in the already cited *Maslov* and *Omojoudi* judgments, in which the ECtHR returned to dedicating more attention to the concrete needs of protecting subjects and the family nucleus, to the solidity of the bonds developed with the country of residence, and to the interests of the minors involved. It is worth adding that such recent judgments as *Slivenko and others v. Latvia*, 9 October 2003, or *Ariztimuno Mendizabal v. France*, 17 January 2006 – as well as the already cited *Rodriguez Da Silva* – appear to express a new tendency to expand

---

prohibition on Austrian territory to be disproportionate, not because of its duration, but because, given the applicant's young age, it concerned a formative period of his life. On this issue, cf. P. VAN DIJK, 'Protection of Integrated Aliens Against Expulsion under the European Convention on Human Rights' (1999) 1 *European Journal of Migration and Law* 301 and C. RAUX, 'Les mesures d'éloignement du territoire devant la Grande Chambre de la Cour européenne des droits de l'homme' (2007) 71 *Revue trimestrielle des droits de l'homme* 850.

13   On the use of the comparative argument in the ECtHR's jurisprudence in the matter of family life, see G. REPETTO, *Argomenti comparativi e diritti fondamentali in Europa. Teoria dell'interpretazione e giurisprudenza sovranazionale*, Jovene, Napoli 2011, pp. 147 ff.

14   Following the same line as *Üner*, see also: *Onur v. United Kingdom*, judgment of 17 February 2009; *Grant v. United Kingdom*, judgment of 23 May 2006; *Cherif and others v. Italy*, judgment of 7 April 2009, also paradigmatic of the consequences that the recent domestic regulations regarding the struggle against international terrorism may have on the situations protected under Article 8 of the ECHR.

the protection under Article 8, guaranteeing protection to long-term resident immigrants regardless of the existence of family bonds, but solely on the basis of the necessary respect for their private life. This broadening of the convention's protection, as recognized by the Grand Chamber in *Sisojeva and Others v. Latvia*, 15 January 2007, appl. no. 60654/00 (paras. 89 ff.), also raises important questions in terms of the relations between the ECHR and the national and Community regulations in this matter, with the Strasbourg judges having in similar cases to draw a careful balance between the applicants' arguments and the preservation of the States' margin of appreciation, and therefore respect for the structure of the national immigration regulations.

Although brief, this examination of the ECtHR's jurisprudence in the matter of immigrants' family life[15] already underscores the picture's lights and shadows, but also its dynamicity, and the presence of diverging thrusts, of trends not infrequently in conflict with one another.

On the one hand, in fact, this oscillating jurisprudence is marked overall by a defensive interpretation of the theory of European consensus, and, especially in some of its recent developments, appears too sensitive to the States' claims – all the more so when obligations of a positive nature are in question. It is also shown to be non-incisive upon the major and often unjustified differences in treatment that mark the European mechanisms for protecting the right to family life, between those who are citizens and those who are foreigners. On the other hand, this jurisprudence has played a leading role in bringing to the table in the European sphere the need to protect immigrants' family life; it has made an important contribution to working out national and Community-level rules and jurisprudence. On the whole, this jurisprudence has also restricted the states' margins of appreciation in the matter – also interpreting this margin as a frame within which to examine the regulations contested in light of multiple judgment criteria[16] – and attributed to its references to 'democratic society' a greater value of protection than its traditional value as a clause legitimating state practices that limit these rights. Lastly, noteworthy is the attention that these rulings have

---

[15] For more detailed reconstructions of the ECtHR's jurisprudence in the matter, see for example F. SUDRE (ed.), *Le droit au respect de la vie familiale au sens de la Convention européenne des droits de l'homme*, Bruylant, Bruxelles 2002; N. ROGERS, 'Immigration and the European Convention on Human Rights: Are New Principles Emerging?' (2003) 53 *EHRLR* 53; A. DEL GUERCIO, 'Il diritto dei migranti all'unità familiare nella giurisprudenza della Corte europea dei diritti umani e nell'ordinamento dell'Unione europea', in A. CALIGIURI, G. CATALDI, N. NAPOLETANO (eds.), *La tutela dei diritti umani in Europa. Tra sovranità statale e ordinamenti sovranazionali*, Cedam, Padova 2010, pp. 387 ff., G. BASCHERINI, *Immigrazione e diritti fondamentali. L'esperienza italiana tra storia costituzionale e prospettive europee*, Jovene, Napoli 2007, pp. 241 ff.

[16] Y. ARAI, 'The Margin of Appreciation Doctrine in the Jurisprudence of Article 8 of the Convention on Human Rights' (1998) 16 *Netherlands Quarterly of Human Rights* 41, and D. THYM, 'Respect for Private and Family Life under Article 8 ECHR in Immigration Cases: a Human Right to Regularize Illegal Stay?' (2008) 57 *International and Comparative Law Quarterly*, especially pp. 103 ff.

for the reality of family relations affected by individual disputes, and to the reasons for protecting the interests of the parties most exposed to the consequences of measures that hamper or break family unity, and particularly that of minors. Similarly, one should not overlook the attention that the ECtHR has, in the absence of a family life, recently devoted to reasons connected with protecting the applicants' private life.

3. THE JURISPRUDENCE OF THE ECJ: IS THE FAMILY GOING TO MARKET?

Originally, in the EC setting, the right to family life was of importance only insofar as it related to the free circulation of workers, as Community law applied only to European citizens that could be called emigrant workers. On the other hand, for other Community citizens, family life was of importance as a situation 'wholly internal to a member state'.[17]

This picture changed with Maastricht, in correspondence with the gradual generalization of the freedom of circulation for European citizens. In fact, the Court of Justice gradually broadened the number of subjects to whom Community law applied – on the one hand by giving broad interpretation to the categories of persons contemplated by it (and thus reinterpreting the very concept of working activity), and on the other by adding categories not contemplated by it. In these ways, the Luxembourg judges made the current Article 45 TFEU (formerly Article 39 TEC) apply not only those working abroad, but also to those going abroad in search of employment;[18] to those who, although continuing to reside in their own state, offer services in other member states;[19] and to those who relocate not as renderer, but as recipient of the service.[20] Similarly, the European Community legislator reached the same result by adopting three directives in 1990 (364, 365 and 366), which extended the right of circulation and stay (and therefore the possibility of resorting to European Community law in the matter of family reunification) to so-called 'inactive' subjects, to workers that had ceased their activity, and to students. This change of orientation in the matter of family life, from instrumental right to subjective right, was later to find confirmation in Article 7 of the Charter of Nice, obviously inspired by Article 8 of the ECHR.

Today, European Community law offers distinct regulations in the matter of family life, depending on whether it is dealing with EU families (in whole or in part) or with families composed entirely of citizens of third-party countries.

---

17   See for example C-180/83, *Hans Moser v. Land Baden-Württemberg* [1984] ECR I-2539.
18   C-48/75, *Royer* [1976] ECR I-497.
19   C-60/00, *Mary Carpenter v. Secretary of State for the Home Department* [2002] ECR I-6279.
20   C-186/87, *Ian William Cowan v. Trésor public* [1989] ECR I-195.

Currently, the norm of reference in the matter of the family life of European Union citizens is Directive 2004/58/EC of the European Parliament and of the Council of 29 April 2004 on the right of citizens of the Union and their family members to move and reside freely within the territory of the Member States. The directive extended to all EU citizens the right to family reunification in the territory of a Member State other than that of which they are a national. The directive also applies to non-Union family members of Union citizens and to citizens of States outside the EU, with which the European Community has reached association agreements.

Limiting the analysis to the jurisprudence regarding the entry and stay of the non-Union family member of the Union citizen, it bears pointing out that this confirms, on the whole, the gradual distancing from the original economic matrices in favour of an approach increasingly centred upon fundamental rights, and in particular on Article 8 of the ECHR, and the corresponding jurisprudence.

In this development of jurisprudence as well, we may identify two major phases, whose turning point may be seen in the proclamation of the Charter of Nice. While in the first phase, as already discussed, it is through the freedom of circulation of workers in the Community that family life is brought under the responsibilities of the ECJ,[21] in the second phase this bond between freedom of circulation and family life is to be gradually supplanted by appeals to the broader guarantees originating from the ECHR, the Charter of Nice, and European citizenship. The passage between the two phases is well attested by such decisions as C-413/99, *Baumbast and R v. Secretary of State for the Home Department* (2002), and the already cited *Carpenter*. In *Baumbast* in fact, the Court of Justice aimed to reconstruct the rights of non-Union family members as rights independent of the movements of the citizen of the Union; in *Carpenter* on the other hand, the judges in Luxembourg for the first time directly addressed Article 8 of the ECHR to resolve the dispute – moreover with a ruling that effectively underscores the complexity of the relationships currently in progress in the European sphere, between productive and reproductive work.[22]

Alongside these two paths in the ECJ's jurisprudence in the matter, a third itinerary is gradually taking shape, in whose frames of argument the centrality taken on by European citizenship and by the need to actually guarantee the

---

[21] Paradigmatic of this initial phase in the jurisprudence is judgment C-249/86, *Commission of the European Communities v. Federal Republic of Germany* [1989] ECR I-1263.

[22] For a critical approach to the idea that 'different social roles pertain to men and women, ordered along the divide between productive and reproductive work', see S. NICCOLAI, 'Changing Images of Normal and Worthy Life. The Constitutional Potential of Economic Sensitivity within EU Gender Policies', in EAD. and I. RUGGIU (eds.), *Dignity in Change. Exploring the Constitutional Potential of EU's Gender and Anti-Discrimination Policies*, European Academic Press, Fiesole 2010 pp. 65 ff., and C. HOSKINS and S.M. RAI, 'Recasting the Global Political Economy: Counting Women's Unpaid Work' (2007) 12 *New Political Economy* 297.

rights connected with it appears to downplay that dialectic between economic matrices and the rights issue that marks out the two previous phases.

Signs of this direction appear in fact to come from *Zambrano* (C-34/2009, *Gerardo Ruiz Zambrano v. Office national de l'emploi (ONEm)*, 2011). Indeed, this judgment, with a bare-bones line of argument, based its recognition solely upon Article 20 TFEU of the right to stay for a non-Union citizen, the father of young children who were themselves European citizens (see para. 45). In this decision, therefore, it would appear that the simple attribution of European citizenship and the need to guarantee the exercise of the rights connected with this status becomes a fundamental factor for distinguishing situations coming under the sphere of application of European Union law from 'purely internal' situations.

However, this ruling cannot be said to mark a paradigm shift. For example, as early as C-148/02, *Carlos Garcia Avello v. Belgian State* (2003), the Court ascribed importance to EU citizenship in a purely internal situation, and, then as now, it is the specific features of the cases coming into relief that provide the key for reading the two decisions. In *Zambrano*, the father's deportation would have deprived the minor children of the possibility of effectively enjoying their rights as European citizens. Moreover, that it is the exceptionality of the concrete case that explains *Zambrano* is confirmed by C-434/09, *Shirley McCarthy v. Secretary of State for the Home Department* (2011) shortly thereafter, which denied Ms McCarthy's husband, a non-Union national, the right to stay recognized by Article 3, no. 1 of Directive 2004/83/EC, since the citizen of a Member State who also possesses citizenship in a different Member State, but has never resided there, does not for this reason alone come under the sphere of application of Directive 2004/83/EC. In this decision, the Community judges reformulated the question set out by the national judges (it was also the first reference for a preliminary ruling raised by the UK Supreme Court), shifting the attention from Directive 2004/38 to Article 21 TFEU. This reformulation, not essential in light of the reference for a preliminary ruling, appears to be explained rather by the ECJ's intent to distinguish Ms McCarthy's situation from that characterizing the *Garcia Avello* and *Zambrano* cases (para. 56 is explicit in this sense) and to return to some issues left open by *Zambrano*,[23] in particular as to the possibility of invoking, in a purely internal situation, the right to stay that European citizens enjoy by virtue of Article 21 TFEU.[24]

---

[23]   See the Editorial 'Seven Questions for Seven Paragraphs' (2011) 36 *European Law Review* 161, according to which the argument's brevity made the decision unclear.

[24]   In fact, for the Court of Justice of the European Communities, 'no element of the situation of Mrs McCarthy, as described by the national court, indicates that the national measure at issue in the main proceedings has the effect of depriving her of the genuine enjoyment of the substance of the rights associated with her status as a Union citizen, or of impeding the exercise of her right to move and reside freely within the territory of the Member States, in accordance with Article 21 TFEU' (para. 49).

Zambrano thus confirms the case-by-case approach[25] of the ECJ in this matter, and does not effectively contribute towards explaining what subjects and cases, in the absence of clear transnational elements, may or may not come under the sphere of application of the relevant EU Law. Despite this, it will at any rate be interesting to understand to what extent, and in accordance with what itineraries, the Court will, on this road, be willing to broaden the sphere of application of the provisions on EU citizenship.

On the other hand, as regards the life of families that are fully non-EU nationals, the trend is to extend to the Community the migratory policies developed from the 1990s onwards, which led the legislator and the ECJ to take action.

An initial important contribution in this regard came from the jurisprudence on association agreements. This jurisprudence in fact helped equalize from a number of standpoints the statute of social rights of workers, and their family members, coming from these countries with that of European citizens, in some cases objectively as well as subjectively reconfiguring these rights and their means of protection with respect to the provisions of some national constitutions, and also on more than one occasion remarking on the importance of substantial and effective integration, particularly of the second generation of immigrants.[26]

In the matter of family reunification, it should be observed that the adoption of Council Directive 2003/86/EC of 22 September 2003 *on the right to family reunification*, despite all its limitations,[27] gave rise to a series of rulings of interest as much for the merit of the solutions they set out, as for the argument sustaining the whole framework.

In C-540/03, *European Parliament v. Council of the European Union* (2006) the ECJ expressed itself in favour of the legitimacy of the norms of Directive 2003/86, which admit more restrictive national disciplines, and therefore declared the European Parliament's application groundless, but at the same time specified that the concept of integration, however 'not defined' it was, 'cannot be interpreted as authorising the Member States to employ that concept in a manner contrary to general principles of Community law, in particular to fundamental rights' (para. 70) and delimited the margin of appreciation enjoyed by Member States, pointing out that 'Article 4(1) of the Directive imposes precise positive obligations [...] on the Member States, since it requires them, in the cases determined by the Directive, to authorise family reunification of certain members of the sponsor's family, without being left a margin of appreciation'

---

25   Cf. S. SPINACI, 'Le sentenze Zambrano e McCarthy e i nodi irrisolti della cittadinanza europea' (2011) *Giurisprudenza costituzionale* 2544.

26   See for example C-65/98, *Safet Eyüp v. Landesgeschäftsstelle des Arbeitsmarktservice Vorarlberg* [2000] ECR I-4747 – for the opening it shows towards *more uxorio* cohabitation arrangements depending on the actual nature of the bond.

27   For more on the adoption and content of this directive, see E. GUILD, *The Legal Elements of European Identity. EU Citizenship and Migration Law*, Kluwer, The Hague 2004, pp. 111 ff.; G. SIRIANNI, *Il diritto degli stranieri all'unità familiare*, Giuffrè, Milano 2006, pp. 34 ff.

(para. 60). More recently, C-578/08, *Rhimou Chakroun v. Minister van Buitenlandse Zaken* (2010) stressed that Directive 2003/86 must be interpreted taking into account that it proposes favouring family reunification and protecting the right to family unity as a fundamental human right, while at the same time demonstrating, on the merits as well as in the arguments, an opening for the instruments forged in the ECtHR's jurisprudence in the matter, and aimed at a careful assessment of the nature and solidity of family bonds.

Likewise, as regards these paths of EU jurisprudence concerning migrations and family life, there is no interest here in going beyond their respective contents[28] so much rather as pointing out the Community jurisprudence in the matter – albeit with a casuistic approach developed in accordance with continuously evolving and not always clear logic that leaves considerable margins of uncertainty and at times leads to conflicting decisions[29] – appears to place its chips on two tables: as a judge of rights, engaged in a constitutional conversation with the Strasbourg court and with common constitution traditions, in the case of entirely non-EU families; or as a judge that tends to act within Community law, and that in a certain way reinterprets its original 'economicist' matrix in the case of families composed of EU and non-EU nationals, as well as showing a capacity to cover demands that the rhetoric of fundamental rights struggles to grasp.

4. CONCLUSIONS. MOVEMENT OF PEOPLE, MOVEMENT OF LAW

In a setting like Europe, in which economic crisis and public order are gradually tending to restrict the concrete possibilities of immigrants' family life and to render their juridical condition precarious – by skewing migratory policies towards limits on entry and repressing irregularities, and by articulating prospects for integration that, in their feebleness and functionalization to narrow national interests, appear to hark back to a return to the historic German *Gastarbeiter* model – the role played by the European courts in matters of

---

[28] Of the recent works on the issue, here are cited only D. SCHAFFRIN 'Which standard for family reunification of third-country nationals in the EU?', in J. CARLIER and P. DE BRUYCKER (eds.), *Immigration and Asylum Law of the EU: Current Debates*, Bruylant, Bruxelles 2005, pp. 90 ff.; S. NINATTI, 'Il diritto alla vita familiare all'esame della Corte di Giustizia', in M. CARTABIA (ed.), *I diritti in azione*, il Mulino, Bologna 2007, pp. 239 ff., and A. TRYFONIDOU, 'Family Reunification of (Migrant) Union Citizens: Towards a More Liberal Approach' (2009) 15 *European Law Journal* 634; E. DE WAELE, 'EU Citizenship: Revisting its Meaning, Place and Potential' (2012) 12 *European Journal of Migration and Law* 319.

[29] The limits on an approach of this kind, with regard to *Zambrano*, were underscored for example by A. WIESBROCK, 'The Zambrano Case: relying on Union Citizenship in "internal situations"' European Union Democracy Observatory on Citizenship, http://eudo-citizenship.eu/search-results/449-the-zambrano-case-relying-on-union-citizenship-rights-in-internal-situations, accessed 20.3.2012.

Gianluca Bascherini

immigrants' rights to family life should not be overlooked, both as regards family reunification, and as concerns the limits that reasons connected with family life place upon the immigrant's expulsion.

Over the past quarter century, the ECtHR has played a decisive role in recognizing and guaranteeing the needs to protect the private and family life of immigrants, devoting particular attention to the concreteness of the interests in play, especially as regards the subjects most exposed to the consequences of measures that impede or break family unity. It is easy to imagine that in coming years, the Strasbourg judges will again be called upon to clarify the interactions between the ECHR and the national and European immigration disciplines. However, in spite of all this, the jurisprudence regarding Article 8 ECHR is 'characterized by a welcome quest for clarity'.[30] In it, the relationships between family life and private life are being redefined, thus laying the foundations for a rethinking of the protection afforded to immigrants by this article. At the same time, the tendency to develop general criteria in the matter both of expulsion and of family reunification bears witness to the Court's openness in articulating a jurisprudence that facilitates the direct application of Article 8 by the national courts, and thus the same Court's willingness to make an active contribution to harmonizing European, national, and Community migration policies.

Nevertheless, the ECJ's jurisprudence in the matter shows interesting dynamics and possibilities. This dynamism of the ECJ is without a doubt linked to the greater pressure exerted on this jurisprudence by the language of fundamental rights, and to this court's tendency to behave increasingly as a judge of fundamental rights, valuing the contributions originating from Strasbourg's jurisprudence and limiting with rights-based arguments the margins of action of the national regulations submitted for its judgment.[31] Nor must it be ignored, however, that this jurisprudential *élan* is nevertheless connected with important disciplines of the phenomena that have appeared in the EU setting in the meantime, and this activism by Luxembourg, in its turn, appears to potentially herald major consequences for national regulations.

The ECHR and ECJ jurisprudences in the matter, especially in their recent developments, in fact appear to pay particular attention to the situation of those immigrants for whom the bonds are strongest in their country of residence, above all as concerns their family life. The 'best interests of the child' constitutes a criterion of ever-increasing relevance to these courts when it is a matter of assessing an expulsion measure or a request for family reunification, and, especially in Strasbourg, the thesis of a tendential non-deportability of second-generation immigrants, and of those arriving in the countries of residence when of a young age, is gradually acquiring importance.

---

30   D. Thym, 'Respect for Private and Family Life', *supra* n. 16, p. 112.
31   A. Vespaziani, 'Tre metafore del costituzionalismo europeo: molteplicità dei livelli, tono costituzionale e ponderazione', in F. Cerrone and M. Volpi (eds), *Sergio Panunzio. Profilo intellettuale di un giurista*, Jovene, Napoli 2007, p. 545.

202   Intersentia

This attention to minors and the younger generation surely bears witness to a more mature awareness of the structural nature of the immigrant presence, and of the role this presence plays in European societies that are older and older, while being less and less enterprising. But this attention, however, also appears to promote an outlook for intergenerational integration that addresses a substantial, far more than a formal, vision of citizenship, and at the same time restores the complexity of the relationships that bind citizenship, rights and family life, the various effects of a family member's rights upon the conditions and rights of another member: at times it is the minor that 'accesses' one of the parent's rights, and at times, instead, it is the reasons of protecting the minor – not infrequently a citizen, or *as if he were one* – that bear retroactively upon the juridical condition of the foreign parent.

At the same time, it should not be overlooked that the paths of jurisprudence examined in summary here make an interesting observation point for the complexity of the relationships that bind together law, economics, society and family life, and appealing to the complexity of these relationships allows me to return, in conclusion, to the reasons for the particular dynamicity that EU jurisprudence expresses on the matter today.

Today, an 'economicist' court like the Court of Justice appears in fact to articulate a more incisive protection of the rights connected with family life, because – where the rhetoric on the fundamental nature of rights pertaining to family life risks, if encapsulated within excessively rigid dogmas, being led to stereotyping visions that are as such ineffective for the concrete demands of justice lying behind the various disputes – affairs regarding family life, and especially involving its interruption, bring with them a mass of questions of undeniable economic importance, which perhaps in the 'economicism' of Luxembourg's jurisprudence, find, if not more suitable instruments, at least a 'context' more equipped to take this component into account 'as well'; to effectively intercept – at least in some of their paths – pieces of reality and demands for justice; and to dynamically identify their forms of protection.

Community jurisprudence clearly highlights a gradual broadening of the sphere of operation of the non-discrimination principle, even making it an open clause[32] directed at removing de facto social inequalities. This jurisprudence, therefore, just as in the matter of immigration and family life, brings up the possibility of 'using the principles of Community "economic constitution" as a framework for opening spaces for freedom outside the area of economic relations'.[33]

---

[32]   On the prospects that these clauses offer to the development of European constitutional law, refer to A.A. CERVATI, 'Diritto costituzionale e impegno etico dei giuristi', in ID., *Per uno studio comparativo del diritto costituzionale*, Giappichelli, Torino 2009, especially pp. 51 ff.

[33]   Thus, P. RIDOLA, 'Diritti di libertà e mercato nella "Costituzione europea"', in ID., *Diritto comparato e diritto costituzionale europeo*, Giappichelli, Torino 2010, especially pp. 155 ff.

This is not the place to deal with the complex issues regarding the interdependence between market arrangements and institutional balances, or the ability of these arrangements to be translated into regulatory orders.[34] Similarly, it is not possible here to reason about the limits of a pluralism built starting from the market paradigm: the ability of the principles of the European economic constitution to articulate a 'neutral framework of "rules of pluralism"' or, to the contrary, the tendency of these principles to condition the spaces of freedom for private powers. These questions in fact touch upon issues central to the reading of the market paradigm, which, moreover, has been historically considered in quite different, if not opposite ways: as a place for spontaneity or of rules; as a factor of social cohesion or break-up; or as grounds for conflict or cooperation.[35] And there is no doubt that post-war constitutionalism expresses in this regard a vision in many ways distant from that characterizing the construction of the EC.[36]

Here, to conclude, I would like only to stress that the disputes in the matter of immigration and family life, like those connected with gender discrimination, today offer an important occasion for reflection regarding those interactions – non-linear, fragmentary, and often conflicting – between law and market, between people, families, economics, and society, that raise questions as to the ability of our interpretative categories to bring out often unprecedented requirements of justice, thus avoiding taking solace in the reassuring presumption that 'the principles and values we have can contain everything, resolve, explain, and define every situation of reality [... and] protect us from everything' and, rather, accept 'that there is always something that goes beyond, that lies outside (and in the case of immigrants and their families, outside is not simply a metaphor), and that is the movement of the law'.[37] It is a movement that, in this as in few other cases, coincides with – or at least is closely linked to – the movement of people in their search for a better quality of life.

---

[34] Of the reconstructions of the debate in this matter, which marked a thread of European thought extending from Adam Smith to Hayek, fertile points for reflection may be drawn from A. GIULIANI, *Giustizia e ordine economico*, Giuffrè, Milano 1997, especially pp. 137 ff. On this important component of Giuliani's reflection, cf. F. CERRONE, 'Introduzione: premesse logiche ed etiche di una comunità civica e del suo ordine giuridico' (2010) 3 *Sociologia* 7 ff., as well as A. BIXIO, 'Retorica e dialettica nell'opera di Alessandro Giuliani', *ibid.*, pp. 33 ff.

[35] For a reconstruction of these different readings, see for example M.R. FERRARESE, 'Immagini del mercato' (1992) *Stato e mercato* 291 ff.

[36] On these issues, in addition to P. RIDOLA's already cited essay, I have gleaned major points for reflection from S. NICCOLAI, 'Trasformazioni del senso del lavoro di cura e argomentazione costituzionale. A margine di una controversia di discriminazione per handicap', in A. CERRI, PETER HÄBERLE, I.M. JARVAD, P. RIDOLA and D. SCHEFOLD (eds.), *Il diritto fra interpretazione e storia. Liber Amicorum per Angel Antonio Cervati*, Aracne, Roma 2010, t. III, especially pp. 420 ff.

[37] S. NICCOLAI, 'Trasformazioni', *supra* n. 36, p. 427.

COOPERATION IN RELATIONS BETWEEN THE ECJ AND THE ECtHR

Angelo Schillaci

1. SEPARATION AND COOPERATION

Before beginning the detailed analysis of the most recent developments in the relationship between the ECJ and the ECtHR, some general remarks on the institutional and juridical framework in which such relation originated and grew might be necessary.

As is common knowledge the EU has not yet in fact acceded to the European Convention on Human Rights (ECHR). The two legal systems are therefore still formally separate and independent: even this very statement, however, must be explained in detail, mostly concerning the presence of references to the ECHR in the fundamental texts of the European Union: consider TEU Article 6, sections 2 and 3 and, in particular, Article 51 et seq. of the EU Charter of Fundamental Rights that – through the so-called 'horizontal clauses' – aim at comprehensively regulating the complex forms of interpretative interaction through which the relationship between the EU and the ECtHR took place, at least as of 1974.[1]

In the context of such preliminary remarks, however, it shall suffice to underline that although the aforementioned norms codify a complex and ever-developing system of relations, they do not allow us to overcome the root

---

[1]   On the evolution of protection of fundamental rights in the EU, see S.P. Panunzio, *I diritti fondamentali e le Corti in Europa*, in S.P. Panunzio (ed.), *I diritti fondamentali e le Corti in Europa*, Jovene, Napoli 2006, pp. 1 ff.; P. Ridola, 'Diritti fondamentali ed integrazione costituzionale in Europa', in P. Ridola, *Diritto comparato e diritto costituzionale europeo*, Giappichelli, Torino 2010, pp. 199 ff.; P. Häberle, *Europäische Verfassungslehre*, Nomos Verlag, Baden-Baden 2011; F. Balaguer Callejón, 'Niveles y técnicas internacionales e internas de realización de los derechos en Europa: una perspectiva constitucional' (2004) *Rev. Der. Const. Eur. (Revista de Derecho constitucional europeo)* 25; G. Cámara Villar, 'Los derechos fundamentales en el proceso histórico de construcción de la Unión Europea y su valor en el Tratado Constitucional' (2005) *Rev. Der. Const. Eur.* 9; A. Rodríguez, *Integración europea y derechos fundamentales*, Civitas, Madrid 2003; C. Pinelli, 'I diritti fondamentali in Europa tra politica e giurisprudenza' (2008) *Politica del diritto* 45; U. Villani, 'I diritti fondamentali tra Carta di Nizza, Convenzione europea dei diritti dell'uomo e progetto di Costituzione europea' (2004) *Il diritto dell'Unione europea* 73.

problem, that is, the persistent separation – at least on a formal level – between the two legal systems.

In other words, the current relationship between the EU and the ECHR, marks – so far, at least – a clean break with the traditional reconstructions about the relations between legal systems.[2] Such reconstructions, in fact, mainly focused on the different forms, techniques and limits of the transposition of norms from one legal system to another, while the relationship between the EU and the ECHR took a very different route.[3]

However, it can only be partially maintained that the traditional reconstruction of the relationship between legal orders is solely focused on the production – within a legal order – of norms whose content reflects that of the norms of the 'external' legal order taken into consideration. This is indeed a legitimate argument for reconstructing the relations between national and international laws, based on the dualistic model of separation. Yet such a paradigm is already questioned by the classic monistic approaches, which trace the relational dynamics – and the very relevance of the norms of international law at a national level – back to a unitary legislative process, averse to any distinction between the legal orders involved.

On the other hand, studies on international private law – and particularly studies on *renvoi* – show that the research on the transposition of 'external' norms has always been completed by research on the application of such norms, and therefore on the relevance of interpretation dynamics in managing the relations among legal orders, even beyond normative references that indicate connecting criteria or even proper 'norms on the production by means of *renvoi*'.[4]

At the same time, it cannot be forgotten that the relationship between the EU and the ECHR will soon be affected by a phenomenon of 'classic' connection and transposition. As a consequence of the expected accession of the EU to the ECHR,[5] in fact, the conventional norms will be subject to the system of validity

---

[2] See the classic reconstructions of H. Kelsen, 'La transformation du droit international en droit interne' (1936) *Revue Générale de droit international public* 5, and H. Triepel, 'Les rapports entre le droit interne et le droit international' (1923) *Académie de droit international. Recueil des Cours* 77. In the Italian literature, see the classic works of D. Anzilotti, *Il diritto internazionale nei giudizi interni*, Zanichelli, Bologna 1905, A. La Pergola, *Costituzione e adattamento del diritto interno al diritto internazionale*, Giuffrè, Milano 1961, and R. Quadri, *Diritto internazionale pubblico*, Liguori, Napoli 1968. More recently, see also G. Tesauro, 'Costituzione e norme esterne' (2009) *Il diritto dell'Unione europea* 195.

[3] On the principle of exclusiveness see, in the Italian literature, C. Pinelli, *Costituzione e principio di esclusività*, Giuffrè, Milano 1989.

[4] On *renvoi* in a general and constitutional perspective, see the classic works of E. Betti, *Problematica del diritto internazionale*, Giuffrè, Milano 1956 and A. Bernardini, *Produzione di norme giuridiche mediante rinvio*, Giuffrè, Milano 1966.

[5] On the accession by the EU to the ECHR after the Lisbon Treaty, see A. Gianelli, 'L'adesione dell'Unione europea alla CEDU secondo il Trattato di Lisbona' (2009), and A. Bultrini, 'I rapporti fra Carta dei diritti fondamentali e Convenzione europea dei diritti dell'uomo dopo

and application of international treaty norms within the EU, on the basis of the scheme that was codified in the Treaties and in the ECJ case law.[6] Nonetheless, it must be pointed out that the formal outcomes of the accession will join an already established sum of relations that originated and developed from case law, through a system of interpretative interactions that has produced progressively integrating effects and that is characterized by cooperative features (at least to a certain extent).[7]

Having said that, one cannot overestimate the existence of various possible approaches to this issue, and particularly the aforementioned dialectic between the principle of exclusiveness of legal systems, transposition processes, and the relevance of interpretation and application dynamics in reconstructing the relationship between legal orders, even beyond formal processes of transposition. It suffices to say that an analysis based on the exclusivist paradigm would entail a reconstruction of relations among legal orders on the level of relations among norms, and would therefore imply referring to criteria for resolving antinomy, that is to the legal standing of such norms. Nevertheless, in the framework of the relations between the EU and the ECHR, such an attempt would certainly fail. On the contrary, an approach based on the interpretation and application dynamics of 'external' norms, even regardless of the existence of formal transposition processes – though raising some methodological issues – has the significant benefit of creating an adequate reconstructive framework for the research subject, which shows an evolutionary dynamic that has gradually prescinded from the existence of a formal connection among legal orders.[8]

In other words, the ECHR has gradually gained importance for the EU legal order beyond the classical transposition processes, by exclusively relying on the initiative of the ECJ, which only afterwards would be transposed in the Treaties' text. Thus, the relationship between the EU and the ECHR seems to have questioned the principle of exclusiveness of legal systems even before this occurred with the national legal order, and in a very different way.

On the other hand, norms like the current Article 6, section 3 of the TEU – let alone the so-called horizontal clauses of the Treaty of Nice – could only with

---

Lisbona: potenzialità straordinarie per lo sviluppo della tutela dei diritti umani in Europa' (2009), both in *Il diritto dell'UE* 678 and 700.

[6] See E. CANNIZZARO, 'Diritti "diretti" e diritti "indiretti": i diritti fondamentali tra Unione, CEDU e Costituzione italiana' (2012) *Il diritto dell'UE* 23. Among the most recent decisions, see *Kadi* (Cases C-402/05 P and C-415/05 P, *Kadi and Al Barakaat v. Council and Commission* [2008], ECR I-6351) and *Intertanko* (Case C-308/06, *Intertanko and others* [2008], ECR I-4057) judgments. More references in A. SCHILLACI, 'Tutela dei diritti e cooperazione tra ordinamenti in due recenti pronunce del giudice comunitario' (2009) *Giurisprudenza costituzionale* 1255.

[7] See P. RIDOLA, *supra* n. 1; M. KOTZUR, 'Kooperativer Grundrechtsschutz in der Völkergemeinschaft' (2008) 35 *Europäische Grundrechte Zeitschrift* 673. See A. TIZZANO, 'Les Cours européennes et l'adhésion de l'Union à la Cedh' (2011) *Il diritto dell'UE* 29, as well as the contribution of S. VEZZANI in this *Volume*.

[8] See, in general, G. TESAURO, *supra* n. 2, 222.

difficulty be traced back to the classic method of normative *renvoi* as a technique of relationship among legal orders. As a matter of fact, such a provision seems to refer to the discipline of interpretation processes and to the shaping of the paramount judgment criterion rather than to the level of relations among norms. That is, Article 6, section 3 did not lead to a *renvoi* to the conventional norms, but to acknowledgement of the possibility of interaction among legal orders, operating exclusively on the level of law interpretation and application, with a more specific reference to the shaping of the paramount judgment criterion, regardless of formal considerations as to the standing, the *status* or – more generally – the derivation of the norms concerned.

2. THE OPENING UP OF THE ECJ AND THE COMPARATIVE METHOD

Besides, the keystone in such a reconstruction could be represented by how dynamics shaping the paramount judgment criterion regarding rights are influenced by comparative operations, whose possible implications on the level of cooperation among legal orders shall be taken into examination.

The possibility of tracing the ECHR's relevance in ECJ case law to the recourse to comparative argumentation seems to be confirmed by a series of elements.[9] Besides the basically unilateral character of *renvoi* operations and the already mentioned absence of a horizontal link between the two legal orders, the feature of such operations that bears highlighting is their finalistic character. The opening of the ECJ to the ECHR legal order was indeed justified, at least in the beginning, by the need to grant the protection of fundamental rights and, at the same time, by the absence of adequate normative references within the EU legal order itself:[10] we are indeed not far from some classic interpretations of legal comparison that underline its functional capacities in approaching the gaps of the legal order of origin.[11]

---

[9]   On the use of legal comparison in case law, see G. Repetto, *Argomenti comparativi e diritti fondamentali in Europa*, Jovene, Napoli 2011; V. Jackson, *Constitutional Engagement in a Transnational Era*, Oxford University Press, Oxford 2010; P. Ridola, 'Il giudice costituzionale e la comparazione', in P. Ridola, *supra* n. 1, pp. 293 ff.; C. Pinelli, 'Trapianti, innesti, dialoghi. Modalità di trasmissione e circolazione del diritto straniero' (2010) *Rivista trimestrale di diritto pubblico* 495; A.M. Lecis Cocco Ortu, 'La comparaison en tant que methode de determination du standard de protection des droits dans le systeme CEDH' (2011) *Rivista dell'Associazione Italiana dei Costituzionalisti* 4 (www.rivistaaic.it); from a different perspective, see G. De Vergottini, *Oltre il dialogo tra le corti: giudici, diritto straniero, comparazione*, Il Mulino, Bologna 2010.

[10]   See F. Sorrentino, 'I diritti fondamentali in Europa dopo Lisbona' (2010) *Corriere giuridico* 146.

[11]   On the evolution of method in legal comparison, see L.-J. Constantinesco, *La scienza dei diritti comparati*, Giappichelli, Torino 2003; Id., *Il metodo comparativo*, Giappichelli, Torino

Beyond the functionalist aspect, the comparative nature of such operations seems to be confirmed when considering other interpretations of legal comparison that focus on the relationship with alterity in the critical approach to the legal heritage of the legal order of origin.[12] From such a perspective, the opening of the EU legal order to the ECHR, though by default a horizontal link, has relevant implications for the construction of a plural system for the protection of rights in Europe. In particular, the circulation of protection standards, of argumentation techniques and even of the various interpretations of the nature and the reach of single rights as to specific requests of protection, is a development factor of that 'open society of interpreters' that feeds on the comparative opening up to other legal heritages and serves as a factor of material integration among legal orders and, perhaps, of gradual (and difficult) emersion of a 'common constitutional law'.[13]

At the same time, we must not lose sight of the fact that, since they concern the protection of fundamental rights, such an opening and interaction also appear to be susceptible to turning themselves into a development factor of self-determination paths based on the conscious exercise of a fundamental right: transferring the protection issue to a supranational level – and opening defence pleas, before the national judge, by considering the norms of other legal orders, be they national or international – stimulates the circulation of different dialectics about rights and constitutes a tool to develop their (self-) understanding, leading to relevant consequences for the political community's own integration processes.

At the same time, the very claim of control of a certain legal order over the level of protection granted in another legal order – which translates the relationship among legal orders into terms that only appear to be conflicting – is the answer to specific, unfulfilled protection claims and may be seen as a factor of gradual integration, stimulating the development of the issue of protection in the legal order of origin. The latter, indeed, is bound to respond to the relationship, both to legitimate and, more broadly, to 'elude' the control of the other legal order, and thus tends to enrich its own norms through the critical opening to the 'other' level of protection.

It is, therefore, a bilateral (where not multilateral), fully dialectical and critical process, characterized by a changeable equilibrium and by the ongoing

---

2000; P. GLENN, *Legal traditions of the world: sustainable diversity in law*, Oxford University Press, Oxford 2010.

[12] See P. LEGRAND, *Le droit comparé*, PUF, Paris 1999; ID. (ed.), *Comparer le droits, résolument*, PUF, Paris 2009; A.A. CERVATI, *Per uno studio comparativo del diritto costituzionale*, Giappichelli, Torino 2009.

[13] See P. HÄBERLE, S.P. PANUNZIO and P. RIDOLA, *supra* n. 1; P. RIDOLA, 'I diritti di cittadinanza, il pluralismo e il tempo dell'ordine costituzionale europeo. Le 'tradizioni costituzionali comuni' e l'identità culturale europea in una prospettiva storica', in P. RIDOLA, *supra* n. 1, pp. 51 ff.; C. PINELLI, *Il momento della scrittura*, Il Mulino, Bologna 2002; A. PIZZORUSSO, *Il patrimonio costituzionale europeo*, Il Mulino, Bologna 2002.

comparison of different levels of protection, and between them and the claims for justice coming from groups and individuals; and, above all, this process – precisely in this complex alternation of setbacks, intermediate answers, attempted reconciliation, closures, elaboration of new claims for justice and their persistent non-fulfilment – shows the extent of the efforts for a cooperative relationship. From this perspective, therefore, comparison as the 'fifth interpretation method' shows its deeper link with the development dynamics of the 'open' and 'cooperative' Constitutional State.[14]

In other words, the shaping of the paramount judgment criterion stimulates relationship dynamics that, mostly with no regard to the classic dogmatic approach based on the principle of exclusiveness, enhance the interpretation phase, appearing to be fully aware of the gradual entrance of the textual references into a hermeneutic constellation characterized by a wide plurality of interpretation options: the aim of such dynamics – as already very well highlighted by the Italian Constitutional Court – can only be the development of the issue of protection (see the decisions nos. 317 of 2009 and 80 of 2011).

3. EU LAW IN ECtHR CASE LAW: RESISTANCE AND (LABOURED) OPENING

With reference to the relationship between the EU and the ECHR, however, the link between such openings and the wider phenomenon of (cooperative) interaction among legal orders on the issue of fundamental rights in Europe becomes more and more complex. Still, analysis of the different development phases of the relationship shows that – in this case, too – it is not possible to speak in undoubted and absolute terms of non-communicativeness between the two legal orders and, above all, it shows that the relationship among them has been subject to a complex development process.

To be sure, at least since the late 1990s – and parallel to the intensification of ECtHR activity and to the growing number of pending suits – the ECtHR has begun, so to speak, to 'become aware' of the Community experience and of its considerable relevance from the perspective of fundamental rights protection as well. The divide seems to have been precisely the proclamation of the EU Charter of Fundamental Rights in 2000: in fact, this clearly showed that the Community law had changed from being a one-dimensional experience oriented towards economic integration to being a 'place' in which to exercise the understanding and management of economic dynamics considering the relationship between

---

[14] See P. Häberle, *supra* n. 1; M. Kotzur, *supra* n. 7, and *Grenznachbarschaftliche Zusammenarbeit in Europa: der Beitrag von Art. 24 Abs. 1 a GG zu einer Lehre vom kooperativen Verfassungs- und Verwaltungsstaat*, Duncker & Humblot, Berlin 2004; A. Di Martino, *Il territorio dallo stato-nazione alla globalizzazione: sfide e prospettive dello stato costituzionale aperto*, Giuffrè, Milano 2010.

market and fundamental rights, between the importance of free competition and the correction of its distorting effects in the light of profound claims for justice.[15]

Obviously, such an evolution could not be ignored by the ECtHR. Bear in mind, then, the evolution of Strasbourg's case law in the great number of cases where a State that is a member of the EU and of the ECHR at the same time finds itself in the role of defendant before the Strasbourg Court for a violation of the Convention due to internal norms or praxis established in order to comply with certain obligations deriving from this State's membership in the EU, with a consequent conflict among mutually exclusive international obligations.

Such a conflict was settled by the ECtHR – after considering various case law positions[16] – in the *Bosphorus* judgment.[17] In this pronouncement, the Strasbourg Court acknowledges that the ECHR does not oppose the intensification of international cooperation, yet it aims to be a tool that can stimulate and orient international cooperation itself towards the protection of rights to its maximum possible extent. In this light, in judging a state action that has been considered prejudicial to norms of the Convention, the Court will give high priority to the fulfilment of the 'competing' international obligation, by verifying whether the legal order that gave rise to such an obligation – in this case, the EU legal order – grants an equivalent (here with the meaning of 'comparable', not 'identical') protection of rights and fundamental freedoms, at the level of both protection tools and of concrete protection granted to the legal position being appealed to. Such a compatibility judgment can be readjusted by the Court at any time, in consideration of possible changes in the circumstances and the concrete peculiarities of each case (*Bosphorus* judgment, paras. 149 ff.).[18]

The *Bosphorus* judgment starts a new phase in the relationship between the ECtHR and the ECJ, as it puts an end to long years of highly frequent – and relevant – references to the ECHR's experience in the Community case law relating to rights – references that were not followed by a corresponding behaviour on the part of the Strasbourg Court. The solution envisaged by the

---

[15] On this evolution see P. RIDOLA, 'Diritti di libertà e mercato nella Costituzione europea', in ID., *supra* n. 1, pp. 139 ff.

[16] See i.e. the Strasbourg Court's decisions in the cases of *Matthews v. United Kingdom* (judgment of 18 February 1999) and *Senator Lines GmBH v. EU Member States* (judgment of 10 March 2004). On this case law, see A. GIANELLI, *supra* n. 5, p. 681, L. M. DÍEZ-PICAZO, 'Le relazioni tra Unione europea e Convenzione europea dei diritti dell'uomo', in S.P. PANUNZIO (ed.), *supra* n. 1, pp. 269 ff.; A. TIZZANO, *supra* n. 7; S.P. PANUNZIO, *supra* n. 1.

[17] ECtHR, *Bosphorus Hava Yollari Turizm Vel Ticaret Anonim Şirketi v. Ireland*, judgment of 30 June 2005. See, in the Italian literature, E. CANNIZZARO, 'Sulla responsabilità internazionale per condotte di Stati membri dell'Unione europea: in margine al caso Bosphorus' (2005) *Rivista di diritto internazionale* 762; M. PACINI, 'Il controllo della CEDU sugli atti nazionali in funzione comunitaria' (2006) *Giornale di diritto amministrativo* 21, as well as A. BULTRINI, *supra* n. 5, p. 702, n. 192.

[18] See an application of the equivalence judgment in the ECtHR decision in the case of *Kokkelvisserij U.A. v. the Netherlands* (judgment of 20 January 2009): on this decision, see D. RUSSO, 'Una decisione della Corte di Strasburgo verso l'affermazione di un controllo sull'operato della Corte di giustizia' (2009) *Rivista di diritto internazionale* 1119.

Bosphorus judgment is in line with developments of the European integration process, which is characterized by a fully dynamic and flowing arrangement, open to change and to progressive adjustment. The fact that Strasbourg can, albeit indirectly, control rights protection at a Community level, far from representing an undue interference or an irreconcilable conflict, could represent a factor of integration among different protection levels and, above all, among legal and argumentative heritages. Furthermore, it facilitates the circulation of specific solutions to concrete claims for justice.

4. THE EU CHARTER OF FUNDAMENTAL RIGHTS IN THE ECtHR'S CASE LAW

EU law – and in particular the EU Charter of Fundamental Rights – has been taken into consideration more and more by the ECtHR in the last ten years, even in cases not involving the indirect relevance of Community law in national conduct prejudicing a fundamental right.

In this case, the opening up is even more complex, especially as regards the argumentation techniques used by the ECtHR to justify its references to the Charter. The integration of the paramount judgment criterion through references to international or supranational norms other than the ECHR is frequent in ECHR case law, and closely linked to the need to ensure that the ECHR – a 'living' text[19] – conforms to the concrete dynamics of international cooperation on rights protection.

In other words, as already made clear by the seminal judgment *Demir and Baykara v. Turkey*,[20] the elevation of international norms other than the ECHR to a paramount judgment criterion is functional to integrating the norms of the ECHR itself, in order to link the extent of the considered right to the level of consensus reached by the States in their cooperative action in the protection of fundamental rights, particularly when the norms raised at the source of integration of the paramount judgment criterion 'denote a continuous evolution in the norms and principles applied in international law or in the domestic law of the majority of member States of the Council of Europe and show, in a precise area, that there is common ground in modern societies' (para. 86).

Analysis of the argumentation of the ECtHR's decisions most open to EU law and to the EUCFR must be traced back to a more general context of interpretational interaction, thus revealing the integration and cooperation implications of the relationship between the two legal orders, from a different perspective but with the same expansive force.

---

[19]   See, among others, the cases *Saadi v. Italy* (ECtHR, judgment of 28 February 2008), *Vo V. France* (ECtHR, judgment of 8 July 2004), *Mamatkulov and Askarov v. Turkey* (ECtHR, judgment of 4 February 2005).

[20]   ECtHR, judgment of 12 November 2008, paras. 65 ff.

Moreover, these decisions mainly concern rights that still raise disputes, and whose protection seems to be more precisely granted by the provisions of the EUCFR. From this perspective, the reference to the EUCFR has the major function of specifying the level of consensus that has been reached in Europe about the protection of a specific right: Consider, for example, the *Neulinger and Shuruk v. Switzerland* judgment on the protection of children,[21] where the reference to Article 24, para. 2 of the Charter is used as a point of closure for the Court's argumentation as regards the child's interest as the supreme judgment criterion in decisions relating to children's rights.

Moreover, in some cases the Court goes even further and, besides the reconstruction of European consensus, it refers to the Charter in order to extend the non-discrimination hypotheses to the framework of the open clause as referred to in Article 14 of the Convention,[22] or even better, to state the content of points of law arising at the trial.[23]

Likewise, as regards the gradual extension of the right to family life for homosexuals and transsexuals, it will be useful to consider first of all the *Christine Goodwin v. United Kingdom* judgment[24] and the *I v. United Kingdom* judgment,[25] where the reference to Article 9 of the EUCFR – but also to the ECJ's case law on the right to social and medical assistance and the right to non-discrimination at the workplace – constitutes the starting point of a case law particularly keen on protecting the rights of transsexuals. The reference to Article 9 – as it lacks any mention of the diversity of the spouses' biological sex in establishing EU citizens' right to family life ('Everyone has the right...') – serves, especially in the *Christine Goodwin* judgment, to base the right to family life on gender alterity rather than on the alterity of biological sex, thus overcoming the past case law on transsexualism (cf. points 97 ff. of the judgment, in particular). A special reference needs to be made to the relevant and well-known *Schalk and Kopf v. Austria* judgment on the right to family life for homosexuals who are denied the right to marry or to recognition of their partnership in their own home state.[26] Also in that judgment, the possibility of applying to homosexuals Article 12 ECHR on the right to marriage – though

---

21   ECtHR, judgment of 6 July 2010.
22   Cf. *G.N. v. Italy* judgment, para. 126, where Article 14 ECHR is construed in the light of Article 21 EUCFR, with reference to the prohibition of discrimination based on genetic characteristics or handicap; likewise, cf. in general, as regards the impact of the prohibition of discrimination on the grounds of sexual orientation as referred to in Article 21 of the EU Charter of Fundamental Rights, the dissenting opinion of judges Bratza, Fuhrmann and Tulkens in the case of *Fretté v. France*.
23   See e.g., ECtHR, case of *Scoppola v. Italy (no. 2)*, judgment of 17 September 2009, paras. 37 ff.
24   ECtHR, judgment of 11 July 2002.
25   ECtHR, judgment of 11 July 2002.
26   ECtHR, judgment of 24 June 2010. On this decision, see G. Repetto, '"Non perdere il proprio mondo". Argomenti dei giudici e matrimonio 'same-sex' tra Corte di Strasburgo e Corte costituzionale' (2010) *Rivista critica del diritto privato* 525.

not questioning the member states' autonomy as to whether and how such an acknowledgement is to be made, and hence dismissing the appeal – is indeed inferred from the interpretation of the conventional norm in light of Article 9 of the EUCFR,[27] whose broader phrasing allows for a more precise identification of the holders of rights.

Remaining within the framework of the material integration of the Convention's contents through its interpretation in light of the EU Charter of Fundamental Rights, consider the *Sørensen and Rasmussen v. Denmark* judgment on negative freedom of association.[28] More specifically, in that judgment the reference to fundamental legal texts of the Council of Europe (the European Social Charter) and of the EU (the Community Charter of the Fundamental Social Rights of Workers and Article 12 of the EUCFR in particular) allows the ECtHR to overcome its interpretation of Article 11, finding in its provisions the guarantee of negative freedom of association (points 33–38 and 66–77). Likewise, the reference to Article 28 of the EUCFR in the aforementioned *Demir v. Turkey* judgment represents a crucial integration source of the paramount judgment criterion (Article 11 ECHR), considering outdated the commonly accepted orientation of the European Court that did not include the right to collective bargaining among the basic elements of the right to freedom of association, which is protected precisely by Article 11 of the Convention (cf. paras. 147 ff., and 153).

Thus, the text of the EU Charter of Fundamental Rights as it is referred to by the ECtHR represents the epiphenomenon of the broadest and deepest experience dynamics, circulation of discourse on rights, and rights awareness.

5. EUCFR AND 'HORIZONTAL CLAUSES' IN THE ECJ CASE LAW: TOWARDS ANOTHER CENTRE OF GRAVITY?

At the same time, however, the EUCFR is the fundamental document of one particular level of protection, the EU level: as such, it does not merely acknowledge the ECtHR's legal heritage and the constitutional traditions shared by Member States, on the basis of the phrasing of Article 6 TEU. The undoubtable influence of such experiences[29] coexists with a distinctive vocation to determine identity traits which, nonetheless, are structurally open to interaction with other levels of protection. From this point of view, the phrasing of the material provisions and the contemplation of norms dedicated to relations between protection levels (the so-called horizontal clauses, Article 51 ff.) perform the

---

[27] See para. 61.
[28] ECtHR, judgment of 11 November 2006.
[29] See P. Ridola, *supra* n. 13, and 'La Carta dei diritti fondamentali dell'Unione europea e lo sviluppo storico del costituzionalismo europeo', in Id., *supra* n. 1, pp. 163 ff.

same function, which is that of keeping unity and diversity together by safeguarding the interaction itself.[30]

In this context it seems necessary to examine to what extent the EUCFR's entry into force affected the ECtHR's relevance in the ECJ case law, and in particular whether the reference to the ECHR still plays a noteworthy role in the ECJ case law, or rather if the EUCFR's vocation to represent a basically absorbing paramount criterion prevailed, leading to a weakening of the ECtHR's role as the centre of gravity of the European system of protection of fundamental rights and freedoms.

The ECJ's case law is not uniform on that point, and reproduces the already mentioned tensions between reassertion of identity and protection of the interaction.

Even before the EUCFR entered into force, the Court used some of its provisions to confirm the convergence among levels of protection, sometimes by simply recording the convergence,[31] sometimes by testing and identifying the margin of autonomy of the Community protection level, then enhancing its interpretation by referring to the Charter: on this point consider the much debated *Viking*[32] and *Laval* judgments,[33] but also the *Dynamic Medien* judgment, on the protection of minors.[34]

Conversely, after the Charter entered into force, the Court's argumentation on rights seemed to grow poorer. In particular, motivations supported by joint reference to different sources of the Community catalogue of rights provided in Article 6 TEU became rarer and the trend was to refer exclusively to the Charter's provisions, though with some important exceptions.

Such a trend appears to be consolidated in the most recent judgments – those of 2011 in particular – while the case law of 2009 and 2010 still shows the 'classical' paths of argumentation: it suffices to recall a series of judgments where reference to the EUCFR does not exclude the mention of the

---

30   On the evolution of the protection of fundamental rights in Europe after the Treaty of Lisbon see, in the Italian literature, P. Ridola, *supra* n. 1; F. Sorrentino, *supra* n. 10; A. Gianelli and A. Bultrini, *supra* n. 5; L. Daniele, 'La protezione dei diritti fondamentali nell'Unione europea dopo il Trattato di Lisbona: un quadro d'insieme' (2009) *Il diritto dell'UE* 645; A. Tizzano, *supra* n. 7; M. Cartabia, 'I diritti fondamentali in Europa dopo Lisbona: verso nuovi equilibri?' (2010) *Giornale di diritto amministrativo* 221; G. Strozzi, 'Il sistema integrato di tutela dei diritti fondamentali dopo Lisbona: attualità e prospettive' (2011) *Il diritto dell'UE* 837; A. Rosas and H. Kaila, 'L'application de la Charte des droits fondamentaux de l'Union Européenne par la Cour de Justice: un premier bilan' (2011) *Il diritto dell'UE* 1.

31   See the decisions C-303/05, *Advocaten von den Wereld* [2007] ECR I-03633, para. 45, and C-450/06, *Varec* [2008] ECR I-00581, para. 48.

32   C-438/05, *International Transport Workers Federation v. Viking* [2007] ECR I-10779, paras. 43 and 44.

33   C-341/05, *Laval un Partneri Ltd contro Svenska Byggnadsarbetareförbundet, Svenska Byggnadsarbetareförbundets avdelning 1, Byggettan e Svenska Elektrikerförbundet* [2007] ECR I-11767, paras. 90 and 91.

34   C-244/06 [2008] ECR I-00505.

corresponding provisions.[35] Also in 2010, however, other judgments[36] confined themselves to referring to EUCFR provisions, followed by the constant case law of 2011[37] and 2012,[38] with some exceptions.[39] Moreover, the aforementioned cases concern rights whose protection by the Community had been traditionally and considerably affected by the interpretation and application experience that had taken shape within the ECtHR (for example, the effective jurisdictional protection, as in *Knauf, Fuß, Gavieiro Gavieiro* and *DEB* judgments).

Hence the Court's orientation on this point does not seem to have reached consolidation, and relevant fluctuations can still be registered. Nonetheless, in two cases the Court provided some further elements – although not going in the same direction – to understand the relations between the EUCFR and the ECHR.

The first reference is to the *Volker und Markus Schecke* judgment,[40] on the right to privacy in the processing of personal data. In this case – though stating that the validity of the challenged norms 'shall be assessed in the light of the Charter's provisions' (para. 46) – the risk of unilateral reference to the Charter leading to a closure of interaction was avoided by mentioning the 'horizontal' clause referred to in Article 52, para. 3 of the Charter. Indeed, by virtue of such a provision, the Court leads its arguments on the path of the 'parallel' interpretation of the provisions of Article 8 ECHR and of Article 7 EUCFR, and by also taking into consideration ECtHR case law (para. 51 and 52 for the general profiles, and para. 87).

---

35   See the ECJ's judgments in the following cases: C-578/08, *Chakroun* [2010] ECR I-01839 para. 63; C-317 to 320/08, *Alassini* [2010] ECR I-02213 para. 61; C-409/06, *Winner Wetten* [2010] ECR I-08015, para. 58; C-145/09, *Tsakouridis* [2010], n.p., para. 52; C-208/09, *Sayn Wittgenstein* [2010], n.p., para. 52.
36   See the ECJ's judgments in the following cases: C-555/07, *Kükükdeveci* [2010] ECR I-00365, para. 21; C-570 and 571/07, *Blanco Pérez* [2010] ECR I-04629, para. 65; C-407/08 P, *Knauf* [2010] ECR I-06375, para. 91; C-211/10 PPU, *Povse* [2010] ECR I-06673, para. 64; C-550/07 P, *Akzo* [2010] ECR I-08301, para. 54; C-243/09, *Fuß* [2010] ECR I-09849, para. 66; C-444 and 456/09, *Gavieiro Gavieiro* [2010], n.p., para. 75; C-279/09, *DEB* [2010], n.p.
37   See the ECJ's judgments in the following cases: C-109/10, *Solvay* [2011], n.p. para 53; C-155/10, *Williams* [2011], n.p., para. 18; C- 447/09, *Prigge* [2011], n.p., para. 38; C-297 and 298/10, *Hennigs* [2011], n.p.; C-391/09, *Runeviç Vardyn* [2011], n.p., para. 43; C-543/09, *Deutsche Telekom,* [2011], n.p.
38   CdGUE, C-172/11, *Erny* [2012], n.p., para. 50; C-141/11, *Hörnfeldt* [2012], n.p., para. 37; C-78/11, *ANGED* [2012], n.p., para. 17; C-292/10, *G.* [2012], n.p.; C-360/10, *Belgische Vereniging van Auteurs, Componisten en Uitgevers CVBA* [2012], n.p.
39   See the ECJ's judgments in the following cases: C-500/10, *Belvedere Costruzioni srl* [2012], n.p., paras. 23–24; C-507/10, *X.* [2011], n.p., para. 43; C-256/11, *Dereci* [2011], n.p. para. 70; see also GC, T-439/07, *Coats Holding Ltd* [2012], n.p., para. 172; T-336/07, *Telefónica, SA* [2012], n.p., para. 81; T-439 and 440/10, *Fulmen* [2012], n.p., para. 87; T-341/07, *Sison* [2011] n.p., para. 81.
40   C-92 and 93/09, *Volker und Markus Schecke* [2010], n.p.

The ECJ's path of argumentation appears even more articulate in the slightly earlier *McB* judgment on the natural father's right of custody.[41] In this case there was also a seminal reference to Article 52, para. 3 of the Charter, on the basis of the correspondence between Article 7 EUCFR and Article 8 ECHR (para. 53), allowing the Court to introduce into its argumentations the ECtHR's *Guichard v. France*,[42] *Balbontin v. United Kingdom*[43] and *Zaunegger v. Germany*[44] judgments. The content of Article 7 of the Charter is therefore determined by complementing it with new interpretations of the paramount judgment criterion in light of Article 52, para. 3 of the Charter, and thus of the Strasbourg Court's case law. The interaction with the ECHR legal order completes an essential step of the judgment, also revealing what we may call cooperative implications, since the reference to the ECHR's experience proves to be of seminal importance in specifying the contents of a Charter provision.

In conclusion, the analysis of application of the EUCFR by the ECJ shows on the one hand a clear tendency to focus EU rights protection on the Charter's provisions. On the other hand, the risk of an 'identitary' withdrawal and for a unilateral standardization on the Charter's provisions appears to have been averted – not only on a textual level, but already with significant application consequences – by the reference to horizontal clauses, and especially in cases where the definition of the law's content is more controversial. From this perspective, the opening of the EU level to contributions from other legal orders helps to dispel uncertainties of interpretation and to specify the content of the protected right: the relationship among legal orders develops through the shaping of the paramount judgment criterion, which becomes the 'place' where the relationship itself is managed in cooperative terms.

6. CONCLUSION

In summary, the analysis of the relationship between the ECJ and the ECtHR shows a chiastic progression, whose main feature is the proclamation (and, afterwards, the entry into force) of the EU Charter of Fundamental Rights. Reference to the ECHR was the main tool for the construction of the EU system of rights protection, but only when such a system delivered a seminal document (the Charter of Nice) did the ECtHR rise above its traditional indifference towards the EU legal order, by acknowledging it was a fitting partner in the dynamics of rights protection, and by acknowledging that the Charter was a

---

[41]   C-400/10, *McB* [2010] ECR I-08965. On this decision, see N. LAZZERINI, 'Il controllo della compatibilità del diritto nazionale con la Carta dei diritti fondamentali secondo la sentenza McB' (2011) *Rivista di diritto internazionale* 136.

[42]   ECtHR, judgment of 2 September 2003.

[43]   ECtHR, judgment of 14 September 1999.

[44]   ECtHR, judgment of 3 December 2009.

possible source of integration of its paramount judgment criterion, which is mostly represented by the Convention. On the other hand, with the implementation of the EUCFR it seems that Luxembourg is starting to adopt a strongly autonomous line of case law, even if the relevance of the horizontal clauses of the EUCFR cannot be underestimated.

Lastly, such a situation will be influenced by the EU's accession to the ECHR, which is being negotiated. Moreover, 2011 witnessed two important signs of progress: the joint statement from the presidents of the two Courts on 24 January[45] and the draft accession agreement on 24 June.[46] The joint statement contained not only the appreciation for the frequent application of the EUCFR by the ECJ – with a concomitant invitation to full compliance with Article 52, para. 3 on the lowering of the protection standards to the ECHR level – but also the seminal statement of principle on the ECJ's precedence over the ECtHR in cases relating to the interpretation of EU law. Such a statement marks the conclusion of years of fears and conflicts, since the contrasts between the two Courts was one of the main obstacles to the EU's accession to the ECHR (cf. ECJ Opinion 2/94),[47] and finds full procedural implementation in the draft accession agreement, whose Article 3, para. 6 states that when, in ECtHR proceedings involving the EU as a party, an act of Community law is claimed not to be compatible with ECHR norms and the ECJ has not yet given its judgment on the point (pursuant to Article 6 TEU), the ECJ has to be given the opportunity to deliver its opinion within a reasonable period of time, without prejudice to the ECtHR proceeding.

This solution is an interesting one, as it expresses a principle of fair cooperation between legal orders. In particular, it allows the EU legal order to provide its own 'point of view' on the matter, contributing to the definition of the concrete protection standard. The 'comparative' vocation of such pronouncement by the ECJ is very clear. The ECJ will be asked to compare the protection standard that had been granted by the EU with the one granted by the Convention.

At the same time, the heralded 'institutionalization' of the dialogue between ECJ and ECtHR seems to identify Luxembourg as the centre of gravity of this relationship and cooperation, thus coming full circle.

---

[45] See E. Chiti, 'Cedu e UE: un comunicato congiunto della Corte di Strasburgo e della Corte di Lussemburgo' (2011) *Giornale di diritto amministrativo* 899; G. Repetto, 'Prove di 'entente cordiale' tra le due Corti europee' (2011) *Diritti comparati* (www.diritticomparati.it), as well as the contribution by S. Vezzani in this *Volume*, and J. P. Jacqué, 'The accession of the European Union to the European Convention on Human Rights and Fundamental Freedoms' (2011) 48 *CMLR (Common Market Law Review)* 995.

[46] CDDH-EU(2011)16.

[47] On the Opinion 2/94, see G. Gaja, 'Opinion 2/94. Accession by the Community to the EC for the protection of human rights and fundamental freedoms' (1996) 33 *CMLR* 973.

But as is common knowledge, in Europe – and particularly when it comes to the protection of fundamental rights – no balance point can claim permanence. The impetus from the concrete and ever-new claims for justice (which are specific to the most complex societies) is too strong to be able to declare such laboured and profoundly dynamic relations concluded, even when using the harmonic imagery of chiasmus. Only a strong emphasis on the cooperative features of such relationships can effectively convey the great effort and deep tension of a process that, precisely because it regards fundamental rights, is controversial by nature.

THE EU AND ITS MEMBER STATES BEFORE THE STRASBOURG COURT

A Critical Appraisal of the Co-Respondent Mechanism

Simone Vᴇᴢᴢᴀɴɪ

1. PRELIMINARY REMARKS ON THE EU ACCESSION TO THE ECHR: THE PROBLEM OF SHARED RESPONSIBILITY

The EU accession to the ECHR will mark an important step in filling the gap of accountability for human rights violations by public authorities in the European legal space. As is known, accession is provided for by Article 59(2) ECHR[1] and mandated by Article 6 TEU, as amended by the Treaty of Lisbon. This Article also introduced the necessary legal basis for accession, which was previously found lacking under Community law.[2] Official negotiations for the elaboration of an international agreement on accession began in July 2010 between the European Commission and an informal working group of the Steering Committee for Human Rights (CDDH) of the Council of Europe.[3] A draft accession agreement (henceforth, the 'Draft Agreement') was adopted in July 2011, and constitutes the basis of discussion for further negotiations which are now underway.[4]

---

[1] Introduced by Protocol XIV, entered into force on 01.06.2010.
[2] ECJ, Opinion 2/94 [1996] ECR I-1759.
[3] On the negotiation process, see S. Dᴏᴜɢʟᴀs-Sᴄᴏᴛᴛ, 'The European Union and Human Rights after the Treaty of Lisbon' (2011) 11 *HRLR (Human Rights Law Reports)* 645, 660–2; J. P. Jᴀᴄǫᴜᴇ́, 'The Accession of the European Union to the European Convention on Human Rights and Fundamental Freedoms' (2011) 48 *CMLR* 995; V. Pᴇᴛʀᴀʟɪᴀ, 'L'adesione dell'Unione europea alla Convenzione europea dei diritti dell'uomo', in N. Pᴀʀɪsɪ and V. Pᴇᴛʀᴀʟɪᴀ (eds.), *L'Unione europea dopo il Trattato di Lisbona*, Giappichelli, Torino 2011, p. 287; P. Iᴠᴀʟᴅɪ and C. E. Tᴜᴏ, 'Diritti fondamentali e diritto internazionale privato dell'Unione europea nella prospettiva dell'adesione alla CEDU' (2012) *Rivista di diritto internazionale privato e processuale* 3.
[4] Cf. CDDH-UE(2011)16, 19.07.2011, available at www.coe.int/t/dghl/standardsetting/hrpolicy/cddh-ue/cddh-ue_documents_EN.asp, accessed 01.07.2012, where all the *travaux*

The EU accession will likely contribute towards consolidating common 'constitutional' values in the European legal space, and will reshape the existing relationship between the two courts in Strasbourg and Luxembourg. The character of this relationship will be dependent upon the changes in the rules governing the proceedings before the ECtHR, to be introduced by way of amendments to the ECHR and, then, to the Rules of Court.

Not surprisingly, one of the most controversial points in the negotiation process remains the drafting of a co-respondent mechanism (CRM), intended to allow, subject to certain conditions, the joint participation of the EU and of one or more member state(s) in the same procedure. As we shall see more clearly later on, this mechanism has three main rationales: (a) to give the EU an opportunity to participate in proceedings questioning the conformity with the ECHR of national measures that apply EU law, and conversely to allow member states to defend the conformity with the ECHR of a provision of the EU constitutive treaties; (b) to ensure an effective enforcement of the Strasbourg judgements, by binding the contracting parties (EU or member states) empowered to modify the act at the origin of the violation found; and (c) to preserve the autonomy of the EU legal order, both by avoiding interference by the ECtHR in the internal division of responsibilities between the EU and its member states, and by allowing the Court in Luxembourg to review the lawfulness of an EU act or omission according to EU law (and indirectly with the ECHR), before the ECtHR adjudicates on the conformity of the same act or omission with the ECHR.

The present paper critically considers the CRM by highlighting some of its major difficulties. Before analyzing the mechanism, as envisaged in the Draft Agreement, some preliminary remarks are necessary concerning the division of responsibility, in the post-accession scenario, between the EU and its member states for breach of obligations under the ECHR.

In the last few years, the apportionment of responsibility between the EU and its member states has been the object of a debate spurred by the works of the ILC, which came to an end in 2011 with the approval of the Draft Articles on the responsibility of international organizations (DARIO).[5] The problem has been tackled several times in international practice, especially in the context of the

---

préparatoires can be read. When the agreement was considered for adoption by the CDDH in October 2011, various states expressed a number of legal concerns and the European Commission noted that further debates were needed in the EU (CDDH(2011)009, p. 3). The negotiation process then stalled for several months, as some governments (*in primis* the UK) seemed to contest the whole outcome. However, in June 2012, the accession talks between the Council of Europe and the European Commission were resumed (cf. Doc. 47+1(2012)R01, 21.06.2012). One should also consider that, after the completion of the negotiation phase, the EU institutions or one or more member states will very likely seek an opinion from the ECJ under Article 218(11), on the compatibility of the accession agreement with EU primary law.

5   Available with Commentary at http://untreaty.un.org/ilc/reports/2011/2011report.htm, accessed 20.06.2012.

WTO.[6] Moreover, some mixed agreements entered into by the EU already provide detailed procedural rules to ensure that arbitral procedures initiated by third states or private parties for breaches of such agreements are directed, depending on the cases, against the EU, a member state, or both of them. The most significant examples are provided by UNCLOS[7] and by the Energy Charter Treaty.[8]

A solution aimed at assuring legal clarity in the apportionment of responsibility for violations of the ECHR has been recently suggested by Gaja, former ILC Special Rapporteur on the responsibility of international organizations. According to his suggestion, the accession agreement should contain a special rule on attribution, 'to the effect that the conduct of a state would be attributed to a Member State when it exercises its discretion and to the EU when the state implements a binding act of the Union to the extent that the act does not leave discretion'.[9] Gaja's proposal would make it possible to hold either the EU or its member states exclusively responsible, in the case of violations of the ECHR caused by state measures adopted in the implementation of EU law. This would be totally in line with Protocol No. 8 annexed to the TEU, requiring the accession agreement to establish 'mechanisms necessary to ensure that proceedings by non-Member States and individual applications are correctly addressed to Member States and/or the Union as appropriate'.[10] However, a rule with this content has not been included in the text of the Draft Agreement and, indeed, no reasonable prospects seem to exist for this proposal to be accepted. This implies that the EU accession will not change the attribution of conduct by state organs in breach of obligations under the ECHR. In the event that an alleged wrongful conduct is taken by the organ of a state in the implementation of an EU act, said conduct will at most trigger an EU additional derivative (or indirect) responsibility.

One should begin by noting that, under customary international law, a state is responsible for a breach of an international obligation committed by one of its organs in the exercise of its functions.[11] The circumstance that a state organ acted in the implementation of an act of an international organization is not

---

6   Cf. F. HOFFMEISTER, 'Litigating against the European Union and its Member States. Who Responds under the ILC's Draft Articles on International Responsibility of International Organizations?' (2010) 21 *EJIL (European Journal of International Law)* 723.

7   Cf. Annex XI to the Convention, in particular Article 6(2).

8   Cf. Article 26(3)(b)(ii) of the Energy Charter Treaty and the Statement submitted by the EU in accordance with it, OJ (1998) L 69/115.

9   G. GAJA, 'Accession to the ECHR' in A. BIONDI, P. EECKHOUT and S. RIPLEY (eds.) *EU Law after Lisbon*, Oxford University Press, Oxford 2012, pp. 180–190. The possibility of special rules on attribution derogating from general international law is also envisaged by Article 64 of the DARIO.

10   Protocol No. 8, Article 1(b).

11   See Article 4 of the 2001 ILC Articles on state responsibility, codifying customary international law.

per se sufficient to preclude state responsibility. This principle has been clearly affirmed by the ECtHR with regard to alleged infringements of the ECHR by states implementing EC/EU law.[12] Several decisions may be recalled in this regard, among which *Procola*,[13] *Cantoni*,[14] *Bosphorus*[15] and *MSS*.[16] It is worth emphasizing that, in accordance with this case law, as a matter of principle states are not exonerated from responsibility when acting as mere executors of an EU law provision that leaves no room for discretion.

After the accession of the EU to the Convention, it will also be possible to hold the EU responsible before the ECtHR in connection with an action or omission by a state. Lacking any indication to the contrary, the responsibility of the EU should be appreciated according to pertinent customary international rules, which have been (to a great extent) codified by the DARIO. According to Article 17 of the DARIO, the EU could bear responsibility because of circumvention of an obligation under the ECHR through adopting a decision that binds, or authorizes, said state to commit the wrongful act. Depending on the specific circumstances of each case, the EU's responsibility may also be triggered on different grounds in connection with the act of a member state: for aiding and assisting,[17] directing and controlling[18] or coercing[19] said state in the commission of the wrongful act.[20]

No problem of shared responsibility will arise, instead, in the case of breaches of the Convention caused by conduct of EU agents without any role being played by state authorities. The *Connolly* case provides an illustration of this situation.[21] The plaintiff, who filed an application with the Strasbourg court against the member states of the EU, was a former official of the European Commission. He alleged that his dismissal had implied a violation of a number of rights guaranteed under the ECHR and its First Protocol, namely the freedom of speech, the right to a fair trial, and the right to property. The ECtHR rightly declared the claim inadmissible *ratione personae*, since the conduct not in

---

[12] Cf. A. BULTRINI, 'La responsabilité des Etats membres de l'Union Européenne pour les violations de la Convention européenne des droits de l'Homme imputables au système communautaire' (2002) 49 *RTDH (Revue trimestrielle des droits de l'homme)* 5; E. CANNIZZARO, 'Sulla responsabilità internazionale per condotte di Stati membri dell'Unione europea: in margine al caso Bosphorus' (2005) *Rivista di diritto internazionale* 762.

[13] ECtHR, *Procola v. Luxembourg*, judgment of 28 September 1995.

[14] ECtHR, *Cantoni v. France*, judgment of 11 November 1996.

[15] ECtHR, *Bosphorus Hava Yolları Turizm ve Ticaret Anonim Şirketi v. Ireland*, judgment of 30 June 2005.

[16] ECtHR, *MSS v. Belgium and Greece*, judgment of 21 January 2011.

[17] Cf. Article 14 of the DARIO.

[18] Cf. Article 15 of the DARIO.

[19] Cf. Article 16 of the DARIO. It is worth noting that in the exceptional case of coercion on the part of an international organization, the wrongfulness of the conduct of the coerced state would be excluded (see the Commentary to Article 16).

[20] As pointed out by the same ILC in its Commentary, overlap between Article 17 and Articles 14–16 of the DARIO is possible.

[21] ECtHR, *Connolly v. 15 Etats membres de l'Union Européenne*, judgment of 9 December 2008.

conformity with the ECHR was carried out by organs of the EU that were not party to the ECHR, and there had been no action by a contracting state's organ.[22] After accession, a complaint of this kind would certainly be admissible and should be directed against the EU as the sole respondent. It is true that in the *Gasparini* decision the ECtHR admitted a collective responsibility of member states for the acts of an international organization, on the basis of the mere transfer of state competences to the organization.[23] Nevertheless, the same Court limited such responsibility to the scenario in which, when the member states concluded the agreement establishing the organization, it was evident that the protection of human rights in the newly created organization was manifestly deficient.[24] Since the Court has already ruled that in the EU's legal order fundamental rights receive an equivalent protection to that granted by the ECHR, it does not seem that member states of the EU might be held responsible for violations committed by EU organs, in the lack of any participation by state organs in the violation of an obligation under the Convention.[25]

2. THE CO-RESPONDENT MECHANISM AS ENVISAGED IN THE DRAFT ACCESSION AGREEMENT

The introduction of a CRM was first suggested in 2002 by the CDDH in a study on accession.[26] Subsequently, it has been supported by the majority of the doctrine, as well as by governmental and EU constituencies. According to the mainstream reading, this mechanism would make it possible to preserve 'the specific characteristics of the Union and Union law', as mandated by Protocol No. 8 annexed to the Treaty of Lisbon. Yet, diverging positions still exist as to in what circumstances, and by whom, such a procedure should be activated.

According to Article 3(2) of the Draft Agreement, when an action has been brought against one or more member states of the EU, 'the Union may become a co-respondent to the proceedings in respect of an alleged violation notified by the Court if it appears that such allegation calls into question the compatibility with the Convention rights of a provision of EU law, notably where that violation

---

[22] *Ibid.*

[23] ECtHR, *Emilio Gasparini v. Italie et Belgique*, judgment of 12 May 2009.

[24] Cf. F. BENOÎT-ROHMER, 'Bienvenue aux enfants de Bosphorus: la Cour européenne des droits de l'homme et les organisations internationales' (2010) 81 *RTDH* 19, 23–4 and 26–7.

[25] Cf. A. POTTEAU, 'A propos d'un pis-aller: la responsabilité des Etats membres pour l'incompatibilité du droit de l'Union avec la Convention européenne des droits de l'homme' (2009) 4 *RTDE (Revue trimestrielle de droit européen)* 697, 706–7.

[26] CDDH, 'Study of Technical and Legal Issues of a Possible EC/EU Accession of the European Convention on Human Rights', DG-II(2002)006 (2003) 24 *HRLJ (Human Rights Law Journal)* 268, 273–4.

could have been avoided only by disregarding an obligation under European Union law'.[27]

The same Article 3 establishes, at para. 3, that member states can become co-respondents to proceedings brought against the EU. This is possible when a conflict is alleged between the ECHR and a provision of EU primary law, notably when the alleged breach of the ECHR could have been avoided only by disregarding this provision. In all probability, this hypothesis is liable to happen rarely, in situations similar to those of the *Matthews* case.[28]

Finally, according to draft Article 3(4), should a complaint be brought against both the EU and one or more member states, each of them can ask the Strasbourg Court that its status be changed from respondent to co-respondent if the conditions in paragraphs 2 or 3 are met. To grasp the rationale for this change of status one should consider that the activation of the CRM implies that different criteria must be used to assess the admissibility of claims and that the proceedings can be suspended to allow the ECJ to intervene in the case (see *infra*, Sections 2.2 and 2.3).

It is important to note that the CRM can be activated only on the basis of a request by the potential co-respondent. It is then for the Court to assess whether 'it is plausible that the conditions in paragraph 2 or paragraph 3 of [Article 3] are met'.[29] The co-respondent takes part in the proceedings alongside the respondent *as a party to the case* and not as an *amicus curiae* pursuant to Article 36(2) ECHR in the case of third party intervention.[30] Accordingly, it is bound by the judgment delivered at the end of the procedure.

Clearly enough, the co-respondent procedure presents several advantages from the perspective of the EU and of its member states. First of all, it allows the EU to express its views in proceedings where the interpretation of EU law is at stake and to ask the Grand Chamber to re-examine a decision unfavourable to it. Secondly, the procedure allows the ECtHR to exercise its functions without having to assess the internal distribution of competences in order to split the responsibility between the EU and the member state(s) concerned. In this regard, the Explanatory Report to the Draft Agreement states (para. 54) that, unless required by the respondent and the co-respondent(s), the ECtHR should

---

[27]   The adverb 'notably' indicates that the EU may also request to be joined to the proceedings in cases different from the one referred to as an example, for instance in cases calling into question the compatibility with the ECHR of a recommendation issued by the EU.

[28]   ECtHR, *Matthews v. United Kingdom*, judgment of 18 February 1999.

[29]   Draft Agreement, Article 3(5).

[30]   Absent any indication to the contrary in the accession agreement, in the event of distinct violations attributable to the EU and to a member state, post-accession it will remain possible to sue both of them as multiple respondents. In such a case, the admissibility of claims should be assessed separately, according to the usual criteria established by the Convention. An intervention of the EU in proceedings calling into question the interpretation of EU law brought against a member state, and *vice versa*, would continue to be possible in the quality of *amicus curiae*, as happened for instance in the *Bosphorus* case.

'ordinarily' establish responsibility *in solido*. Several authors have emphasized that the most important advantage of the CRM would be precisely that of relieving the ECtHR of distributing responsibility between the EU and its member states.[31] In any case, there would be sound policy reasons for further specification in the accession agreement of the Court's power to deviate from the rule of joint liability.[32]

After accession, the EU would have to establish an internal mechanism to solve problems connected with the implementation of the Strasbourg judgments, notably those establishing joint liability. In particular, EU law should establish who has to adopt the required measures of *restitutio in integrum* and how the just satisfaction to be paid to the victim has to be apportioned. It is premature to make predictions on the possible content of this mechanism.[33] In any case, a pivotal role will be played by the ECJ, which will be called upon to apportion responsibility among the EU and its member states when deciding infraction proceedings, actions for annulment or actions for failure to act, relating to the implementation of the ECtHR's decisions.[34]

2.1. EXCLUSION OF *INTERVENTION FORCÉE*

During the negotiation process, the possibility has been excluded of empowering the ECtHR to oblige the EU, or a state, to join the proceedings as a co-respondent. In this author's view, this circumstance can severely impair the effectiveness of the procedure. A better solution to serve the proper administration of justice would be providing the possibility of *intervention forcée*.[35] In other words, it would be advisable to empower the ECtHR to compel the EU, even against its own will, to participate as co-respondent in any proceeding calling into question the compatibility of EU law with the ECHR, at the request of the state against

---

[31] J.P. JACQUÉ, *supra* n. 3, p. 1016; O. DE SCHUTTER, 'L'adhésion de l'Union européenne à la Convention européenne des droits de l'homme: feuille de route de la négociation' (2010) 83 *RTDH* 535, 555.

[32] One may wonder whether such a power should possibly be attributed to the Court given that it will be called to evaluate compliance with its judgment under Articles 46, paras. 4 and 5 ECHR.

[33] Cf. O. DE SCHUTTER, *supra* n. 31, pp. 560–1.

[34] The introduction of a new procedure before the ECJ, through an amendment of the Treaties has been proposed by T. LOCK, 'EU Accession to the ECHR: Implications for Judicial Review in Strasbourg' (2010) 35 *ELR (European Law Review)* 777, 787. In my view, existing procedures before the ECJ would be sufficient after the adoption of an EU decision or regulation establishing the criteria for the implementation of the ECtHR's judgment by member states and the EU (legislative and administrative authorities).

[35] This solution has been proposed by O. DE SCHUTTER, *supra* n. 31, p. 556. Partially different is the position of Lock, who deems it appropriate to grant the respondent state the right to designate the EU as a co-respondent, but not to allow the ECtHR to compel the EU to join the proceedings (T. LOCK, 'Walking on a Tightrope: The Draft ECHR Accession Agreement and the Autonomy of the EU Legal Order' (2011) 48 *CMLR* 1025, 1045).

which the application was initially brought, or even at the Court's initiative. The Court should be also empowered to add member states as co-respondents even against their will, should a complaint be brought against the EU for violations that have their origin in EU primary law.

Two main objections have been voiced against *intervention forcée*. On the one hand, it has been contended that it would undermine the autonomy of the EU legal order, by making the ECtHR interpret EU law in order to establish whether a certain EU act afforded the sued state enough leeway to comply with the ECHR.[36] On the other hand, it has been argued that it would place an excessive burden on the applicants, forcing them to face two counterparts, in contrast to the equality of arms principle.[37] Both objections are not, in this author's view, well founded.

As far as the first objection is concerned, the point has been made that a determination by the Strasbourg Court that a state had no margin of discretion in implementing an EU act would be incompatible with the principle of the autonomy of the EU legal order. Indeed, the ECJ has consistently held it incompatible with the Treaties for the EC to conclude an international agreement which empowered an external judicial body to rule on the respective competences of the EU and its member states, as regards the matters governed by this agreement.[38] However, it seems that the situation is significantly different in the case of the ECHR, since accession to the Convention is mandated by the Article 6 TEU. This article may be interpreted as playing a permissive role, so as to allow EU participation in the Strasbourg judicial system, without the need to amend some EU primary law provisions that may be affected.[39] Apart from this observation, it is argued that the introduction of *intervention forcée* represents the better solution for preserving the autonomy of EU law.

---

[36] One author has even criticized the current formulation of Article 3, insofar as it entrusts the ECtHR with the duty to assess whether a certain state conduct is (at least *prima facie*) necessitated by EU law (or whether an alleged violation of the ECHR by the EU could have been avoided only by disregarding a provision of EU primary law), before granting permission to use the CRM (J.P. Jacqué, *supra* n. 3, p. 1015).

[37] According to one author, the applicants should be given a veto power (C. Ladenburger, 'Vers l'adhésion de l'Union européenne à la Convention européenne des droits de l'homme' (2011) 47 *RTDE* 25).

[38] Cf. Opinion 1/91, [1991] ECR I-6099, para. 34; Opinion 1/00, para. 16. On this case law see A. Potteau, 'Quelle adhésion de l'Union Européenne à la CEDH pour quel niveau de protection des droits et de l'autonomie de l'ordre juridique de l'UE?' (2011) 115 *RGDIP (Revue générale de droit international public)* 77, 105–10; M. Parish, 'International Courts and the European Legal Order' (2012) 23 *EJIL* 141.

[39] Article 2 of Protocol No. 8 requires that the agreement on accession 'ensure that accession of the Union shall not affect the competences of the Union or the powers of its institutions'. Nonetheless, this provision should be interpreted in keeping with its object and purpose, i.e. precluding only an extension of the competences and powers of the EU institutions *par rapport* to those of member states.

One should not forget that in situations where the CRM could apply, the possibility remains for an applicant to sue the EU, a member state, or both.[40] For instance, possibly because of a lack of knowledge of EU law, a plaintiff may sue a state which has adopted a measure infringing one of his rights, whose content is necessitated by an EU law provision leaving no discretion. Should the EU decide not to appear as a co-respondent, the ECtHR could not avoid going into a detailed analysis of EU law. Notably, the ECtHR would have to interpret EU law in order to establish whether the alleged violation of the Convention could have been avoided only by disregarding an obligation under EU law: according to the *Bosphorus* jurisprudence, this operation is necessary to establish whether the 'equivalent protection' doctrine applies.[41] In any case, the ECtHR would be called upon to inquire into the allocation of competences between the EU and its member states when deciding upon the measures of a general or individual character to be adopted by the responsible state. Something similar would happen under a *Matthews*-like scenario, if the member states did not ask to join the proceedings and the Court had to decide the admissibility of a complaint against the EU. The Court would be called upon to interpret EU primary law to evaluate whether the alleged violation of the ECHR had its origin in EU law, or whether the state which adopted a concrete measure acted in the exercise of its margin of discretion.[42] In all these situations, the *mise en oeuvre* of the CRM

---

[40] Some doubts may be raised concerning the possibility for an applicant to sue the EU as the sole respondent, alleging its responsibility for having issued an act on the basis of which a member state has adopted a concrete measure. According to the 'monetary gold' principle, an international tribunal should reject an application which would require determining the rights and obligations of a state not party to the proceedings (ICJ, *Monetary Gold Removed from Rome in 1943*, ICJ Reports 1954, p. 19). One may argue that, in a scenario like *Bosphorus*, an application lodged exclusively against the EU should be declared inadmissible, as it would require the Court first to establish whether a member state not party to the proceedings has violated the ECHR. It should be noted that, so far, the ECtHR has avoided considering the 'monetary gold' objection when it has been raised before it (in the *Banković* and *Behrami and Saramati* cases), declaring the applications inadmissible on different grounds. Most importantly, in the *Gasparini* decision (involving the question of the responsibility of member states for the conduct of an international organization) the Court clearly affirmed the possibility of deciding the merits of cases implying the prior assessment of the respect for fundamental human rights by an international organizations not party to the proceedings.

[41] There has been a lot of discussion as to whether this doctrine should be abandoned post-accession. However, the terms of the discussion have often been confused. If one believes that EU member states will continue to be responsible for breaches of the Convention exactly as they were before EU accession, one should conclude that the doctrine will not be affected by accession. Of course, this does not mean that it should be relied upon by the Court to exclude the EU's responsibility, which would introduce a totally unjustified privilege.

[42] It should not go unnoticed that, according to the voluntary approach of Draft Article 3(3), it would be up to each state to decide whether to join the proceedings as a co-respondent. The participation of only a group of member states would undermine the efficacy of the judgement issued in Strasbourg, the implementation of which required the amendment of the EU constituent instruments.

would allow the Court in Strasbourg to render a decision without having to engage in a thorough discussion of the internal division of responsibilities.

The second objection mentioned above is not devoid of interest, in that it arises from an often neglected perspective: the applicants' viewpoint.[43] However, it seems once again that, overall, the introduction of the CRM would rather favour the interests of the victims of breaches of obligations under the ECHR. In the event the mechanism is not activated, it would be extremely difficult for a victim to obtain the execution of a decision issued against a state, when the source of the violation lay in an EU act, in the implementation of which the state did not exercise a margin of discretion. On the other hand, it would be difficult for the EU institutions to abide by a judgment finding that a provision of primary law is in contrast with the European Convention, as any amendment to the Treaties would require an approval by all member states. Furthermore, the burden for the applicant deriving from the activation of the CRM is clearly overestimated, if one merely considers that a similar burden may stem from the participation of the EU (or interested member states) in proceedings as *amici curiae*.[44]

This leads us to make a step forward, by questioning the appropriateness of the conditions for triggering the co-respondent mechanism. This mechanism has been elaborated because, in situations such as those of the *Bosphorus* and *Matthews* cases, the joint participation of the EU and its member states in proceedings before the ECtHR is deemed useful. The aims pursued are to guarantee that all the interested parties have the opportunity to have their reasons heard, to avoid an inquiry by the Strasbourg Court into the apportionment of responsibility between the EU and its member states and, finally, to favour the enforcement of the judgments by binding all the parties in a position to remedy the ascertained violations. If this is true, the co-respondent mechanism should be devised so as also to be applicable in the event that the plaintiff sued the EU in a *Bosphorus*-like scenario,[45] or conversely one or more member states in a situation like *Matthews*. This is not possible under the strict triggering test outlined in the Draft Articles. A better model was unfortunately dropped during the *travaux préparatoires*. According to this model, '[i]n cases in which there seems to be a substantive link between the alleged violation and a provision of EU law, and in which the application is directed against one or more member State(s) of the European Union, but not against the European Union itself (or *vice versa*), the co-respondent mechanism would allow a High Contracting party which is substantively implicated by the application to join the proceedings as a full party'.[46]

---

[43] The opportunity of assessing the efficacy of all possible solutions on the basis of the needs of the applicants has been particularly emphasized by T. Lock, *supra* n. 35.

[44] Cf. Article 36(2) ECHR.

[45] Cf. G. Gaja, *supra*, n. 9, p. 191.

[46] CDDH-UE(2010)16, 2. See also CDDH-UE(2011)94, Article 4; an even broader formula had been proposed by the Italian delegation (CDDH-EU(2011)09, 5). The modification introduced in the Draft Articles has been rightly criticized by V. Petralia, *supra* n. 3, p. 308.

2.2. ADMISSIBILITY CRITERIA FOR APPLICATIONS

Some considerations are now needed concerning the admissibility of applications in cases where the CRM applies. One should preliminarily observe that, once the accession process is completed, the prior exhaustion of the local remedies rule will also apply when the respondent party is the EU. Judicial remedies accessible to the individual before the EU jurisdictions include: the action directed to obtain the annulment of an act of the EU whose illegitimacy is alleged (Article 263 TFEU); the action directed to obtain a reparation for extra-contractual liability of the EU (Articles 268 and 340 TFEU); the action for failure to act (Article 265 TFEU); petitioning the Tribunal of public function in the case of employment disputes; and petitioning the General Court on the basis of an arbitration clause in the case of contractual disputes (Article 272 TFEU).[47] According to Article 274 TFEU, disputes to which the EU is a party are not excluded from the competence of domestic courts. As a consequence, before suing the EU in Strasbourg in some cases an applicant may be asked to institute proceedings before competent domestic courts for contractual liability.

After accession, the Court will be faced with the difficult task of assessing which judicial remedies may be qualified as accessible to individuals, and capable of providing effective means of redress against EU measures. It should be added that disagreement persists on whether the preliminary reference procedure under Article 267 TFEU should be considered as a remedy to be exhausted.

With specific regard to the CRM, under the Draft Agreement a new Article 36, para. 4 would be added to the ECHR, establishing that the applications' admissibility must be assessed only in the light of the original application, 'without regard to the participation of a co-respondent in the proceedings'.[48] This solution is certainly intended to favour the applicants. It derogates from the rule under customary international law according to which, in cases where two subjects of international law are deemed jointly responsible in connection with a certain act, the admissibility of claims must be assessed separately, having regard to the local remedies offered in each domestic legal order.[49]

From a systematic point of view it seems questionable to extend the international control of the Court, in contrast to the subsidiarity principle underlying the judicial supervision mechanism put in place by the Convention. In this author's view, a preferable solution would be a minor adjustment concerning the application of the six month rule established by Article 35(1). In cases where a violation is alleged, deriving from a state measure carried out in

---

[47] Obviously, since an appeal from the decisions of the General Court lies with the ECJ, should an action before the court of first instance fulfill the requirements provided for by the prior exhaustion rule, an appeal should also be filed with the ECJ.

[48] Draft Agreement, Article 3, para. 1(b).

[49] Cf. R. PISILLO MAZZESCHI, *Esaurimento dei ricorsi interni e diritti umani*, Giappichelli, Torino 2004, p. 134.

the implementation of an EU act, it would be unreasonable to understand the six month rule as referring to the adoption of the EU 'final act'. The accession agreement may specify that, in cases where the EU is deemed responsible for an act that provides the legal basis of a state act or omission, an application should be filed within six months of the measure by means of which the state concerned has implemented the controversial EU act.[50]

2.3. PRIOR INVOLVEMENT OF THE ECJ

According to Article 3, para. 6 of the Draft Agreement, when the EU is a co-respondent in a proceeding and the ECJ has not previously had the opportunity to assess the compatibility of the controversial provision of EU law with human rights standards, the time needed is given to the ECJ in order to examine expeditiously the issue before the external review takes place.

The introduction of a mechanism intended to allow the ECJ to exercise its powers to examine the validity of an act of the EU, before any decision is rendered by the ECtHR, was advocated by the former judge of the Court in Luxembourg, Timmermans,[51] and later by the Presidents of the two Courts in a joint statement released in January 2011.[52] Once again, the involvement of ECJ is intended to avert the risk that the decisions of the ECtHR threaten the autonomy of EU law, or better the prerogatives of the ECJ.[53] It is worth noting that a similar involvement of the ECJ is not provided by the Draft Agreement for cases where the EU has been sued as a respondent.[54]

The Draft Agreement does not elaborate on how the ECJ would exercise this new power, leaving this issue to be resolved by EU law. The alternatives considered include the possibility of allowing the ECtHR to make a preliminary reference to the ECJ[55]; other authors have proposed allowing involvement by

---

[50] The same considerations apply, *mutatis mutandis*, to the scenario where an alleged violation of the ECHR has its sources in a provision of the EU Treaties.

[51] C. TIMMERMANS, speech during the hearing organized by the European Parliament's Committee on Constitutional Affairs, 18 March 2010, available at www.europarl.it, accessed 01.07.2012.

[52] Joint Communication of Judges Skouris and Costa, reproduced as Appendix III in CDDH-EU(2011)03. See also ECJ, *Discussion Document of the Court of Justice of the European Union on Certain Aspects of the Accession of the European Union to the European Convention for the Protection of Human Rights and Fundamental Freedoms*, 10 May 2010, points 11 and 12.

[53] A. POTTEAU, *supra* n. 38, p. 104.

[54] It should be noted in passing that, because of the limitations of the right of individuals to challenge EU acts, cases may quite easily be imagined in which an application in Strasbourg may call into question the compatibility of an EU provision with the ECHR, without the Court in Luxembourg having had the opportunity to rule on the issue.

[55] See European Commission, working document DS 1930/10, para. 5.

the ECJ through a sort of appeal for annulment sought by the European Commission.[56]

In my view, it seems difficult to find a basis in the Treaties for this new competence of the ECJ. This basis could not certainly be Article 263 TFEU, as it provides a short time limit for the impugnation of EU acts. Even Article 267 TFEU does not appear to offer *per se* an adequate legal basis. If it is not possible to qualify the ECtHR as an organ common to the member states, competent to make a reference to the ECJ under Article 267 TFEU, the ECJ has consistently held that an international agreement concluded by the Union may confer new judicial powers in the Court. However, this is possible only 'provided that in so doing [the agreement] does not change the essential character of the function of the Court as conceived in the EU and FEU Treaties'.[57] The ECJ has already held that the very nature and purpose of the preliminary reference would be distorted if the answers given by the Court were not binding upon the judge who requested the preliminary reference.[58] That would be precisely the effect of the ECJ's pronunciations towards the ECtHR.[59] In sum, it does not seem that Article 6 TEU, read in conjunction with Protocol No. 8,[60] could allow the introduction of the CRM without the amendment of the Treaties.[61]

Apart from this, it is argued that the introduction of this mechanism is not legally required, inappropriate or ineffective. As far as the first aspect is concerned, the mistaken assumption is made that the lack of a prior involvement of the ECJ would adversely affect its exclusive task of reviewing the legality of EU acts.[62] The ECtHR has no jurisdiction to interpret in a binding way the domestic law of the Contracting Parties – which, from its perspective, comes into consideration as a mere fact – nor is the Court competent to annul an EU act.[63] The ECtHR would be allowed to indirectly assess the compatibility of an EU act

---

[56]   C. Timmermans, *supra* n. 51; T. Lock, *supra* n. 35, pp. 1049–53.

[57]   Opinion 1/09, 08.03.2011, para. 75; see also Opinion 1/92, I-2843, para. 32.

[58]   Cf. Opinion 1/91, *supra* n. 38, para. 61.

[59]   Cf. CDDH-UE(2011)16fin, 19 July 2011, *Draft Explanatory Report*, para. 60.

[60]   See *supra* n. 39.

[61]   A Treaty amendment is deemed necessary by G. Gaja, *supra* n. 9, p. 194. Conforti agrees that the Draft Agreement introduces a new competence for the ECJ. However, he believes that the agreement may modify every provision of the Lisbon Treaty, without any need to amend the TFEU according to the procedure *ex* Article 48 TEU (Conforti, 'L'adhésion de l'Union Européenne à la Convention Européenne des Droits de l'Homme', available at www.sidi-isil. org/wp-content/uploads/2010/02/Conforti-Ladh%C3%A9sion-de-lUE-%C3%A0-la-CEDH. pdf, accessed 01.10.2012).

[62]   See accordingly S. Douglas-Scott, *supra* n. 3, p. 663; A. Potteau, *supra* n. 38, pp. 101–3; O. Quirico, 'Substantive and Procedural Issues Raised by the Accession of the EU to the ECHR' (2010) 20 *IYIL (Italian Yearbook of International Law)* 31, 47.

[63]   As rightly observed by Group II of the Convention on the Future of Europe on Incorporation of the Charter Accession to the ECHR, 'the principle of autonomy does not place any legal obstacle to the accession by the Union to the ECHR', as 'the Court of Justice would remain the sole supreme arbiter of questions of Union law and of the validity of Union acts' (doc. CONV 354/02, 22.10.2002).

with the ECHR, exactly as it can do regarding domestic law. After said assessment, it would remain up to the ECJ to eventually draw conclusions from the judgment issued in Strasbourg, for instance when subsequently requested by a domestic court to give a preliminary ruling on the interpretation or validity of the controversial EU act.

Moreover, the introduction of the mechanism would set up a double standard, putting the EU in a privileged position compared to that of the other contracting parties.[64] No similar mechanism is envisaged to guarantee to the highest domestic courts the opportunity to provide a ruling on the interpretation or constitutionality of a domestic statute (and indirectly its conformity with the ECHR), whose application has given rise to an alleged violation of the Convention, before the ECtHR carries out its external review.

In addition to further extending the length of the proceedings before the ECtHR, the envisaged mechanism is not likely to produce effective results. It should not go unnoticed that the legal consequences of the ECJ's pronouncements in this new procedure remain unclear.[65] In any case, it may be safely concluded that a ruling by the ECJ – in which the controversial EU act is interpreted consistently with the ECHR or declared invalid – would provide no reasonable prospect of removing the violation. In fact, the ECJ could only adjudicate on the legal basis for the state act (or omission) causing the violation alleged by the applicant in Strasbourg. The person claiming to be a victim of a violation of the ECHR may find it difficult to have his position reinstated by resorting to domestic courts, because the withdrawal of the state measure on the basis of the alleged violation would generally collide with the *res judicata* principle.[66] As a consequence, the special procedural means for the prior involvement of the ECJ would not generally render the application inadmissible for the loss of victim status.[67]

A simpler alternative to the proposed procedure would be, in the author's view, a modification of Article 35 ECHR. A new paragraph should clarify that the request for a reference to the ECJ constitutes a requisite for the admissibility of claims. Whilst doubts persist concerning the application of the prior exhaustion of remedies rule to the EU under customary international law, such doubts could be solved by an amendment to the Convention. Except for some pathological cases – constituting a violation of Article 6 ECHR by the state court omitting to

---

[64]   A. POTTEAU, *supra* n. 38, p. 105.

[65]   Cf. N. O'MEARA, "A More Secure Europe of Rights?' The European Court of Human Rights, the Court of Justice of the European Union and EU Accession to the ECHR' (2011) 12 *German Law Journal* 1813, 1824–5; V. PETRALIA, *supra* n. 3, p. 320.

[66]   This problem is hinted at by J.P. JACQUÉ, *supra* n. 3, p. 1022.

[67]   *A fortiori*, this would be evident should the Court decide to differ the effects of its decision for reasons of legal certainty. As is known, this possibility is envisaged by Article 264 TFEU (concerning the action directed to obtain the annulment of an act) and has been extended, in the ECJ's case law, to the preliminary reference procedure.

make the preliminary reference[68] – a prior ruling by the ECJ would thus be guaranteed. This line of argument has been endorsed in the doctrine[69] and, during the negotiation process, put forward in a proposal by the Italian delegation.[70] According to Italy, the accession agreement should specify that '[w]hen the applicant has no right of direct access to the European bodies, but only to the domestic bodies of the Member States, the applicant shall exhaust all domestic remedies, including a request for preliminary referral to the Court of Justice of the European Union'. Unfortunately, in the end, the opposite view has (so far) prevailed. Thus, according to the Explanatory Report to the Draft Agreement, the preliminary reference procedure 'cannot be considered as a legal remedy that an applicant must exhaust before making an application to the Court'.[71]

3. CONCLUSION

A complete assessment of the co-respondent mechanism will be possible only after the adoption of the final text of the Accession Agreement and of the internal rules adopted by the EU to implement it. As of now, it may be emphasised that the planned mechanism raises several difficulties and risks giving rise to more problems than it will solve.

Quite regrettably, the Draft Agreement establishes a very strict test for triggering the co-respondent mechanism and precludes the Court in Strasbourg from adding, *proprio motu*, the EU or its member states as co-respondents. Paradoxically, for the reasons we have discussed above, the procedure may, as a consequence, turn out to be incapable of pursuing one of the main aims it was developed for, i.e. guaranteeing the autonomy of the EU legal order. Many problems are also raised by the envisaged procedure to guarantee a prior involvement of the ECJ before a decision is rendered in Strasbourg. A simpler alternative would be represented by a modification of Article 35 ECHR, specifying that a request for preliminary referral to the ECJ constitutes a remedy to be pursued in domestic courts, before suing the EU in Strasbourg.

---

[68] Cf. *Ullens de Schoote et Rezabek v. Belgium*, judgment of 20 September 2011, paras. 52–67. See also M. Broberg and N. Fenger, *Preliminary References to the European Court of Justice*, Oxford University Press, Oxford 2010, pp. 271–2.

[69] O. De Schutter, *supra* n. 31, p. 566; Meijers Committee, Doc. CM1105 (23 May 2011), www.commissie-meijers.nl, accessed 02.05.2012.

[70] *Supra* n. 46, p. 5.

[71] *Supra* n. 59, para. 57.

CONCLUDING REMARKS

THE CONSTITUTIONAL RELEVANCE OF THE ECHR IN DOMESTIC AND EUROPEAN LAW
General Assessments

Cesare PINELLI

1. 'CONSTITUTIONAL JUSTICE' WITH REFERENCE TO THE STRASBOURG COURT: A PRELIMINARY ASSESSMENT

The constitutional relevance of the ECHR in domestic and European law due to the Strasbourg Court's influence is increasingly admitted by scholars, although its significance is far from being settled. The fact that, in the current literature on the ECtHR's evolution, 'constitutional justice' is opposed to both 'individual' and 'international justice' suffices to demonstrate how scarce is the agreement on the meaning of 'constitutional'.

The 'individual'/'constitutional' dichotomy refers to the opposition between a casuistic method, with a view to providing sufficient answers to all disputes, and a principled approach, centred on cases raising substantial or new and complex issues of human rights law.[1] The ECtHR's shift from individual relief to general development, and therefore to 'constitutional justice', is associated with its reliance on leading judgments, whose standards or principles are likely to relieve the Court of its heavy backlog.[2] Here, the 'constitutional justice' formula outlines a trend emerging from the ECtHR's case law that relies more on internal concern than on the Court's relationship with national courts, and depends on functional, rather than on normative, reasons.

---

[1] See *inter alia* J. CHRISTOFFERSEN, 'Individual and Constitutional Justice: Can the Power Balance of Adjudication be Reversed?' in J. CHRISTOFFERSEN and M. RASK MADSEN (eds.), *The European Court of Human Rights between Law and Politics*, Oxford University Press, Oxford 2011, pp. 181 ff., and L.R. HELFER, 'Redesigning the European Court of Human Rights: Embeddedness as a Deep Structural Principle of the European Rights Regime' (2008) 19 *EJIL* 127 ff.

[2] J. CHRISTOFFERSEN, *supra* n. 1, p. 183.

The 'international'/'constitutional' divide refers instead to the question of whether the ECtHR's role corresponds to that of an international court as provided in the ECHR, or appears closer to that of a constitutional court as understood in national contexts. Here, a shift towards the latter is likely to be noted as well. While in 1978 the Strasbourg Court admitted that, unlike international treaties of the classic kind, the Convention 'creates, over and above a network of mutual, bilateral undertakings, objective obligations which, in the words of the Preamble, benefit from a collective enforcement',[3] in 1995 it added that the ECHR's 'special character' consisted of being 'an instrument of European public order for the protection of individual human beings', and that, according to Article 19, its own mission was 'to ensure the observance of the engagements undertaken by the High Contracting Parties'.[4] The mission of maintaining a 'European public order' for the protection of individuals revealed a constitutional character that was immediately appreciated by scholars, arguing that the ECtHR had transformed itself into a regional constitutional court.[5]

This meaning of 'constitutional' differs from the previous one on at least three grounds. First, it might co-exist with a casuistic method, whereas 'international justice' might be driven by a principled approach. Second, while the shift from 'individual' to 'constitutional' justice has primarily to do with an issue, such as the backlog, arising within the ECtHR's activity, that from 'international' to 'constitutional' justice directly involves the ECtHR's relationship with national authorities, and with constitutional courts in particular. Lastly, such a relationship poses normative, rather than functional, issues, including that of whether constitutionalism ought to be after out of the old state setting.[6]

In the following pages, as well as in the other essays in this volume, the constitutional character of the ECtHR's case law is intended in the latter meaning, to the extent that it sheds light on the ECHR's relevance in domestic and European law.

On the other hand, this relevance needs to be ascertained through analysis of the different ways in which national legal systems react to the exigencies of the ECHR.[7] In this respect, one should resist the temptation 'to conceive of these issues in a reductionist-linear fashion, with national courts going from a 'conservative' and 'sovereignty-based' position to one of openness towards

---

3   ECtHR, *Ireland v. United Kingdom* (1978), para. 239.

4   ECtHR, *Loizidou v. Turkey* (1995), para. 93.

5   e.g. E.A. ALKEMA, 'The European Convention as a Constitution and its Court as a Constitutional Court' in P. MAHONEY et al. (eds.), *Protecting Human Rights: The European Perspective. Studies in Memory of Rolv Ryssdal*, Carl Heymanns, Cologne 2000, p. 41.

6   For an important account see recently N. WALKER, 'Beyond the Holistic Constitution?' in P. DOBNER and M. LOUGHLIN (eds.), *The Twilight of Constitutionalism?*, Oxford University Press, Oxford 2010, pp. 291 ff.

7   See e.g. G. MARTINICO and O. POLLICINO (eds.), *The National Judicial Treatment of the ECHR and the EU Laws. A Comparative Constitutional Perspective*, Europa Law, Groningen 2010.

Strasbourg and the dynamics of the ECHR system'.[8] Such a fashion does not only risk neglecting the deep structural differences that might occur in constitutional comparison,[9] it also removes both the sense of the ECtHR's aforementioned evolution and the problems that it engenders. A caveat of this sort appears particularly necessary with respect to those national contexts, including the Italian one, in which a narrative has widely developed that the influence of the ECtHR's case law is distancing the Constitutional Court from 'formalism'.

2. TWO VERSIONS OF 'FORMALISM'

Two versions of 'formalism' should be distinguished for the sake of our inquiry: formalism as conceptualism, or *Begriffsjurisprudenz*, and formalism as allegiance to rules even at the expense of principles.

The former, rooted in the positivistic scholarly tradition of continental Europe's countries, reflected the ideological claim of the absolute power of the State over citizens ('internal sovereignty') and of its unconditioned will *vis-à-vis* that of the other States ('external sovereignty' or independence). International law was involved in that conception no less than constitutional law, both being conceived as instruments of the State's will, and at the same time reciprocally connected as the two faces of Janus. These covered under the veil of 'objective law', and thus legitimated, any decision by public officers, irrespective of infringements of the individual's rights, and of the threats to peace and international security, that it might entail.

Such a conception of the law was discredited for its formalism, and definitively supplanted by that encapsulated in the constitutions of post-totalitarian democracies. These were not simply superimposed on the other sources of law as the highest expression of the State's will: in that case, the system would be changed only on formal grounds, and confirmed in its abstractedness, with the effect of leaving the ultimate ends of the national community at the disposal of the State, the omnipotent sovereign of the continental tradition. In post-totalitarian democracies, on the contrary, any subject, including the State, is prevented from determining the community's ultimate ends. These ends correspond to substantive principles enshrined in the Constitution, and are intended to endure irrespective of the contingent actions of public powers, including the political decisions of the majorities in a given legislature. Public powers are rather asked to protect or to promote these principles, according to

---

[8] E. BJORGE, 'National supreme courts and the development of ECHR rights' (2011) 9 *Int'l J. Const. Law* 7.

[9] E. BJORGE, *supra* n. 8, p. 7.

whether prevalence is given to the rule of law or to democracy, namely the negative or the positive side of constitutionalism.[10]

On the other hand, both the 'openness' to international law provided in the European Constitutions, and international agreements such as the UN Treaty, the Universal Declaration of Human Rights, and the ECHR, were grounded on the idea of limited sovereignty. While confirming the sovereignty of States over the respective territories, such agreements imposed on them the burden of maintaining peace and respect for human rights. The international/ constitutional law divide, that the formalist view tended to exacerbate, was thus substantially re-defined with a view to ensuring the common pursuit of these fundamental values. A *telos*, rather than their own free will, would orient the reciprocal States' behaviour, and lay the foundations for an international community composed of individuals and international organisations together with States.

Accordingly, both constitutional adjudication and the new international human rights adjudication issued with the ECHR reflected the aim of ensuring the primacy of the respective charters over the States' sovereignty. The former corresponded to a sophisticated version of the rule of law, overriding the myth of parliamentary sovereignty: while remaining at the centre of democratic life, Parliament was no longer conceived of as the exclusive, or even the highest, institution capable of granting fundamental rights. On the contrary, these should bind not only administrative bodies and the judiciary, but also the representative assemblies. The same occurred under the ECHR. Although its original design did not yet provide compulsory jurisdiction and individual petition, the sole hypothesis of adjudicating human rights internationally posed a fundamental challenge not just to the Westphalian tradition, but to liberal ideas of direct democratic legitimacy and self-determination.[11]

However, after the demise of the State's absolute sovereignty, a weaker version of formalism could survive, resulting from judicial deference towards the popularly elected authorities' will as legally enacted. While restricting themselves to interpreting the scope of legal texts, constitutional courts as well as the ECtHR would content themselves with giving the correct meaning of objective law, thus maintaining a deferent attitude towards, respectively, the legislature and the High Contracting Parties. This version of formalism corresponded partly to the fact that, in the original intent of the framers of most European post-totalitarian constitutions, the notion was seldom acquired that constitutional courts were primarily called to ensure the effective protection of human rights.

---

[10]   C. PINELLI, 'The Combination of Negative with Positive Constitutionalism in Europe. The Quest of a "Just Distance" Between Citizens and the Public Power' (2011) 13 *European Journal of Law Reform* 37.

[11]   A. MORAVCSIK, 'The Origin of Human Rights Regimes: Democratic Delegation in Postwar Europe' (2000) 54 *International Organisation* 218.

3. THE PARALLEL EVOLUTION OF THE STRASBOURG COURT AND THE CONSTITUTIONAL COURTS

In Germany, where the formal conception of *Rechtstaat* had been discredited since the Nazi regime, and supplanted by the longing for a substantive conception of legality, access before the *Bundesverfassungsgericht* was given to the individuals, and the pervasive influence of fundamental rights further reduced the practical significance of the principle of *Rechtstaat* as a separate legal concept. Elements such as the requirement of legal certainty, or the ban on retroactive legislation, were closely linked to the effective protection of fundamental rights, helping to secure a stable legal environment where these rights could be enjoyed in security.[12]

Constitutional courts were elsewhere called to exert functions differing from those provided for in the German system. In particular, the establishment of the *Conseil Constitutionnel* under the 1958 French Constitution was not intended to remove the 1789 tradition, according to which judges had no right to set aside the legislative will of parliament. The main original function of the *Conseil* consisted simply of ascertaining whether statutory law exceeded the bounds reserved to Parliament by Article 34, thus encroaching on the governmental power of regulation. The judicial features of the *Conseil* emerged rather from the development of its jurisprudence after a creative decision of 1971 on freedom of association, followed by constitutional reforms that gradually enlarged the possibility of protecting fundamental rights before that court.

In turn, the provisions concerning the Italian Constitutional Court were close to the Kelsenian model, which was grounded in 'objective legality', although totally different from the kind of formalism affecting the conception of the absolute sovereignty of the State. The fact that, contrary to the German and, later on, to the Spanish system, access before the Court was denied to individuals and reserved to ordinary judges whenever they doubted the law's compatibility with the Constitution, demonstrates *inter alia* that constitutional adjudication was meant to submit the legislation to a superior legal order. According to these provisions, the Court was therefore, and still is, in the condition of protecting fundamental rights only indirectly, namely through constitutional review of statute law. Nevertheless, the Court soon left aside the Kelsenian premises of the model, proving that its paramount function lay in protecting these rights.[13]

---

[12]   R. GROOTE, 'Rule of Law, Rechtstaat and État de droit', in C. STARCK (ed.), *Constitutionalism, Universalism and Democracy – a comparative analysis. The German Contributions to the Fifth World Congress of the International Association of Constitutional Law*, Nomos, Baden-Baden 1999, pp. 289–290.

[13]   A. PIZZORUSSO, 'Constitutional Review and Legislation in Italy', in C. LANDFRIED (ed.), *Constitutional Review and Legislation*, Nomos, Baden-Baden 1988, pp. 109 ff.

The question should thus be posed of how the Italian Court, the *Conseil Constitutionnel*, as well as other European courts, succeeded in shifting their mission from the quest for objective legality to that of ensuring citizens' fundamental rights, sometimes greatly enhancing the reforms that provided the institutional devices that were necessary for that end. Their success was essentially achieved through constitutional interpretation. While leaving aside criteria such as the literal rule and the original intent of the framers, these courts emancipated themselves from deference towards the legislature, relying rather on the teleological or the systematic method, which corresponded to a greater extent to the scope of making the protection of the individual effective. Standards of reasonableness, tests of proportionality and constitutional balancing were accordingly adopted in scrutinizing statutes.[14]

The Strasbourg Court was meanwhile undergoing a fairly similar evolution. This concerned both the methods of interpretation,[15] and the attempts to reduce the weight of the international features affecting the adjudication system, namely the optional character of the Commission's competence to deal with individual applications, and the optional nature of the Court's jurisdiction. These attitudes laid the groundwork for the approval, on 11 May 1994, of Protocol No. 11 of the ECHR, which not only substituted the two pre-existing organs, the European Commission and the ECtHR, with one permanent court, but added that the ECtHR may receive applications from any person, NGO or group of individuals claiming to be the victim by one of the High Contracting Parties of the rights set in force in the Convention or the Protocols thereto (Article 34). For the purposes of this inquiry, it should be stressed that Protocol No. 11 enhanced the Court's role not by superimposing a reform of the control machinery, but by reflecting the perspective of its enduring case law, founded on the complainer's guarantees.

Efforts were thus made in parallel by national courts and by the ECtHR to leave aside the residual sovereignty features affecting the original institutional design, respectively founded on the quest for objective law and on the tradition of international adjudication, to the extent that these were incompatible with the constitutional aim of ensuring effective protection of fundamental or human rights.

---

14   A. VON BRUNNECK, 'Constitutional Review and Legislation in Western Democracies', in C. LANDFRIED (ed.), *supra* n. 13, p. 251.

15   F. MATSCHER, 'Methods of Interpretation of the Convention', in R. ST. J. MACDONALD, F. MATSCHER and H. PETZOLD (eds.), *The European System for the Protection of Human Rights*, Martinus Nijhoff, Dordrecht 1993, p. 68.

4. IS THE ECtHR CHALLENGING THE NATIONAL SYSTEMS OF CONSTITUTIONAL ADJUDICATION?

The elements reported above suffice to deny the assumption that national courts are moving, or perhaps should further move, from a position of defence of the State's sovereignty to openness towards Strasbourg. The idea of a one-sided movement of the former towards the immovable seat whence adjudication on human rights is dispensed throughout Europe misconceives the parallel engagement of national courts and the ECtHR in enfranchising themselves from deference towards the legislature and/or from the residual legacy of the State's sovereignty. Nor could national courts be reproached for limited openness towards non-national law in general, given their longstanding intense interactions with the Luxembourg Court.

In what sense, then, are we able to describe the evolution of the constitutional courts' rulings on fundamental rights in terms of a progressive, but perhaps still too restrained, acceptance of the ECtHR's case law? Is there still something, on a national scale, that impedes a true dialogical attitude towards Strasbourg? Or should we rather admit that that relationship already consists of a process of mutual influence?

While answering these questions, we should first take account of the diverse systems of constitutional adjudication. When coping with the ECtHR's case law, those that grant direct access to the Court for the protection of fundamental rights, such as the German or the Spanish, appear prima facie better equipped, both in technical and in cultural terms, than those the deny such a possibility. Caution is thus needed whenever the former are compared with the latter with respect to the related attitudes of the Courts towards Strasbourg. However, we might already be convinced of the structural inadequacy in dealing with the ECtHR's case law of the systems that make the protection of fundamental rights conditional upon the legislation's scrutiny. The very system of constitutional adjudication should then be deemed an obstacle, grounded on the State's sovereignty, barring the possibilities of a true dialogue with Strasbourg. The suggestion may follow of overriding it by judicial means.

The issue is not merely hypothetical: it lies at the core of the controversy arising from the Italian Constitutional Court's rulings on the ECHR, which I will discuss given its implications for other continental European systems of constitutional adjudication.

Before 2007, the Court held firmly that the ECHR was to be treated as ordinary law in spite of its content and spirit, with the consequence that the Strasbourg case law was scarcely significant in the scrutinies concerning fundamental rights. In the meantime, however, Strasbourg's growing influence on the case law of national judges, including the Italian ordinary courts, led them to set aside the laws whenever they were deemed to counter the ECHR. This gave rise to a circuit connecting together such courts with the ECtHR, from which the Constitutional Court was correspondingly insulated. This situation was likely to weaken the Court's role in the very field of fundamental rights on which, as we have seen, it had established its core mission.

So far, the Court's overruling (decisions no. 348 and no. 349 of 2007) should be viewed as a reaction against such a threat. It relied on the construction of the ECHR as 'interposed norm' between the law and the Constitution, integrating the constitutional parameter in the scrutinies over the law, with the effect that ordinary judges were urged to put before the Constitutional Court any question concerning the law's conformity with the ECHR. This objective has been achieved. Since 2007, ordinary judges have indeed complied with those decisions,[16] and the Court's rulings concerning fundamental rights regularly deal with, and are sometimes heavily conditioned by, the Strasbourg case law. The Court has thus maintained its core mission, but not without significantly changing the approach to it.

In spite of its acceptance by judges, the Court's solution met scholarly criticism on the grounds that the construction of the ECHR as an 'interposed norm' revealed a formalistic approach to human rights issues, being grounded on a theoretical account of the sources of law. However, the connection between the 'interposed norm' category and the sources of law theory is rather doubtful, since the cases falling within the former do not always, or necessarily, correspond to the scenario of sources of law acquiring an intermediate rank between the Constitution and ordinary legislation.[17] Rather than a dogmatic figure, such a category is a judicial doctrine set out for practical reasons.[18]

Apart from this specific aspect of the Italian constitutional experience, criticism of the Court's solution might claim that the ECtHR's treatment of human rights issues is likely to challenge the adequacy of any system of constitutional adjudication based on review over the legislation in force, and, therefore, to ensure only indirectly the protection of fundamental rights. Such a claim rests on the premise that ordinary judges are better equipped than the Court to deal directly with the ECHR by disregarding national laws that conflict with the Strasbourg case law, and looks to the evolution of the national courts/

---

[16]   The few exceptions enumerated by G. MARTINICO, 'Is the European Convention Going to be 'Supreme'? A Comparative-Constitutional Overview of ECHR and EU Law before National Courts' (2012) 23 *EJIL* 415, are likely to confirm that ordinary courts tend on the whole to comply with the Constitutional Court's rulings.

[17]   See M. SICLARI, *Le "norme interposte" nel giudizio di costituzionalità*, Cedam, Padova 1992, pp. 141 ff.

[18]   It concerns cases in which the Constitution entrusts the legislature with the task of establishing principles and standards binding on the government, the regions or other institutions that are in turn constitutionally able to legislate. These correspond to an interposed parameter integrating the Constitution for the sake of the Court's scrutiny over the legislation, and result in fact in their pivotal benchmark exactly as in the ECHR's case law.

ECtHR relationship as if the former should 'go' towards the latter, conceived of as 'Supreme'.[19]

This account appears at least disputed. Other scholars note that, while '[c]onstitutional courts have a consistent track record of taking Strasbourg case law seriously', the opposite is true for lower tribunals,[20] and argue that the ECtHR's jurisprudence follows a trajectory analogous to that of the Italian Constitutional Court in the past decades, with a view to embedding itself more firmly in the national legal systems.[21] A research work concerning the UK Supreme Court, the *Conseil d'État* and the German Federal Constitutional Court confirms that these 'do in fact play an active role in the development of the Convention by way of expanding rights, each one of them in their own way and as a function of national legal jurisprudence', and adds that the Strasbourg Court 'in no way conceives of evolutive interpretation as its prerogative', looking 'at the development of rights by central European courts, and not only in "present day conditions" headcounts'.[22] The same can be said of the 'growing awareness of the principled interaction between domestic and European law',[23] for which the Italian Constitutional Court's 2007 decisions paved the way in its relationships with the ECtHR.

These developments demonstrate that the dynamics actually affecting the ECHR's constitutional relevance in domestic and European law are not one-sided, nor do they challenge the very structure of constitutional adjudication as provided in some countries; lastly, they have little to do with a simple investment in the ECtHR's supremacy. Rather, a mutual influence is emerging between the Strasbourg Court and national judges, fairly corresponding to what twenty years ago was predicted as 'a form of ordered pluralism', namely 'a Europe/States relationship which is neither reduced to the primacy of European norm over national rules, nor broken down in a juxtaposed collection of national and European norms which do not form a unitary system'.[24] In the same vein, the metaphor of 'Europe's constitutional mosaic', also including EU developments,[25] has recently been drawn. It is a kind of pluralism that is not merely compatible with, but stems from, the premises of constitutionalism, and, to that extent, contributes towards demonstrating that the latter is conceivable out of the old state setting.

---

[19] See *inter alia* G. MARTINICO, *supra* n. 16, pp. 422 ff.

[20] L.R. HELFER, *supra* n. 1, p. 137.

[21] L.R. HELFER, *supra* n. 1, p. 141.

[22] E. BJORGE, *supra* n. 8, p. 30.

[23] See G. REPETTO, 'Rethinking a Constitutional Role for the ECHR. The Dilemmas of Incorporation into Italian Domestic Law', in this *Volume*.

[24] M. DELMAS-MARTY, 'The Richness of Underlying Legal Reasoning', in EAD. (ed.), *The European Convention for the Protection of Human Rights: International Protection Versus National Restrictions*, Martinus Nijhoff, Dordrecht 1992, p. 321.

[25] See N. WALKER, J. SHAW and S. TIERNEY (eds.), *Europe's Constitutional Mosaic*, Hart, Oxford/Portland 2011.

It is true that, in European constitutional scholarship, this position remains controversial. It differs not only from that which still relies on the co-essential reciprocal connection between constitutionalism and the state, but also from precisely the opposite claim, echoing post-modernity motives, that the dawn of legal pluralism amounts to the twilight not just of the myth of sovereignty, but of statehood as such. Both these positions fail, however, to capture the sense of the evolution affecting the ECHR's system no less than national constitutional orders in the past decades, thus misconceiving their perspectives.

The question should rather be how ordered the 'ordered pluralism' is, or how it addresses its inner tensions. Questions are involved here that are both factual and normative. An account will given of the most relevant, with a view to affording a tentative approach to the issue.

5. HOW ORDERED IS 'ORDERED PLURALISM'? A TENTATIVE APPROACH

While treating the ECHR's issues, we should first be aware of the 'legal geography' with which they are deeply connected on various grounds. Western European scholars frequently forget that such Member States as Russia and Turkey also adhere to the Convention, and that they raise serious compliance problems for the ECHR, in turn raising rule of law concerns.[26] A striking example arises from the cases of human rights abuses by military and police officials in the Kurdish region and in Chechnya, in which governments failed to investigate alleged human rights abuses or to provide a judicial forum for applicants to substantiate their claims. Since respect for the subsidiarity principle would have in these cases paralyzed its action, the ECtHR decided to disregard it, with the effect of functioning as a first-instance tribunal.[27] Being restricted to situations of evident governmental inertia, if not complicity with gross human rights violations, this exception to the subsidiarity principle should not be taken as a threat to the regular functioning of the ECHR's adjudication system. It serves rather as a caveat, demonstrating that significant asymmetries might be related to the 'legal geography' factor.

On the other hand, such a factor is likely to have played a role in the activist trend affecting the ECtHR's case law in the last decade, with the accession to the ECHR of Eastern and Central European States. Their weak concern for national identity in the field of human rights might have paved the way for a reduction of

---

[26]   S. DOUGLAS-SCOTT, 'Europe's Constitutional Mosaic: Human Rights in the European Legal Space – Utopia, Dystopia, Monotopia or Polytopia?', in N. WALKER, J. SHAW and S. TIERNEY (eds.), *supra* n. 25, pp. 99 ff.
[27]   L.R. HELFER, *supra* n. 1, pp. 143–4.

the margin of appreciation by the Strasbourg Court, together with the assertion of a more pronounced constitutional and centralized role.[28]

'Legal geography' appears prima facie as a matter of fact, although corresponding to tensions that the ECtHR is called to handle on normative grounds. A further factor of tension reveals instead immediately normative features, pertaining to the relationship between the principles on which the ECHR is grounded and their institutional realization. As already mentioned, the ECtHR case law's evolution is marked by the refusal of a blanket deference towards the legislature, with a view to ensuring an effective protection of human rights as conventionally provided for. However, here lies the greatest constitutional challenge: that of 'how responsibility for rights protection and the democratic pursuit of the public interest can be distributed between judicial and non-judicial institutions, each acting in accordance with the rule of law'.[29] Such a challenge is greater than that concerning the distribution of competence between national institutions and the ECtHR, 'because the function of national non-judicial bodies is different under the Convention from that of both national courts and the European Court of Human Rights, which together share similar, though not identical, responsibilities'.[30]

While a structural tension between rights protection and the democratic pursuit of the public interest does inhere to constitutional democracies, the more the Strasbourg Court's constitutional relevance emerges, the more the question of how and to what extent such tension might affect the ECHR's system comes to the fore. Rather than a domestic analogy, what is at stake here is whether and how an 'ordered pluralism' is likely to consolidate.

6. EXAMPLES FROM THE STRASBOURG CASE LAW

The issue should deserve attention on various grounds, among which the ECtHR's increasing deliberate activism might particularly be taken into account.

In *Costa and Pavan v. Italy,*[31] the Court dealt with the prohibition of pre-implantation genetic diagnoses (PGD) as provided in the Italian law no. 40/2004, a masterly example of how a parliament should not behave in regulating artificial reproductive techniques. The law had already been partly struck down by the Constitutional Court, and the unreasonableness of the PGD's prohibition as such was widely held among scholars and the public opinion at large. The ECtHR

---

[28]   On this, see O. POLLICINO, 'Toward a Convergence between the EU and the ECHR Legal Systems? A Comparative Perspective', in this *Volume.*

[29]   S. GREER, *The European Convention on Human Rights. Achievements, Problems and Prospects,* Cambridge University Press, Cambridge 2006, p. 196.

[30]   S. GREER, *supra* n. 29, p. 196.

[31]   ECtHR, *Costa and Pavan v. Italy* (2012).

preferred instead to argue that Parliament had not been consistent in prohibiting PGD while tolerating therapeutic abortion (para. 71).

Although a proportionality test was likely to lead to the conclusion of declaring the provision incompatible with the principles enshrined in the ECHR, departing from human dignity, the Court embarked for a far more perilous approach: that of examining the abstract consistency between various provisions of domestic law which separately are not contrary to the Convention. What about its well-established case law, according to which 'it is not the role of the Convention institutions to examine *in abstracto* the compatibility of national legislative or constitutional provisions with the requirements of the Convention'?[32]

Such a question should *a fortiori* be posed on the ground that the ECtHR judged the application admissible although the applicants did not submit the case to the domestic courts, thus attempting directly and abstractly to question the law itself. While rejecting the exception of inadmissibility laid down by the Italian government on the ground that some domestic courts had recognized the rights of the applicants in similar cases, the Court held that these rulings did not amount to a case law. The Court here left aside the subsidiarity principle not because of a compelling 'state of necessity' such as that emerging in the Kurdish region and in Chechnya, but simply because of the alleged absence of a case law. Does it suffice to disregard what, in the opinion of a former President of the Court, is 'probably the most important of the principles underlying the Convention'?[33] And, most importantly, to the extent that '[t]he Court may only deal with the matter after all domestic remedies have been exhausted, *according to the generally recognised rules of international law*, and within a period of six months from the date on which the final decision was taken' (Article 35, para. 1, ECHR), should scholars congratulate the Court on having taken a step forward in the process of going from an 'international' to a 'constitutional' figure, or should they ask themselves whether it enhances the reasons of an 'ordered pluralism'?

A further example is provided by *Scoppola v. Italy (no. 2)*, where the Court interpreted Article 7, para. 1, ECHR, in the sense that it encompasses the principle of retroactive application of the more lenient penalty,[34] in spite of the fact that such a provision recognizes only the principle *nullum crimen nulla poena sine praevia lege poenali*, and the fact that the solution of the case could fully rely on Article 6, para. 1, ECHR. These elements lie at the core of a dissenting opinion that does not question the notion that 'the Convention is a living instrument requiring a dynamic and evolutive approach that renders

---

[32] See *inter alia* ECtHR, *McCann and others v. United Kingdom* (1995), para. 153.
[33] R. RYSSDAL, 'Opinion: The Coming Age of the European Convention on Human Rights' (1996) 1 *European Human Rights Review* 24.
[34] ECtHR, Grand Chamber, *Scoppola v. Italy (no. 2)* (2009).

rights practical and effective, not theoretical and illusory', but adds that 'no judicial interpretation, however creative, can entirely be free of constraints. Most importantly it is necessary to keep within the limits set by Convention provisions [...] And yet, although the present case does not require it, the majority has gone on to examine the case under Article 7(1) and, in order to apply it, has had it re-written in order to accord with what they consider it ought to have been. This, with respect, oversteps the limits'.[35]

Drawing the line between the need for creative interpretation and respect for legally provided limits to it is of course a difficult task. But such a task occurs provided that the protection of human or fundamental rights requires from the court a choice of that sort. Otherwise, insistence on creative interpretation amounts to a self-referential exercise. Furthermore, the notion fully belongs to constitutional interpretation that 'no judicial interpretation, however creative, can entirely be free of constraints'. In *Scoppola* the Court seems too assertive, and at the same time unconvinced of its constitutional role.

These examples are by no means the end of the story, but should demonstrate that assessments are needed, not only from national courts, in building what should be a common constitutional enterprise.

---

[35]   ECtHR, Grand Chamber, *Scoppola v. Italy (no. 2)*, partly dissenting opinion of judge NICOLAOU, joined by judges BRATZA, LORENZEN, JOCIENÉ, VILLIGER and SAJÓ.